W9-AJM-643

# Vineyard Voices

*Words, Faces and Voices
of Island People*

# Vineyard Voices

## Words, Faces and Voices of Island People

Excerpts from
Interviews by
Linsey Lee

Portraits by
Linsey Lee and
Mark Lennihan

Published by the
Martha's Vineyard
Historical Society

© 1998 Linsey Lee

No part of this book may be used or reproduced in any manner whatsoever
without written permission except in the case of brief quotations embodied in critical
articles and reviews. For information, address the Martha's Vineyard Historical Society,
Box 927, Edgartown, MA 02539.

Printed in the United States of America

Library of Congress Cataloging in Publication Data

ISBN 0-9665253-0-2

ISBN 0-9665253-1-0 (cloth)

Published by the Martha's Vineyard Historical Society

# Dedication

*For Brendan*
*Whose strength, patience, humor and love*
*led me and guided me*
*the whole way through.*

# Contents

Photo Credits . . . . . . . . . . . . . . . . . . . . . . . . . . . . . . . . . . . . . . . . . . . . . . . . . . . . . . . . xiii

Acknowledgments . . . . . . . . . . . . . . . . . . . . . . . . . . . . . . . . . . . . . . . . . . . . . . . . . . . . . xiv

Introduction . . . . . . . . . . . . . . . . . . . . . . . . . . . . . . . . . . . . . . . . . . . . . . . . . . . . . . . . . . . xvi

Map . . . . . . . . . . . . . . . . . . . . . . . . . . . . . . . . . . . . . . . . . . . . . . . . . . . . . . . . . . . . . . . . . xx


GRATIA HARRINGTON
    We Loved to Go Out in Storms . . . . . . . . . . . . . . . . . . . . . . . . . . . . . . . .2
        *The Gale of 1898*

HAM LUCE
    I Guess That's What They Call Progress . . . . . . . . . . . . . . . . . . . . . . . . .4
        *Farming at Farm Neck*

BETTY ALLEY
    So Many Customs . . . . . . . . . . . . . . . . . . . . . . . . . . . . . . . . . . . . . . . . . .8
        *Portuguese Customs*

BETTY MARCHANT SANCHEZ
    Let Her Go, Gallagher! . . . . . . . . . . . . . . . . . . . . . . . . . . . . . . . . . . . . .12
        *Growing Up at the* Gazette

ERIC COTTLE
    I Shut My Eyes and See Them Now . . . . . . . . . . . . . . . . . . . . . . . . . . .14
        *Menemsha and Swordfishing*

MARGUERITE COTTLE
    I Like to Think Ahead All the Time . . . . . . . . . . . . . . . . . . . . . . . . . .18
        *Growing Up on the Bassett Farm in Chilmark*

ERIC AND MARGUERITE COTTLE
    A South Roader and a Cricker . . . . . . . . . . . . . . . . . . . . . . . . . . . . . . .21
        *Two Chilmarkers Chat*

MILTON JEFFERS
    From a Little Different Viewpoint . . . . . . . . . . . . . . . . . . . . . . . . . . . .26
        *Island Blacksmith's Childhood on Chappaquiddick*

SIDNEY HARRIS
    I Knew All the Paths . . . . . . . . . . . . . . . . . . . . . . . . . . . . . . . . . . . . . . .30
        *Growing Up at the Chilmark Brickworks*

DOROTHY WEST
    I Think Writing Is a Compulsion . . . . . . . . . . . . . . . . . . . . . . . . . . . . .34
        *Writing on the Vineyard and New York*

GLADYS LEWIS
    We Had a Very Happy Time . . . . . . . . . . . . . . . . . . . . . . . . . . . . . . . . .38
        *East Chop Summers*

POLLY HILL
    T-i-i-i-i-n Type! . . . . . . . . . . . . . . . . . . . . . . . . . . . . . . . . . . . . . . . . . .40

**LEONARD VANDERHOOP**
The Old Ways . . . . . . . . . . . . . . . . . . . . . . . . . . . . . . . . . . . . . . . . . . . . .42
*Gay Head Life, Neighbors and Ways*

**CONNIE LEONARD**
I Remember Just How It Smelled . . . . . . . . . . . . . . . . . . . . . . . . . . . . . . .46
*Vineyard Haven Childhood, The Grocery Wagon and the Gay Head Light*

**LEONARD ATHEARN**
They Lived off of the Pond to Quite an Extent . . . . . . . . . . . . . . . . . . .50
*Tisbury Great Pond People*

**NANCY WHITING**
We Had a Chance to Influence People . . . . . . . . . . . . . . . . . . . . . . . .54
*Five Vineyard Women and the Civil Rights Movement*

**PAT WEST**
Land a Big Swordfish . . . . . . . . . . . . . . . . . . . . . . . . . . . . . . . . . . . . .58

**HENRY BEETLE HOUGH**
That Was the Paradise in Which We Grew Up . . . . . . . . . . . . . . . . . .60
*North Shore Memories and the Vineyard Gazette*

**LORRAINE ARMITAGE**
We Moved to Indian Hill . . . . . . . . . . . . . . . . . . . . . . . . . . . . . . . . . .66
*The Farm, Locust Grove School, and Fifty Years at Mosher Photo*

**ERFORD BURT**
I Started Building My First Boats . . . . . . . . . . . . . . . . . . . . . . . . . . . .70
*An Island Boatbuilder and Designer*

**ROSE GOUVEIA**
Never Use Metal with Water-glass . . . . . . . . . . . . . . . . . . . . . . . . . . .74
*A Portuguese Family and Forty Years with the Telephone Company*

**ELISHA SMITH**
I Guess I Knew Just About Everybody Who Lived on This Island . . . . . . . . . . .78
*Farm Life at the Head of the Lagoon and Thereabouts*

**MILDRED WADSWORTH**
There Were Hundreds and Hundreds and Hundreds of Lanterns . . . . . . . . . . .82
*One Hundred Years on the Camp Meeting Grounds*

**FANNIE JENKINSON**
We'd All Pile in the Feather Bed Come the Tempest . . . . . . . . . . . . . . . .88
*Chilmark Chores*

**FREEMAN LEONARD**
They Call It a Morale Builder . . . . . . . . . . . . . . . . . . . . . . . . . . . . . . .90
*Film Operator at the Island Movie Theaters*

**JANE NEWHALL**
Handing Out Ribbons . . . . . . . . . . . . . . . . . . . . . . . . . . . . . . . . . . . .94
*The Family and the Fair*

**ALFRED K. WILDE**
Edgartown Was My Town . . . . . . . . . . . . . . . . . . . . . . . . . . . . . . . . . .94
*The Edgartown Postmaster*

**ROBERT JACKSON, JR.**
Rum Running . . . . . . . . . . . . . . . . . . . . . . . . . . . . . . . . . . . . . . . . . .100

**JOHN WHITING**
I Had to Turn It Upside Down . . . . . . . . . . . . . . . . . . . . . . . . .102
*An Anthropologist's Early Life on a West Tisbury Farm*

**LOIS MAILOU JONES**
My Career Was Really Formed on This Island . . . . . . . . . . . . . . .106
*A Painter's Love for the Vineyard*

**ANNE CRONIG**
They're Hard-Working Young Men; They'll Make a Go of It . . . . . . . . . . . . . .110
*The Cronig Family*

**PAT WEST**
A Very Reasonable Cow . . . . . . . . . . . . . . . . . . . . . . . . . . .114
*A Cow in a Catboat — Island Transport*

**DIONIS COFFIN RIGGS**
I Have the Bottle — Minus Champagne . . . . . . . . . . . . . . . . . . .116
*A Pet's Childhood in a Whaling Family*

**PEG KNOWLES**
We Decided We Would Bushwhack . . . . . . . . . . . . . . . . . . . . .120
*Edgartown Summers and a Walk Around the Island*

**BARBARA MEDEIROS**
Great Doings Years Ago . . . . . . . . . . . . . . . . . . . . . . . . . . .124
*Chilmark Childhood*

**HENRY P. SMITH**
A Farmer and a Fisherman . . . . . . . . . . . . . . . . . . . . . . . . . .130
*The Mattakesett Creek Company*

**LE ROY GOFF**
Clambake at Normandy . . . . . . . . . . . . . . . . . . . . . . . . . . . .132

**MARGOT WILKIE**
You Can be in Touch with All That's Good Here . . . . . . . . . . . . .134
*Seven Gates Farm Summers*

**CLAIRE DUYS**
I Raised Horses Always . . . . . . . . . . . . . . . . . . . . . . . . . . . .138
*The Putnam Pony Farm and the Sinfonietta*

**EDWIN NEWHALL WOODS**
This Was Home . . . . . . . . . . . . . . . . . . . . . . . . . . . . . . . .142
*Family, Farm and Fair in West Tisbury*

**HOLLIS SMITH**
Old Booming Ben . . . . . . . . . . . . . . . . . . . . . . . . . . . . . . .146
*The Last Heath Hen*

**IDA KARL**
I Was Crazy About Salesmanship . . . . . . . . . . . . . . . . . . . . . .148
*Oak Bluffs Memories and a Full Life of Work*

**POLLY HILL**
You Have to Observe . . . . . . . . . . . . . . . . . . . . . . . . . . . . .152
*Polly Hill's North Tisbury Arboretum*

**ARNOLD FISCHER**
Here on the Farm . . . . . . . . . . . . . . . . . . . . . . . . . . . . . . . . . . . . . . . . . .154
*Flat Point Farm, West Tisbury*

**ARNIE AND PRISCILLA FISCHER**
Sign Her Up Quick! . . . . . . . . . . . . . . . . . . . . . . . . . . . . . . . . . . . . . .157
*Teaching and Farming in West Tisbury*

**DEAN K. DENNISTON, SR.**
Thank God for the Change . . . . . . . . . . . . . . . . . . . . . . . . . . . . . . . .162
*The Bradley Memorial Church*

**SARAH JENKINSON**
We Had Everything We Needed . . . . . . . . . . . . . . . . . . . . . . . . . . . .168
*Life on an Oak Bluffs Farm*

**TOM TILTON**
You Might See Some Rum Floating . . . . . . . . . . . . . . . . . . . . . . . . .172
*Rum Running*

**MARY BROOKS GRISWOLD**
Life Was a Bowl of Cherries . . . . . . . . . . . . . . . . . . . . . . . . . . . . . . .174
*East Chop Summers*

**ALFRED VANDERHOOP**
And There He Was — Right There . . . . . . . . . . . . . . . . . . . . . . . . .178
*Training Oxen in Gay Head*

**GALE HUNTINGTON**
Right Fal Da Da Diddle Day . . . . . . . . . . . . . . . . . . . . . . . . . . . . . . .182
*Music, Fishing and Farming in Chilmark*

**MILDRED HUNTINGTON**
The Harbor Was Full of Boats . . . . . . . . . . . . . . . . . . . . . . . . . . . . .186
*The Seaman's Bethel and Sailing with Zeb Tilton*

**DAVID WELCH**
You Help Me — I Help You . . . . . . . . . . . . . . . . . . . . . . . . . . . . . . .190
*Pig Slaughtering and Farms in Oak Bluffs*

**FRANKLIN BENSON**
They Don't Let Go 'Til Thunder . . . . . . . . . . . . . . . . . . . . . . . . . . .192

**ROBERT NORTON**
There Were a Lot of People Peddling Milk . . . . . . . . . . . . . . . . . . .194
*Buttonwood Farm Milk Run*

**ALICE PURDY RAY**
My Father was a Lighthouse Keeper . . . . . . . . . . . . . . . . . . . . . . . .196
*Childhood at the East Chop Light*

**JOHN COUTINHO**
I Worked Right From the Beginning . . . . . . . . . . . . . . . . . . . . . . . .200
*A Workingman's Life*

**ALICE COUTINHO**
If You Don't Put Mint in It, Forget It . . . . . . . . . . . . . . . . . . . . . .204
*A Portuguese Family*

**NELSON COON**
I'm a Noted Person and I Don't Know Anything . . . . . . . . . . . . . . . . . . . . . .208
*Horticulturist and Gazette Garden Columnist*

**HELEN MANNING**
I Knew That We Had a Special Place . . . . . . . . . . . . . . . . . . . . . . .210
*Childhood in Aquinnah*

**FRED FISHER**
They Drew in the Horse Pull and They Did Pretty Good . . . . . . . . . . . . . . .214
*Nip 'n' Tuck Farm, West Tisbury*

**ROSALIE SPENCE**
He Didn't Care for Land Work . . . . . . . . . . . . . . . . . . . . . . . . .218
*Sailing with Zeb Tilton*

**HAROLD ROGERS**
A Little of This, a Little of That . . . . . . . . . . . . . . . . . . . . . . . . . .222
*Farm Life and House Moving*

**ALICE BURT**
It Was Sort of Like a Family . . . . . . . . . . . . . . . . . . . . . . . . . . . . .224
*A Vineyard Haven Childhood and the Baptist Church*

**DONALD VOSE**
In the Center of Town . . . . . . . . . . . . . . . . . . . . . . . . . . . . . . .228
*An Edgartown Childhood and the Edgartown National Bank*

**DANIEL ALISIO**
Name It, We Had It . . . . . . . . . . . . . . . . . . . . . . . . . . . . . . . .232
*The John Hoft Farm*

**MAXEMENA MELLO**
Too Many Manuels . . . . . . . . . . . . . . . . . . . . . . . . . . . . . . . . .236
*A New Bride's First Day in Edgartown*

**MANUEL CORRELLUS**
I Came Here for Forestry . . . . . . . . . . . . . . . . . . . . . . . . . . . . .240
*Supervisor of the State Forest*

**LE ROY GOFF**
The Lighthouse Was a Noisy Neighbor . . . . . . . . . . . . . . . . . . . . . .244
*West Chop Days*

**SHIRLEY KAEKA**
I Knew All the Neighbors . . . . . . . . . . . . . . . . . . . . . . . . . . . .246
*A Childhood in North Tisbury*

**FRANKLIN BENSON**
I Put a Lot of Ice in There . . . . . . . . . . . . . . . . . . . . . . . . . . . .250
*Cutting Ice on Old House Pond*

**MILDRED HUNTINGTON**
Oh, the Boots! . . . . . . . . . . . . . . . . . . . . . . . . . . . . . . . . . .252

**LYDIA CLEVELAND**
Just to Get Ready for the Next Day . . . . . . . . . . . . . . . . . . . . . . . .254
*Growing Up on a Farm in West Tisbury*

### ROBERT JACKSON, JR.
The Only Job in Town . . . . . . . . . . . . . . . . . . . . . . . . . . . . . . . . . . . . . .256
*Edgartown Swordfishing*

### MARY LOUISE HOLMAN
I Had My Opinion and I Spoke My Mind . . . . . . . . . . . . . . . . . . . . . . . .260
*A Black Woman's Experience in Oak Bluffs*

### ALICE CLEVELAND
The Way of the World Has Changed . . . . . . . . . . . . . . . . . . . . . . . . . . . .264
*A Life of Farming, Whaling Wives, Nursing and the Grange*

### ETHEL WHIDDEN
A Trunk Full of Trees . . . . . . . . . . . . . . . . . . . . . . . . . . . . . . . . . . . . . .268
*Journeying Up to Quitsa Circa 1908*

### ALFRED EISENSTAEDT
Everything Was Like the Beginning of the World . . . . . . . . . . . . . . . . . . .270
*The Vineyard Through the Photographer's Eye*

### JOHN COUTINHO
We Had Snow! . . . . . . . . . . . . . . . . . . . . . . . . . . . . . . . . . . . . . . . . . . .272

### WILLIS GIFFORD
'Twas a Very Essential Get-Together . . . . . . . . . . . . . . . . . . . . . . . . . . . .274
*Gifford's Store and Doings at the Fair*

### MARY COLES
I Was Crazy About Anything to Do With Painting . . . . . . . . . . . . . . . . . .278
*Art, Edgartown and Blindness*

### CRAIG KINGSBURY
I Didn't Bring Any Skunks to the Island . . . . . . . . . . . . . . . . . . . . . . . . .282
*Chestnuts, Critters, Cranberries and the Noble Experiment — Tales from an Island Legend*

Index . . . . . . . . . . . . . . . . . . . . . . . . . . . . . . . . . . . . . . . . . . . . . . . . . . .289

# The Following Photographs Were Taken By:

## *Linsey Lee*

Daniel Alisio
Betty Alley
Lorraine Armitage
Leonard Athearn
Franklin Benson
Alice Burt
Mary Coles
Eric and Marguerite Cottle
Eric Cottle
Marguerite Cottle
Alice Coutinho
John Coutinho
Anne Cronig
Dean K. Denniston, Sr.
Alfred Eisenstaedt
Arnold and Priscilla Fischer

Arnold Fischer
Fred Fisher
Le Roy Goff
Rose Gouveia
Mary Griswold
Sidney Harris
Polly Hill
Mary Louise Holman
Mildred Huntington
Sarah Jenkinson
Ida Karl
Craig Kingsbury
Peg Knowles
Connie Leonard
Freeman Leonard
Gladys Lewis

Ham Luce
Helen Manning
Barbara Medeiros
Jane Newhall
Alice Purdy Ray
Elisha Smith
Alfred Vanderhoop
Donald Vose
Mildred Wadsworth
David Welch
Pat West
John Whiting
Nancy Whiting
Alfred Wilde
Margot Wilkie
Edwin Newhall Woods

## *Mark Lennihan*

Erford Burt
Lydia Cleveland
Alice Cleveland
Nelson Coon
Manuel Correllus
Claire Duys
Fred Fisher
Willis Gifford
Gratia Harrington

Henry Beetle Hough
Robert Jackson, Jr.
Milton Jeffers
Fanny Jenkinson
Shirley Kaeka
Maxemena Mello
Robert Norton
Dionis Coffin Riggs
Harold Rogers

Betty Marchant Sanchez
Hollis Smith
Henry Smith
Rosalie Spence
Tom Tilton
Leonard Vanderhoop
Dorothy West
Ethel Whidden

## *Nina Bramhall*

Gale Huntington

## *Ellen Sudow*

Lois Mailou Jones

## *Brendan O'Neill*

Linsey Lee

# Acknowledgements

*With all my thanks to the people of the Island
who have so generously shared their stories, reflections, humor and wisdom.
They are the people who created this book.*

Many people have given so richly of their time and talents to help assemble this book. I am deeply grateful for their help, interest and enthusiasm.

Fan Ogilvie provided the full range of her organizational, editorial, inspirational, and fundraising skills, for which I am deeply indebted. Karin Stanley, Brendan O'Neill, Annie Fischer, Susan Phelps, and William Stewart should rightfully be co-authors for their invaluable assistance in assembling pieces, editorial and emotional support throughout. Many thanks to Cori Field, Jeff Rossman, Pat Sullivan and Rachel Orr for their editorial skills and helpful critiques. And to Kate Scott for her thorough editorial assistance.

To Adelaide Cromwell and David McCullough, for their guidance and words of support.

Special thanks to Dana Gaines, who designed and drew the map, as only Dana Gaines can. Thanks to Nina Bramhall, whose wonderful photo of Gale Huntington adds greatly to the book. And to Ellen Sudow for her photograph of Lois Jones.

To Kathy Rose and the Wooden Tent Photo Service, for the lovely and professional job she did printing all the photos taken by Linsey Lee. To the Tisbury Printer — Chris Decker and Janet Holladay — for their great skill, hard work and patience in printing and designing this book, and to Steve and Peggy Zablotny, Z Studio, for designing the book cover. And thanks to Karen Huff, Cowgirl Graphics, for her time entering corrections.

Thanks to those who skillfully transcribed the tapes — Sarah Crafts, Veronica Jahne, Ashley Strong, and Caroline Mecum. Thanks too, to those who gave their time to proofread — Veronica Jahne, Fan Ogilvie, Anita Knight, Janet Sylvia, Lisa Morrison, D.J. Young, Pat Reinhardt, Hertha, Nancy Tutko, and Erin Hickey.

Many thanks to the Martha's Vineyard Historical Society, for their support of this book and of the work of the Vineyard Oral History Center. Thanks to Director Bruce Andrews, for his willingness to assist wherever help was needed. To Chris Morse, for his assistance in fundraising. Thanks to Nancy Safford, who generously allowed the use of lines from her 1979 interview with Leonard Vanderhoop. For interns Dana Costanza, for help with typing and cataloguing, and Erin Hickey, for help proofreading, compiling and organizing the index, and for her enthusiasm and hard work.

And thanks to the *Vineyard Gazette* for the invaluable and frequently-visited file archive in their library. With special thanks to librarian Eulalie Regan, whose knowledge of the files, her good spirits and her unfailing willingness to help with details have been such a gift.

Finally, thanks to my family — my mother and my father, whose unfailing support and encouragement helped me all along the way. My cousins, Cass and Abigail Canfield, who so generously gave us their lovely, big house where we could live in comfort in the winter and spread the photos and pages of the book all across the tables and floor. And my husband, Brendan O'Neill, who was there always.

*With special thanks to those whose support made this book possible:*

Anonymous
Richard and Kathleen Emmet Darman
Bliss and Brigitte Carnochan
Deanne Lemle Bosnack
Fred and Jeanne Barron
Robert and Stacey Schmetterer
Tess Bramhall
Alita M. Stange
Dr. Maurice and Nettie Vanderpol
Doran Family Charitable Trust
Ralph and Eleanor Graves
Lucille Kaye
David and Joan Smith
Dr. Leonard and Barbara Scherlis
Cyrus and Peg Vance
Pat Sullivan
Barry Stein and Rosabeth Moss Kanter
Chris Morse
Tom Hale
Ed Cohen

I also want to thank the earliest supporters of my oral history collecting — Mary Wakeman, whose generous and enthusiastic support got the project started in 1981, an anonymous donor to whom I'm always indebted, the Martha's Vineyard National Bank, which provided the funding for my beloved Sony TCD-5 tape deck, and Chris Decker from the Tisbury Printer, who designed and donated the first stationery for the Martha's Vineyard Oral History Project.

The work of the Vineyard Oral History Center has received support from the Massachusetts Cultural Council, a state agency receiving support from the National Endowment for the Arts.

All proceeds from the sale of *Vineyard Voices — Words, Faces and Voices of Island People* will go to support the continued collection of oral history, the Vineyard Oral History Center, and the Martha's Vineyard Historical Society.

# Introduction

The splendors of Martha's Vineyard are many — an empty expanse of windswept beach, the aerial dance of swallows over a still pond at dusk, the smell of sweet fern in the hot sun on a dusty road, the song of pinkletinks on a spring evening. But the people and their vital bond to the Island around them give voice to what is so special about the Vineyard: centuries of men and women depending upon the land, the sea and their neighbors — fishermen, farmers, whalers, boat builders, merchants. Because of the relative isolation of the Island until the middle of the twentieth century, this heritage has not totally disappeared. It lives on in the memories and reflections of older Vineyarders and is maintained by those few Islanders who continue to lead their lives in a traditional way. However, with the rapid pace of change on the Island, traditional lifestyles are lost and there are fewer and fewer people who remember "how it used to be."

Oral history interviews capture the memories, reflections and traditions of life on the Vineyard in all their vibrancy. They tell of the calamitous, joyous and commonplace details in the lives of everyday people. These stories are singular and subjective, full of connections and contradictions. They offer a level of intimacy not found in more traditional histories. These are the voices of the Vineyard: mothers, fathers, school teachers, summer people, shop keepers, artists, writers, sailors and others. In *Vineyard Voices,* you will not find a comprehensive history of the Vineyard. You will find engaging stories from seventy-five Vineyarders, stories full of life, stories that open a window on the past.

I began collecting oral histories from people of the Vineyard in the late '70s. I had been coming to the Vineyard all my life in the summer and I moved here year-round in 1970. In the various projects I undertook and jobs I had — working at the Scottish Bakehouse, writing a book on plants of the Vineyard, shucking scallops at Poole's Fish Market,

designing and researching exhibits for the Historical Society — the people I met and the stories I heard them tell brought the Vineyard of the past and present alive for me in new and wonderful ways. I thought, "These are stories that need to be gathered and saved for everyone to hear." This book contains excerpts from interviews I conducted between 1980 and 1998. The stories are from people who lived from the 1890s to the present, with their grandparents' memories reaching back to the middle of the nineteenth century.

These stories display the rich tapestry of life on the Vineyard, individual threads, yet lives intertwined. They are voices of Yankees, Portuguese, Wampanoags, African-Americans and immigrants from many places. These are people whose spirit is enduringly independent, who live in balance with the natural resources around them, and are conscious of the give-and-take of the sea, the ponds and the land. They form their own strongly held opinions and depend on their own devices. The stories are of Martha's Vineyard, but the themes are universal — change and continuity, racial struggles, women's roles, immigration, the impact of technology, struggle against adversity, family joys and sorrows.

In my years of interviewing I have found much to admire and respect. I see in older Islanders an inner strength, a center of calm. For much of this century and before, life on Martha's Vineyard was not easy. Money was scarce, luxuries few. One "made do." People accepted life as it unfolded, taking the bad with the good, the hardships with the joys. These Vineyarders approach life with a wonderful sense of humor, an indispensable and engaging survival technique which shines through in their stories.

The immense generosity and graciousness of people, sharing their lives, their time, and their stories has so impressed and inspired me. I am constantly awed by the wealth of wisdom and humor each person has to share. And most people seem to enjoy being interviewed. Certainly, in me, they find a rapt audience. Many of the people I interview are in their eighties and nineties, some over one hundred. The eagerness and engagement with which these individuals approach life are a gift and a lesson to us all.

There is a beauty in the way people of the Vineyard speak; their stories told with a cunning turn-of-phrase, a rapier wit, an economy of language usually absent from modern discourse. For generations, talking was the way most Vineyarders entertained themselves — Sunday visiting and gathering around the post office or the general store. As these people speak, their cadence and inflection can be so measured and lyrical, their voices seem almost song-like.

To me, a fascination of oral history is to hear many varied recitations of the same story or conflicting descriptions of the same event from different people. In this sense, the Vineyard becomes a wonderful laboratory for investigating the nature of "truth." The "true" versions of the story can be as numerous as the individuals asked. Each person brings their own bias and outlook on life to the processing of any event. They take ownership of the story, make it theirs, infuse it with subjective reality. Reading these excerpts from oral history interviews is like looking through facets of a diamond, seeing the richness and complexity of life on the Vineyard through the reflections of many perspectives.

Each piece in *Vineyard Voices* is excerpted from an interview or, more often, several interviews I have done with each person. A piece may have been culled from two hundred pages of transcript, but I have tried to keep each story as told, with as little editing as possible, to capture the unique signature of each voice. I have taken the pieces, when I can, to the person I have interviewed for their review and approval. The pieces vary in length and emphasis. Some cover just one incident in a person's life;

others offer more of an overview of someone's life. Some of the shorter pieces were prepared for Vineyard Voices exhibits that have hung at the Martha's Vineyard Historical Society, the Steamship Authority, the Agricultural Fair and Island libraries.

The criteria used in selecting people to interview are broad. Older members of the community are a priority, as are those who have lived or are living traditional Vineyard lifestyles, those who have made significant contributions to life on the Island, and those who have a good stock of Vineyard lore. I have interviewed more than 180 people of the Vineyard, and still my list of people who must be interviewed is in the hundreds.

In preparing for an interview, I do as much research as possible about the person I will be interviewing and on related topics I think might arise. The library at the *Vineyard Gazette* and the library at the Historical Society have been invaluable resources. Most interviews last about an hour-and-a-half to two hours, although they can run as long as six hours. I try to interview each person at least two or three times. With some people, I'm fortunate to be able to conduct five or six interviews.

When I conduct interviews, I use audio tape and take black-and-white photos. I am drawn to the way that listening to or reading a transcript of a voice prompts one to create visual pictures. The black-and-white photo format I find especially evocative, capturing a sense of character which engages the imagination.

Occasionally, when I call to ask someone if they would be willing to do an interview with me, they will say, "But I haven't done anything special." I need to explain that what I really want to hear is stories of day-to-day life — what games they played as children, how they used to conduct household chores, their hopes and dreams — that these are the details that help us understand the past and bring it alive. For me, the high point of my work is having someone who was hesitant about being interviewed say to me, half an hour into the interview, "I didn't realize how interesting my life has been."

These stories remind us of what is special about the Vineyard. They will challenge you, they will make you laugh. You will travel the Vineyard roads with eyes transformed — Peaked Hill becomes an open landscape covered with hundreds of sheep; Duarte's Pond becomes a cultivated cranberry bog full of pickers; a house on North Road becomes a one-room schoolhouse overflowing with children rushing out to recess; the Vineyard Sound becomes a busy thoroughfare filled with three-masted schooners.

Today, people of the Vineyard are continually faced with decisions that impact the quality of life on the Island. As the Vineyard weighs the conse-quences of those decisions, there are lessons to be learned from these stories. The memories and observations preserved through oral histories deep-en our understanding and appreciation of the past and its connection to the present. They illuminate those qualities that make the Vineyard unique. If people listen, these histories can inform the choices that determine the future of our Island.

There are many, many other Vineyard voices we are not hearing from in this volume, and my inten-tion is that there will be *More Vineyard Voices*. Here are just some voices to enchant and inform. With all my thanks to the people who give us these stories, I leave it to each reader to discover their own special treasures in these stories.

Linsey Lee
Tashmoo, June 1998

# The Vineyard Oral History Center of the Martha's Vineyard Historical Society

The stories in *Vineyard Voices* are just a small sampling of the wealth of information to be found in the complete transcript and tape of each interview. In the archive of the Vineyard Oral History Center at the Martha's Vineyard Historical Society are interviews with over 350 people collected over the last forty years by a number of collectors — myself, Bob Post, Nancy Safford, John Leavens, Stan Lair, Basil Welch, Connie Sandborn, Art Railton and others. These interviews are archived at the Gale Huntington Library of the Historical Society. Other oral history collections are housed at the West Tisbury Library and with the Wampanoag Tribe of Aquinnah.

Transcripts and tapes of interviews are available to the public for education, research, enjoyment and other non-commercial purposes. A catalogue of the collection is being prepared to facilitate the use of the archive. It will include topical indexes, an outline of each interview and photographs of the speakers.

. . . .

The Vineyard Oral History Center was established at the Martha's Vineyard Historical Society in 1994 to promote the preservation and collection of Vineyard history, past and present, through oral histories and related materials. The Oral History Center continues to conduct interviews with people of the Island and holds workshops to encourage members of the community to collect oral histories.

Working with the Vineyard schools is a priority of the Center. Using oral history techniques, students have the opportunity to work with primary sources and to realize the richness of their community as a classroom. Their interviews provide a wonderful addition to the archive, and the exhibits they create from their work are displayed in the Historical Society's Childrens' Gallery. The Center also works with Vineyard Senior Centers, Camp Jabberwocky, and Windemere long-term care facility.

The Oral History Center welcomes new additions to the archive of audio and video oral histories with people of the Vineyard, along with photographs and related materials. The Center also welcomes volunteer help with the work of cataloguing and transcribing the collection.

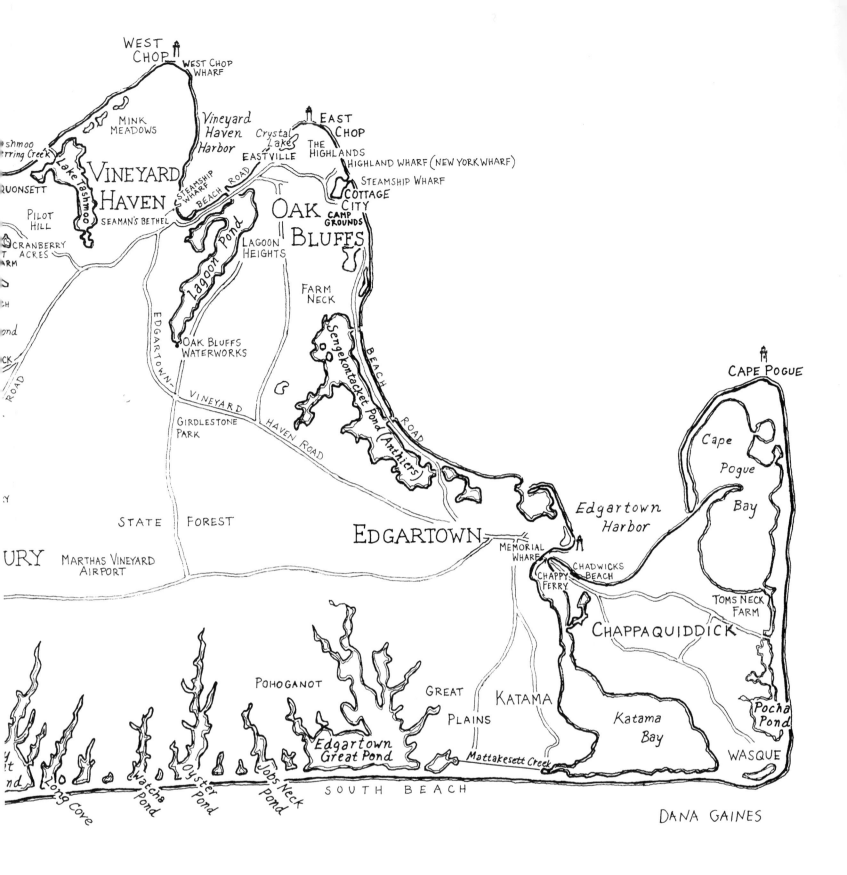

## GRATIA HARRINGTON
1885 – 1987 · Tisbury
Hospital Volunteer Coordinator, Physical Education Teacher
Daughter of George W. Eldridge, Creator of the *Eldridge Tide and Pilot Book*

# We Loved to Go Out in Storms

### The Gale of 1898

You see, we loved to go out in storms, my sisters and myself. And it was a Sunday morning, the last of November. It wasn't cold, but there was this terrific wind and the snow.

And so we told Mother we should go out and see if there was Sunday school. Of course I knew there wouldn't be any, but we wanted to get out.

Mother came from the Middle West, and she never could understand why we liked to go out in storms. All I could think of was a hen who had hatched a bunch of ducklings.

So we went out and went down to the church. Of course it was closed. And then we went down to the shore, about where Owen Park is. And you couldn't see. There was just this snow, just this blizzard of snow, you know.

But there was a funny thing. There was a two-masted schooner right up on the beach. And the name of it was the *Mary Eldridge*. And of course, that was my sister's name. Isn't that a queer thing!

But then the most extraordinary thing happened. The sun came out for about five minutes. And shut right down again. The most extraordinary thing! And it meant that the men — the Vineyard Haven sailors — saw the condition of the harbor. And we did, too.

All those wrecked ships with just their topmasts sticking out of the water. And of course, the *Newburg* had come around and gone through the wharf. And her bowsprit was sticking out the other side. You can't imagine what it was like.

And so we went home after we had seen all we wanted to see.

Mr. Edwards at the Seaman's Bethel had a daughter about my age, a friend of mine. Mrs. Edwards said to me "Can Mary" — her name was Mary, too — "come up and spend the night with you? She's so troubled about this storm, and she's so nervous and upset."

The Vineyard Haven men got an old whaling dory and patched it up. And they went off and rescued a lot of men. All the dory could carry. And the men came into the Bethel and they were taken care of and given a place to sleep and eat and so forth.

Mary had seen them come in and she was in such an awful state that she came up and spent the night. I remember sleeping with her and she having trouble going to sleep and so forth.

And so all these men were there at the Bethel.

They sent them home as soon as they could. But there were seventy-five men that were there for some time. Of course, the village helped feed them. But I suppose they slept on the floor. I don't know how they managed.

Mr. Edwards used to come up and say to Mother, "Well, we've done all we can, can't you help us out? Can't you get up a little entertainment? We're going to have ice cream and cake. Have a sociable." And so my mother said, "All right."

Two of my sisters played the violin and one sister sang, more or less indifferently. And she had friends; they had a little quartet that used to sing.

And I spoke pieces, and we handed around the ice cream and cake.

So we went down to the Bethel when they had all those shipwrecked sailors.

I remember very well. The terrible experience. Looking into the faces of all those men and thinking what they had been through.

*Interviewed 1983*

## HAM LUCE

b. 1905 • Oak Bluffs
Farmer, Hunter
Caretaker for Flynn Property, Pohogonot, Edgartown

# I Guess That's What They Call Progress

## *Farming at Farm Neck*

That area where we had our farm is now called Farm Neck. And when I was young, and more so before my time, there were a great number of farms out there with cattle on them and that sort of thing.

We were dairy farmers at the time. We kept twenty head of cattle. We had about two hundred acres of land, probably fifty of it was tillable, the rest was pasture. And like all farmers, we got up about four or five o'clock in the morning. Growing up on a farm you become pretty close to nature. I love that farming life. You worked hard, but you felt good about what you got done. It was beautiful out there on the farm. In the morning you'd wake up and the first thing you would do is look out over the farm and down across the meadows and over across Nantucket Sound.

We were on Sengekontacket Pond. Everyone called it Anthiers then. That pond is a tidal pond and there was, of course, a great abundance of shellfish: clams and quahogs and oysters and scallops and that sort of thing. So we derived a great deal of our living right from the pond. Used to have milk on one side of the yard and clams and shellfish on the other. It was a happy combination of farming and fishing. And there were swarms of ducks, waterfowl of all kinds at that time. It was the most natural thing in the world that we gravitated toward the pond to shoot ducks. You know, it's surprising how much stuff we got off the land, between the pond and the fields. We'd pick huckleberries by the bucketful, and beach plums, all that sort of thing. You get eight kids out there picking and you get quite a lot of berries!

In the pond, all around it there are freshwater springs, and in fact some are covered by saltwater at high tide. We'd be working in the corn fields that were within a few feet of the salt water pond. On a hot day, when you were thirsty, you would go down and scoop a little hole out on the beach and let it stand or settle a few moments and get excellent fresh water. You could see the stuff bubbling, fascinating thing.

We had a market garden. We used to all work at it and peddle vegetables in town, to the hotels and markets. There was a good market for all that stuff in the summer. We raised an awful lot of sweet corn. Everybody likes sweet corn. That was probably the best cash crop because you could harvest an awful lot of corn on two or three acres. Of course tomatoes was a crop that was much in demand, too. Turnip was one thing we used to grow a lot of, and now they don't sell that well. But one reason we grew turnips was you fed them to cattle. You used to grind them up. Another crop was the cattle beet, almost identical to the sugar beet. They grow out of the ground, about two feet out of the ground, immense things. And pumpkin's another thing, these huge pumpkins, you know. We had a machine to grind them up for cattle feed. Cows loved them.

We used to cart hundreds of loads of seaweed because that had a lot of plant food in it and helps to bring your soil up. That was one of the fall chores after harvesting. If we didn't have anything else to do, we'd go and bring home seaweed from the pond. And sometimes we'd go to the Beach Road and get it. Eel grass, mostly.

I still love to work in a garden. I've been on my knees since I was seven years old, and I still love doing it. It's just fascinating to watch things grow.

In the winter we did a lot of wood cutting and that sort of thing. We had woodlots of our own that we used to cut. Because we burned wood entirely up to 1940. That's all we did use for fuel. And we needed plenty of it. We had plenty of time in the winter to cut it, which wasn't one of my favorite chores. We cut by hand, we had no machines then. We would use, I guess, seven to ten cords of wood for a year, according to the severity of the winter, of course.

In the living room we had, what you would call an Airtight, that you could burn logs in. In the kitchen was the big Glenwood Cooking Range, and it also had a water compartment on one end where we could heat water. And, of course, the kitchen was the focal point of everything. You studied there, you ate there, and everything else. You only ate in the living room around holidays, whenever you had company, you know. Took Saturday baths there! It was the one place to be, you know. And when we kids'd all play in the snow, you'd get your feet wet and come in and then stick your feet in the oven. That was ritual. And people say, "How'd you ever cook on a fire?" I say, "We used to cook pretty darn well." All in knowing how to handle it.

We also had a smokehouse. It was just a little shack, and it had a trench in it. We used to use corncobs. They were sweet and gave a better flavor to the meat. Besides, we had lots of them. You'd have a smoldering fire there, and you'd string the stuff up a ways off it. And you did it over a period of several days, a couple of hours each time. It had to be salted first because that's what preserved meat.

You'd salt it in a stone crock. Salt, according to how much weight you had in there. The way we could tell if we had enough density was to put a raw potato in there. If it floated, it was dense enough.

We used to salt herring. Spring of the year, we'd go to where the Oak Bluffs pumping station is. The herring would come in the thousands. And we'd go up there and scoop them out. We'd put them in brine and then hang them outside to dry. They'd keep indefinitely.

We'd do the same thing with hake and frost fish. We used to go over to these docks in winter, in the night, and we'd catch hake. Bring them home, and then we'd gut them and clean them, and put them in brine. You'd see all these roofs would be plastered with fish drying, like you used to see in Gloucester. And you'd use them like cod, to make fishcakes, creamed fish, or whatever. We all used to go nights with carts, pushcart or wheelbarrows.

And the frost fish. Small fish, maybe weigh a pound or so. We'd go down on the beaches with a lantern and a rake. You could rake them up with a rake. With a rake! I don't know if they were attracted by the light or they were feeding inshore, but we'd rake them in by the bushel.

That was one of the standbys for the winter food. A lot of things like that we could do. And, as I say, it was not only food, but it was fun, too. It was part of the fun of a kid growing up on the Island. I think we had an enchanted childhood. The beaches were so easily accessible if we wanted to go swimming, and we weren't that far from the woods. Never that far from nature. We were so close to it all the time.

I'm just as enthused about what is going on outdoors as I ever was and I enjoy every minute of it. There's so much to see and hear. I love to hear the surf and walk the beach. There's something wonderful about living near salt water. You know, the ocean is almost like a living thing in a way. It has so many moods. It can be placid some days, and other days it's ugly-looking and mean. But what a tremendous thing it is.

But, you know, I've been very fortunate. I've done all the things I've wanted. I liked what I was doing, working around the animals and growing things. I worked a lot of hours, but it didn't seem that way because I really liked what I was doing. I lived on and worked the farm. After my father died I took it over and continued. And, of course, my father had taken it over from his father.

It was always a dairy farm. My grandfather had a milk route. That's the way we all did it. We didn't do any wholesale at all. It was just house to house. We had a horse and cart to deliver milk. Our route was in Oak Bluffs. We lived about a mile and a half out of town and it would take most of the morning. The customers would be all over the place, anywhere from Main Street to East Chop. We finally bought a pickup truck back in 1932. Then you'd get around quickly.

In the fall of the year after everyone left, the summer resort, you know, was closed down, really, and you had too much milk, too much, then we'd make butter and that sort of thing from the surplus milk. And a lot of it went into the pigs because you just had so much milk that there was no place to sell it.

The number of farms diminished when Oak Bluffs became a summer resort. A lot of those people moved into town and became carpenters and painters and that sort of thing. They could make a lot more money working for the summer people. They deserted the farms or moved away. When I was growing up, it had gotten to be where there used to be a dozen farms or fifteen farms, there were only about three that were really active. It was cellar holes where there once were farms.

Now I don't like to go out there. All I see is houses all over the place. I don't see any meadows or the pastures where we would keep our animals. Houses and new roads. I guess that's what they call progress.

*Interviewed 1984*

# BETTY ALLEY
b. 1912 • Oak Bluffs
Homemaker
Secretary, Dukes County Extension Service
Secretary, Oak Bluffs Tax Department

# So Many Customs

## Portuguese Customs

My mother came over here when she was seven years old, from the Azores. She was born in St. Michael, one of the islands in the Azores. My father was thirteen when he came from St. George. And they came here and settled right here on the Island, on Martha's Vineyard.

My grandmother lived just down from where we lived. When my mother had all her children, she never had any doctors or anything. She had them all at home, you know, and I used to go down to call my grandmother to come up to assist. I always had to run through the fields and say, "Come to the house, Mother's having another baby!"

My grandmother always made cookies. She made tremendous molasses cookies. I never saw any, any bigger, and when you would go down to see her she would have a plateful on her table. You always had to have a cookie before anything else, and I used to say to her to come up with me through the fields. And she would say, "Don't you want a cookie first?" But she would say it in Portuguese. You know, because she only spoke Portuguese. I had to have a cookie before we went back up through the fields. And then she would go up with me, and after a little while we would have a new baby.

I remember a lady living a little way from us up on the hill, like, and she had one room dedicated just to the Holy Ghost, all decorated. She'd decorate it for days and it was a privilege for us to be allowed to go in and see it. They used tinsel, and all kinds of paper flowers and real flowers and — they were beautiful. They'd do the whole wall. And they'd have a little statue of the Baby Jesus right in the middle of all this decoration.

And then Christmas Eve they used to go around and sing Portuguese songs. They'd go from house to house and sing. They'd go to the different houses where Portuguese families lived. The men would play their banjos and the mandolin. And you could hear them play all the way down the street. And it would be pretty to listen to them. I remember standing upstairs at my bedroom listening out the window.

And the *chamarita* — that was a beautiful dance. There was a lady down the end of our street where I lived and she was one of the best dancers. Little old lady, too. Everybody used to go to her house at Christmas. They always dropped in and they danced the *chamarita* there. And from our house we could hear them singing and dancing.

Her name was Caroline Pachico. We used to call her Tia Carlinda, which is — everybody had to be a *tia* because *tia's* aunt, you know, in Portuguese. For an older lady, someone you knew, you always had some sort of respect. So they were all *tia*. So, she was Tia Carlinda.

All the older people, like the older ladies that lived around — the little Portuguese ladies, you know — we had to call them all, *tia*, too. My mother's name, maiden name, was Pachico. Her first name was Mary. She was Tia Maria Chic, and that's what they used to call her. My husband's grandmother was named Lina, but she wasn't Portuguese. But she was Tia Lina just the same, and she learned how to speak Portuguese with all these little old ladies up here.

In my family we never went to bed that we didn't ask my father and mother to bless us before we went upstairs. And they would say their little thing in Portuguese that they were blessing us before we went up the stairs. And if you got halfway up the stairs and you didn't ask, you came back down again. And we always had to, when we finished eating, we always had to stand by where we sat and say a prayer, and we all had to do that before we could leave the table.

Too many of those customs are gone from everything.

Killing the pig, that was a big day. I remember that. Everybody took part in that, we all had to.

Because we used every part of the pig, you know.

Up at the top of the hill there was a man who used to do the slaughtering. So we didn't have to do it right in the yard. They would take the pig up there. Children used to hate to see them go because he was like a pet, you know. Anyway, so we had to go up there and we all had to take part in making everything. My mother made the sausages and linguica and made the blood pudding. I remember that when they made the blood pudding, oh, I never could stand it. They'd go up with a pan to get the blood and we used to disappear when we knew that was happening. They had to grind all the meat, do all of that. People used to come and help; come around, and then you'd give them a part of the pig, to take home and everything. My mother always had these great big crocks that I remember, that she'd keep the pig parts in with vinegar and spices.

My father had a cellar. The cellar that you could put vegetables in, to stay for the winter. He had a root cellar too. It was all cement, all around. And then in one corner there'd be sand. The turnips and the cabbage, you can plant them right in there. Keep them all winter. We used to have to go down and get a cabbage or kale. We had a lot of kale. My mother always made kale soup. She made a kettle about this big. Everything she did was big.

And we had a lot of grapes. And my father made wine. When the grapes were ripe, he had a wooden grape vat, with slats and you had to turn it to get the juice to come out from the bottom. It was a big wooden thing, I remember, and it was always in the cellar. And when he was making it, every time anyone went down to the cellar, they had to give a turn to the top crank, so the juice would go through. And my brothers, of course, were teenagers. They'd always go down and taste it, you know. We always used to kid them. But we always had a bottle of wine at the table at holidays, or Sundays. My father always used to let us have a little bit. Because he made it all himself and I doubt that he put anything that was too sharp in it, if we were going to have any. So he made it only for the family, for holidays or special occasions.

I was thinking the first day of May; we used to go and hang May baskets every year when we were growing up. We'd take weeks to decorate a May basket — we used to spend hours and days decorating these cardboard boxes with crepe paper, pink and blue and white, and put handles on them. We'd make beautiful ones. We'd save all our pennies and we'd get candy and an orange or an apple and we'd go around and hang May baskets at our friends' houses. And our teachers' too. It was a big thing. Just before it got dark you could go and do this. You'd go and hang it and then you'd go and hide, see, and then they'd have to find you.

And, by the way, if it was a girl and you hung it to a boy, if he caught you he could kiss you and something like that. And we didn't only do it the first day of May. We did it anytime through the month of May.

And my brothers used to be quite the devils. They didn't only put candy in the baskets they did, they'd put in all the stuff that they'd pick up from the ground or anything like that, you know. Coal and polliwogs and ... Just to be devilish.

It was a good family. We didn't have an awful lot, but we had what we needed, and we never went hungry. And we got taught what should have been taught at home, I think. But I think of those days a lot. I'd just as soon be back there, to tell you the truth.

I always remember we had a big oak table, a round one, you know, with the big pedestal underneath. And we all sat around it. We had to put extra leaves in the middle to take care of all of us, there were nine kids. We all ate when it was time to eat. We didn't eat, you know, and run. We all sat at the same time and then my father would sit down last. And, like I told you, we all had to say a prayer before we left the table.

My father, when he'd get home at night, he'd be tired and we'd have supper. My father couldn't read or write, you know. He could read just a little bit of English, because he only went to school until about the fourth, fifth grade, you see. So, my sister would read to him every night for a whole hour. She would read all the news from the newspaper for him. He always kept up on all the current events.

We had to be quiet. That's when we went in the parlor and did our homework. He had sort of like a routine. He liked music. He'd say, "What's the matter, no music tonight?" After he had his paper read, I had to go play music for a half an hour for him. By that time it was seven or eight o'clock. And then after that, you did your homework and you went to bed. And that was it, you know.

We made our own fun, like I say, but we got along pretty well. You have a big family like that, you have to. Because we all stayed home, you know, in those days, with our families. Many of the fami-lies we knew were big in those days. If they had ten or eleven children in a family, that was nothing. When we'd walk to school, we'd have a whole school walking. We all kind of enjoyed our lives, you know?

But I was thinking, so many customs that the kids don't do today. I tell my great-grandchildren about them on Sundays. I tell them all this. They love to hear.

*Interviewed 1995*

## BETTY MARCHANT SANCHEZ
b. 1901 • Edgartown
Linotype Operator for *Cambridge Chronicle*
Proprietor Marchant House Bed and Breakfast, Edgartown

# Let Her Go, Gallagher!

## *Growing Up at the* Gazette

The *Vineyard Gazette* was owned by my father for over forty-six years. It had been founded by his great-uncle. He was editor and publisher and the head of every department for a while. Then he had one foreman, and after a while he took in a young girl who was quite happy to learn the mechanical part of a newspaper.

I was all enthusiasm about the newspaper business. So from the age of twelve, I'd go down there after school most every day, do a little puttering, but it all helped in teaching me things.

I remember when I was doing that at my very youngest age, they sat me up on a big stool at what used to be called the bookkeeper's desk, built up high, you know, like Scrooge. I'd be on the stool and I'd put all the addresses on the wrappers for the outgoing papers. I did that first of all.

Then I got interested in the proofreading part. I suppose it started very simply. I suppose my father passed me a little article and said, "Girlie, read that over and see if you see any bad errors." So that taught me bookkeeping or copy reading. And also at the very beginning, I learned to set type by hand.

As I look back at the way some of those older people worked, can you imagine, even an article four inches long, every single letter of that had to be picked up and put into a metal stick, leads between the lines to keep them upright. If you touched one letter wrong at the wrong moment, they'd all fall down like a line of dominoes.

I remember after the whole week's work came the noontime or early afternoon of putting on the last forms of the *Gazette* which would be out the next morning.

An old-time press was driven by a big wheel; a man about town would come in for so much an hour and turn that wheel, and I'd stand up on a platform almost as high in feet as the papers.

You see, that's what I mean. I learned everything there. Anything I ever did afterward came from my knowledge around there.

So I'd be up there on this platform. Well, you fed those papers in much the same way as a woman in a laundry — a laundry of the past, anyway — would feed the sheets into the gauge. Well, that's the way you would feed a paper. So the first thing we'd do, we'd run off two or three papers and pass 'em to my father, and then to the other girl and to me and I suppose the foreman. We'd all scan it quickly as we could, and say, "Uh-oh, there's a boo-boo there." Well, if it was minor, sometimes we'd let it go.

But if it was really important, we'd say, "Stop the press. There's an error." And then when we found everything was all right and it could roll, my father would stand up there ... He always had a certain dignity. He might have printer's ink on his pants, they might have become very smudgy, but he had a certain dignity as he stood there. And he'd say, "Let her go, Gallagher! Once more the Thunderer goes forth to the world."

My father was conscientiousness itself. He didn't ever want to hurt people's feelings. I suspect he would not have been too good on a bigger paper.

He was awfully good to people who ran up a bill ... who couldn't always pay it. And of course we didn't have too much of this world's goods, either. We used to begin the winter with a barrel of apples and a barrel of potatoes in the cellar because some poor farmer or somebody who carried on farming on his property was better able to pay in that way than in cash.

*Interviewed 1984*

## ERIC COTTLE

b. 1917 • Chilmark

Fisherman

# I Shut My Eyes and See Them Now

## *Menemsha and Swordfishing*

I grew up in Menemsha. So did my parents and grandparents. They went to school together. Same as Marguerite and I. We did the same thing. Our house had kerosene lights and a kerosene stove. Had a coal stove too, and in the living room we had a wood stove. It was my job on Saturdays to cut enough wood to last a week. My father had a woodlot up on the Crossroad. He would get it cut and bring it down in eight foot lengths that I had to cut up into foot lengths with a buck saw. I thought I was put upon. I'm sure it didn't hurt me a bit.

Knew everybody that owned here. Actually there was more people that lived in the Creek then than there is now, year-round. I suppose there was thirty-five, forty people. There was somebody in just about every house all year. And everybody, the older people, we always called them "uncle" and "aunt." There was a Dan Vincent and his wife was Georgie Vincent and it was Uncle Dan, Aunt Georgie. We didn't call him Mr. Vincent, always uncle. Everybody was uncle and aunt. I don't think I was related to any of them. Everybody looked out for us. They were good to us, good to the kids, the older people were. They really were.

I used to go over to Aunt Georgie's and play Flinch. I don't remember how to play it now, but she loved to play Flinch. She'd flinch me. Then she'd laugh, got a great charge out of flinching. And I used to go over to Willy Mayhew's, stop in there, and he'd make some tea and I used to have some tea and crackers with him.

I used to borrow David Butler's skiff. Uncle David. He said, "There's a skiff. Anytime you want it, take it." So I'd go down, get the skiff, and row around the Basin. Told all the kids the same thing. "You want a boat? Nobody's using it. Take it. The oars are in it. Take it. Just tie it up when you're through, that's all I ask." They treated us good.

A lot of the houses didn't have any insulation. You had outside walls was all you had. See the nail heads. Now, down in the house, cold morning, you'd see every nail head, white. Frost on it. Break ice in the bucket if you wanted to wash your face before the stove was going.

Didn't have any running water at all. We'd get our water from the brook. Sunday afternoon, it was my job to lug about twenty buckets of water for Mother to wash clothes and rinse them in. Took quite a few trips. My father dug a hole and put a barrel down in there and we'd dip it out of that. Good water, great water. That's before they built any houses on the brook, see?

Didn't have any electricity. Didn't think anything about it. Thought everybody did the same thing. I didn't know I was poor until they came from the mainland and told me. Some of these summer people come, said, "My God, you folks are some poor." I didn't know it. I was happy.

My father's grandparents were both deaf-mutes. His mother wasn't very well after he was born so he went to live with his grandparents. And of course they didn't speak. So everybody thought he was a deaf-mute because he never spoke, because he didn't hear anybody speak. And somebody went there one day and said his name, and he turned his head. And they said, "I believe he can hear." He could hear all right. But his grandparents didn't speak, so he didn't know how to talk 'til he was, well, three or four years old. I don't say that's the absolute truth, but that's what I've always heard.

He knew all the signs. He could talk good using both hands. Everybody did. I knew quite a few signs then, but I've kind of forgotten them now. I don't remember too many, but I remember some.

There was three or four people in Chilmark that were deaf-mutes when I was young. Fellow by the name of Josie West who loved to play cards. We'd go over to the post office. It's where that Lombardi's is now. The mail come in there and we'd go in there and Josie would be there, playing cards. So I knew the signs for suits. He was a good card player, too. I could talk to him. Of course, it was hard because most of them couldn't spell. So you had to guess. They'd have two or three letters, then you'd have to guess. If you were carrying on a conversation, you could pick it up. You could figure out what they were talking out. But it was a language all their own. Different language. They had a different language on the mainland than they did around here.

They had signs for most of the people. Now Ernest Mayhew, that was a sign! Because they hung a May basket on something, and he had run right into a clothesline, come right across there and thrown on his back. And that was Ernest Mayhew's sign — go like that — grab your neck, and let's talk about Ernest Mayhew! And then his father, he lost his hand when he was a kid in a threshing machine. That was always the sign for Benny Mayhew, going like that — covering one hand. They had signs for a lot of different people.

I went to the Chilmark School. It was called the Chilmark School then. No self-respecting Menemshan would call that Menemsha over there. That's Chilmark and this is Menemsha, see? Because Menemsha runs from top of the hill down to the Creek. Rest of it is Chilmark. We walked to school. It was just one room, eight grades. One teacher. That was Maude Reed. And don't look cross-eyed or she's got you. She was hard. She was good, though. If you couldn't learn with her, there was no hope for you. Good teacher. There was about thirty, thirty-five students in school. Somebody would be reciting all the time, you know. You learned to concentrate.

After school I would come home, and usually I'd go down to the Creek. In the wintertime, the men would be in the different shacks, shucking scallops, and I'd go down, go from one shack to another and see what they were doing until dinnertime, then I'd come home. I spent most of my time down to the Creek. Summertime, I was wet all summer, because I'd go down there and play in the water. Loved to be around the water.

I wanted to go fishing. I always wanted to. From the time I could walk and talk, I wanted to go fishing. All I wanted to do. Get out of school to go fishing. That's what I did, too.

My father was a lobsterman. He went lobstering. When I got old enough to go, I went with him, but we didn't get along. I didn't think he knew much about lobstering. Well, I was that age, you know, fourteen, fifteen. I was pretty smart, so I knew all there was to know. So he says, "You know, I don't think you and I better go together anymore." Says, "One of us is going to get thrown overboard. So," he says, "I guess you better go." So then I went with my uncle. Got along with him all right.

Then one summer I went down on Georges Bank swordfishing with Bob Jackson from Edgartown. On the *Hazel M. Jackson*. And then I went back with Benny Mayhew again and went with him for quite a while. I went scalloping quite a few years, then several winters I went quahogging all winter with a bull rake. Then I went with Jimmy Morgan, and in 1961 I got into lobstering. I started lobstering and that went for twenty years; lobstering on my own, had my own boat.

I never learned to swim. I played around the water, but I never went to the beach. I always played with the boats. I had boats on a string and played boats and didn't think about swimming. Go in up to my knees. Then soon as I was fourteen, I was fishing all summer. I didn't get a chance to go to the beach. I fell over several times, but I always managed to get hold of something, haul myself out. Never thought anything about it. Really never did.

I'd start swordfishing about the first of July and go until I started school. I went with Carlton Mayhew. Went with him a couple of years. I did all the steering. You could steer from the mast. Could stop the engine from up there. I could open her up or slow her down from there. They had all the controls up there on string, just all strings. Didn't have anything fancy like they got now.

I would steer him on the fish and he would harpoon them. You look at the end of the pole and never look at the fish, just look at the end of the pole. Wherever that pole goes, you steer that boat to go with the pole. If he wanted you to go that way, he put the pole that way. Once he's harpooned the fish, he would run aft and throw the keg over. Then he had to get another lily on the harpoon, get it ready, so if they see another one they're set. I'd slide down the stay. Had a piece of garden hose, cut off and split, that was over the head stay. Then I'd grab the line and they'd drop me off in the dory.

Well, sometimes you get the fish in fifteen minutes, sometimes takes you four hours. Depends. You're just hanging on to the rope. And they're kind of hauling you. He's full of fight. Sometimes you can go fast. There was one kind of scary fellow, he come up through the bottom of the boat with a sword. Stuck up by the side of the boat. He was in there that deep, the sword. There was a weight aft, I went back and got that. Then I come up front and pounded on the sword to drive it out. Then took my shirt off and put it in the hole, so it wouldn't fill up with water. Best I could. It leaked, of course, but I stopped most of it. He was all done then.

Then, you put what they call the fluke rope, put that on the fish. Tie it up to the side of the dory. And then they pick me up. I throw them the rope, then we hoist him aboard. He's still shiny and beautiful looking. They stay that way for fifteen, twenty minutes as a rule. That's it. Then you cut the sword off and all the fins and tail. So that they bleed. And lay them on their backs so all the blood settles right down on their back bone. Then, coming in you clean them.

As you was going around, you might strike another one, put a keg on it with a flag and leave it. Then you go back and find and haul that one. Some of them big boats, they have ten or fifteen out one time. If you got too many out, you know, before you even get to them, sometimes you get one that had a bite taken out of him. Sharkie had a bite.

When that happened, we'd usually cut it up and gave it away. You know, cut that piece out and cut it up for ourselves and give it away.

When I was on the *Hazel M. Jackson* one day we got twenty-eight. Big fish, too. I think they averaged two hundred and fifty pounds. The biggest fish we ever got was four-eighty, I think. That was on the *Priscilla*. I've seen one or two at five hundred somebody else got, but I never got a five hundred pounder. It was off Noman's. Benny Mayhew harpooned it. Now they catch a lot of ten pounders now, on long lines. That's what's ruined the business. And long lines, they catch everything. They're indiscriminate, those hooks. They started long-lining probably about 1949, '50, along in there. They thought there was an unlimited supply, apparently.

Oh, I wouldn't have missed it for the world. Soon as it come January, I was ready to go swordfishing. It was a disease. Yes, it was. It was a disease. Everybody felt the same way.

Everybody looked forward to swordfishing. Oh, it was great fun. God, I loved to look out and see their two fins going along — their tail and their front fin, you know? Man, I shut my eyes and see them now. You ask anybody if they ever went swordfishing and they loved it, really. You've got to like it or you wouldn't go. It's too damned hard an existence, really. It really is.

I don't know of anybody that ever got rich fishing. You could make a good living, but I don't know of anybody ever retired in good shape from fishing. I really don't. You know, when you go fishing, you think you're going to get rich, but you don't. Then you think you're going to starve to death, but you don't do that either.

*Interviewed 1998*

## MARGUERITE COTTLE
b. 1919 • Chilmark
Homemaker
Conservationist

# I Like to Think Ahead All the Time

## *Growing up on the Bassett Farm in Chilmark*

I grew up on the South Road. My father was John Bassett. He was a farmer and he owned a lot of land off Tea Lane, on Middle Road, and South Road. He used the South Road land for farming. He grew up there. Now, all the Bassetts seem to have left the Island, most of them. Norton Bassett was an ancestor and he came back, but he was the only one. My father, he went west — they all went west — and he was out in Oregon state and Washington for quite a few years. But his mother got into financial difficulties and he came back to save the farm and to help her.

My mother was born in England. She was married before. I believe her husband was in the Navy and he died. And she had this little baby boy, so she came to this country with a sister or aunt, we never were sure. She lived around Boston and then she got a job with the Blackwells, who came down to Chilmark in the summers. And she met my father. So I had a half brother, and then when he was eight, she had my sister. And when my sister was eight, she had me. By that time she was forty-five and my father was fifty-five.

When I was young my grandmother lived with us. My grandmother and grandfather went to California in a covered wagon. They were going to raise sheep. She didn't tell me much about it. She used to talk about Californ-I-A. She would tell about the roses she grew there. She brought some of them back in a bucket. They said they wouldn't grow, but they grew and we all have transplants from them. It's a rambler and it was quite a large, pink rose and very fragrant. She had a green thumb. She had a beautiful garden.

Oh, we had quite a farm. It was at least a hundred acres. It was on both sides of the road. My father had cows, and the sheep, and oxen and the horse. We had ducks. There were turkeys. He used to sell turkeys, ship them off-Island Thanksgiving and Christmas. I remember him crating them up. I suppose Bart Mayhew picked them up and took them to the steamship wharf.

My father had a wonderful garden, potatoes and corn and carrots and beets and all the vegetables. Of course, he used to grow field corn, too, and lots of stuff. He had a little plot separate for me. I always had a flower garden. I always loved to plant flowers. And not a weed would show. And we had apple trees and pear trees and cherry trees. Beautiful cherries. Well, of course, the cherries didn't keep. We'd eat them as soon as they ripened, but my father used to have barrels of apples down cellar, and they'd last all winter. He was great for Russet apples.

My mother used to have lots of chickens. She used to sell eggs and raise chickens. The mailman would bring them, and those chickens would arrive and she didn't have an incubator. She had a big box, and in the middle would be a stone jug with hot water for warmth and had blankets all around them. It kept them warm anyway.

And then there were hens. She had her chickens and raised those and the hens. People would stop by and buy the eggs. I used to gather eggs in the chicken house. Had a pet chicken.

My father took care of the cemetery. Did the burials and did the mowing. He used to go up there with the old horse. I used to be able to drive the horse and wagon and, you know, we'd get to that cemetery and that horse — I guess he was tired from climbing Abel's Hill — he would just drop in the traces. Lie right down in the shafts. He was just tired. He was all right. He just rested.

And my father used to fish Chilmark Pond. He used to seine it for perch and used to ship the perch to New York. He put them in barrels, and they must have gone on the steamship. I remember the seining, pulling the seine net around. And I remember when my mother, if there was any smelts, she would get them and cook them up in the frying pan, the spider, we called it. I never hear that fish mentioned now.

My father used the horse for haying. The field, it's at the foot of Abel's Hill on the right, and you can see through there now. That was a hay field, the whole thing. There were nice marshes then around the pond, down by Chilmark Pond, right down by our house. That was salt marsh hay that they used a lot. The marshes, they're practically all gone now. We used to mow that. Now, of course, you can't touch the marshes. But they used to mow them. And I used to stow hay in the wagon. Ten cents a load I got. It all went into the barn. It was a beautiful barn. The '44 hurricane took it.

We had a woodshed. And there was a corn crib, but it burned down because my father was smoking herring and it caught fire. But it used to be full of ears of field corn.

We used to take the ox cart to go berrying out on King's Highway. It was quite clear then. There was nice berries, blueberries. And my father used the oxen for getting wood and hauling rocks when he was making stone walls.

We did a lot of walking. My mother and I used to go to West Tisbury a lot to visit people, but we always walked. We never had a car. We'd walk to Chilmark Center. They used to visit a lot, visit back and forth. People don't do that so much anymore, you know. And when I was a teenager I used to walk up to Menemsha to visit with friends and go to the beach.

When I was a teenager I worked at the Blue Barque. It was a tea house on the South Road. The Cavert sisters had it when I worked there. There were three sisters, Cora, Mae and Helen. Helen had a shop in Oak Bluffs. Cora had this tea room and Mae helped her. And Leitha was the cook. I always liked her. She came from the South. She was a wonderful cook. Cora had a tea room out in the little barn and she sold gifts, too. Dishes and things. I have some. A few things I still have, including one of, well, he was supposed to be King of England, but he abdicated. The Duke of Windsor.

I'd work about two or three hours or I'd work nine or ten hours. It depended. Sometimes she'd have a dinner party. It was a four-course dinner. And apt to be lobster. At tea it would be little tiny sandwiches. Sometimes it was lobster, sometimes cucumber, you know, little things like that. And small cupcakes. Or sometimes it was cinnamon toast with the tea. She had nice things. Nice china, a silver teapot.

The people who came there were very nice. Mainly the ladies from Edgartown like Emily Post and some of those people. Got a lot of those. We got some men, but it was mostly women. They would have card parties sometimes in the big house. All women. I suspected that they were gambling, but I wasn't serving. Leitha took care of them in the house.

We always had summer people, you know, and there were some rich people who used to come and buy some of the products from the farm. They were always very good to me, gave me things, gave us things for Christmas. And I never resented it. I mean, I never felt that they had everything and I didn't have very much. Never felt that way. I must have known I wasn't rich. The big cars and the chauffeurs, and I had an ox cart.

I always was a bit of a homebody, I guess, and I liked to keep house. I kept house for my father after my mother died. When we were married we lived with my father. He was all alone. There was an awful lot of things we didn't have, but we managed. You made do, you know. I didn't even have an ironing board. We used to have a little blanket and a cloth and laid it out on the dresser and ironed. We had flat irons. We'd put them on the hot stove, the woodstove. Had a dry sink. You had to cart all your water outdoors. Great big tall pump on the floor. The pump was taller than I am. Heat your water on the stove. Wash everything by hand and had two babies. Did that. Didn't have anything. No electricity. No running water.

You know, I like to think ahead all the time. Don't want to go back. Don't even want to think about it. They can have the old houses and the outhouses and the kerosene lamps and all that. Anybody wants it, they are welcome to it. I don't want it anymore. I like the easier living.

*Interviewed 1998*

## MARGUERITE COTTLE
b. 1919 • Chilmark
Homemaker
Conservationist

## ERIC COTTLE
b. 1917 • Chilmark
Fisherman

# A South Roader and a Cricker

## *Two Chilmarkers Chat*

ERIC: Well, we grew up together. Went to the same school, just like my parents. She was a grade or two behind me, but we went through grammar school together. Then I went to high school and the next year or two she come down. Went through high school together.

MARGUERITE: I don't remember you especially in grammar school.

EC: I remember you being around there, but that's all I remember. I wasn't interested in girls.

MC: We didn't get to be friends until high school, did we?

EC: Yeah.

MC: Different parts of town. The towns were kind of divided, you know. There were South Roaders and North Roaders and Crickers.

EC: Didn't get along too good.

MC: No, no. It wasn't so much with schoolchildren. But some of the grown-ups.

EC: When there was shellfishing up in the Pond, the Crickers thought the Pond belonged to them and the guys from the South Road had no right to be there. They were madder than hell; they didn't want them up there catching their scallops. But they paid taxes just the same. They had just as much right. So the Crickers wouldn't pay much attention to them. They kind of ignored each other. But you go to town meeting and somebody from the South Road proposed something, those from the North Road and the Crick, they said, "No way, we won't go for that." And somebody from the Crick proposed something and the South Roaders says, "No, we're not going to vote for that."

MC: The Crickers and the North Roaders wouldn't get along either.

EC: Well, none of them got along too good. Kind of clannish.

MC: Yeah, there was different factions. Of course, I had a favorite North Roader. That was — wasn't Welcome, wasn't Zeb...

EC: George Fred.

MC: George Fred Tilton. Oh, I thought he was wonderful. When I was a kid, you know. Well, he paid lots of attention to me, I suppose. I was just a little kid. And he knew I had five or ten dollars in a New Bedford bank, so he was always going to go rob the bank, get my money. It was stuff like that. You know, he was full of fun. And he used to tell some pretty good stories. One was, they wanted to fix the North Road because it was just ruts, pretty poor travelling. So he got up in town meeting and he said the way the road was now, when two cars met, they just exchanged cars, went into reverse and kept going. That was the kind of humor that he had. You remember that?

EC: He sounded like that. They were some family, them Tiltons. I knew Zeb, George Fred and Welcome. There were those three. Don't remember the rest.

MC: You remember William.

EC: Yeah, he lived down here summers.

MC: He was our neighbor down on the South Road, he and his wife Rebecca. They were a great old couple. She used to make the best fudge. My mother and I used to visit them.

EC: We started going together after I got out of school. She and my sister were in the same class. And they were practicing for graduation, so I'd take them down there and go pick them up. First, I'd leave her off and bring my sister. Then I said, "This is dumb." Then I'd bring my sister home and take her home!

MC: That was when we were still teenagers.

EC: Well, I was going down there every night when they lived on the South Road, and I stayed there until half-past eleven or twelve, half-past twelve, then I came home. Coming home one night, I says, "I think we better get married and I'll stay down there! Don't have to come clear back to Menemsha every night." So the next night I went down, I said, "We gotta get married. This is bizarre! Me riding back and forth to Menemsha down here every day." Well, we decided to get married.

MC: When we were married we lived with my father. He was all alone. And then we had two sons. And when my father died in '46, we moved to the Crossroad and the old farmhouse was sold. We didn't have the money, my sister didn't have the money to work on it, you know. It needed some — it needed a rich man, it really did. And I didn't marry a farmer, I married a fisherman.

EC: No. All I ever wanted to do was go fishing.

MC: Well, you helped out at the farm a bit. I can remember them going, rounding up the sheep and shearing them.

EC: I remember, I helped him one or two years. Pen them up. Then you had to take them out of the pen after they were sheared. Took two or three people to do the job.

MC: We had some blankets made from the wool. Where did the rest of the wool go?

EC: Sent it off-Island, I think, same as Arnie Fischer does.

MC: And then the ox cart we used.

EC: Carting hay.

MC: There were horses for that.

EC: He used the horses for that, huh?

MC: I stowed the hay for ten cents a load. I remember my father building a stone wall. He used oxen to pull a stone boat that carried the rocks up next to the wall. I remember being fond of the oxen. They were very slow, moderate creatures, you know.

EC: Some strong, though. They were strong. They were slow and steady. They'd move ahead slow where a horse was liable to jump, you know? They used to use them to move houses. They moved a lot of houses on the Island.

MC: They moved a lot up here.

EC: They moved houses from Chilmark to West Chop. A lot of houses around here were moved from one place to another. Planks and rollers, with a pair of oxen. Of course, them days they could go down the road and when it come night, they unhook the oxen and go home and leave the house there, right in the middle of the road.

Nobody going up and down the road. I'm told they moved quite fast. They get a gang of men, just move the rollers, keep laying the plank and put the rollers, the plank and rollers, and the oxen just kept plodding along. They moved quite fast and moved quite a ways in a day.

MC: And they moved the Coast Guard Station over from Cuttyhunk.

EC: I'll tell you, it was interesting to look out and see this big building coming across the Sound on a barge. It was quite a feat, really. It looked some strange to look out in the middle of the Sound, here was this great big house floating across.

MC: It was a beautiful day. There was a big crowd down there on the jetties.

EC: They had a tractor to move it when it came ashore, of course, instead of oxen, and went along, moved the plank, then the rollers, the plank, the rollers. Took it up where it is now. That was after the war, in the '50s.

MC: By the Second World War, we were married and had the two children. There were the blackouts. You know, it was pretty dismal. Eric was in the fishing industry, and they never called him because they needed the fishermen. So I was down in the old house with my father, and Eric was fishing most of the time. He was away a lot. And at night we'd hear the planes going, searching for saboteurs on the beaches. You couldn't go on the beach. Were we allowed on the beaches during the war?

EC: No, they were patrolled. Patrolled clear around the Island as far as I know.

MC: The beaches were patrolled by the Coast Guard. And they would take turns coming down through. They were looking for saboteurs all the time. There were always rumors going that they were coming ashore. And there was a summer man who wrote a letter to the *Gazette* complaining about the noise of the planes. And I thought, "Gee, it helps me to keep my sanity to know that there's somebody around watching out." I can't imagine why he felt like that. I think they were patrolled constantly. And Eric had to have a pass to get even on the dock.

EC: We had to go to the Coast Guard before we went out, report to them and report to them when we come in. We'd usually go for three or four days at a time. So when we went out, they looked the boat all over and when we come back they'd search again.

MC: It was scary. Of course, I was young, you know, and there were rumors. We never knew what was true and what wasn't because it was just rumors. They claimed that saboteurs were coming ashore.

EC: They claimed they did, but I don't know. They sunk one or two submarines off of here, or so they said. Boy, it was some dark. They cut the lighthouse, the power to the lighthouses way down, you could hardly see the lights. You couldn't have any light shining on your windows. It was all blackout curtains. I used to go out and patrol up on the North Road, make sure nobody was on the road who wasn't suppose to be. I'd go up there, sit in the car and see a car coming, I'd stop them. Find out what they were doing out. Had to have special dispensation to get anywhere.

MC: When we were first married I remember we used to play cards a lot. And go dancing.

EC: Oh, yes. Many times. We used to go dance once a week anyhow. Over at the Tavern. Just this side of the schoolhouse. They used to have dances every Thursday. Once they had it year-round, dances every Thursday night, nine to one. They had a lot of midnight dances, starting five minutes past twelve and going to five minutes past four.

MC: Oh, that was fun.

EC: Yes, 1935 to '40.

MC: And in the '40s.

EC: Oh, yeah. Albert Huntington played the piano. Osborne Tower played the saxophone. Brownie played the drums. They had more, but I don't remember. There was four or five pieces, yes. Had a nice orchestra.

MC: There was that fellow that worked — did he work for Eddie Cottle? He used to play.

EC: Oh, yeah, the two of them, the brothers, the Baptistes, Lester Baptiste and Snooky Baptiste.

They played trumpets. No, trombones. They played trombones, they did. Oh, it was always a good orchestra.

MC: They'd do fox-trot, waltz, polka. All kinds of dancing. Two-step.

EC: Except square dancing. I never cared for square dancing. When I dance, I want to hang right on and dance. I loved to dance.

MC: You're being recorded! Oh, dear!

EC: I love to dance. Well, before we was married, one week, Christmas week, I went every night of the week. Went to Gay Head, went to Edgartown, went to the Katharine Cornell Hall. Used to go there, didn't we? Dance there, and then the Odd Fellows Hall in Oak Bluffs, torn down now. Tivoli, used to go dancing at the Tivoli. All over the Island dancing. Loved it.

MC: They had a lot more dances than they do now.

EC: Oh, yeah. Probably went more after we was married than we did before. We used to go every night, every Thursday night over to the Tavern. We lived right there on the Crossroad. I used to start fishing about half past five in the morning and I'd fish 'til five o'clock or six o'clock in the evening and then I'd go home and clean up and have something to eat and go dance at nine o'clock, dance until one o'clock, and then go fishing next morning half past four, five o'clock.

MC: Lots of energy. I'd go dancing with him, always. The dances, yeah. But not the fishing.

EC: No women went fishing then. Wouldn't have a woman aboard a boat. Claimed it was hard luck.

MC: There were some women who was fishing back then.

EC: That was Ingrid. Ingrid Olsen. Come down with her husband swordfishing from Block Island. I think that was the first one I knew aboard a boat. Then Gus and whatever-her-name-was. They were the next ones, I think. There wasn't very many. I wondered how they was going to make out. But they were all right. They were good. Marguerite went with me lobstering once and never wanted to go again. Boring, she said. Too repetitious. Haul a lobster pot, turn it back, go to the next, haul it and turn it back. Haul the next one.

MC: I was thinking of all the things I could be doing at home.

EC: She didn't enjoy it at all. I thought she'd enjoy it. She didn't care about it at all.

MC: I like the water and the boat, but it's kind of a long haul. No, I'm a farmer, see.

EC: And I'm a fisherman. A South Roader and a Cricker. When we were in grammar school she couldn't stand me and I thought she was terrible. I don't know what happened.

*Interviewed 1997*

## MILTON JEFFERS
b. 1922 • Edgartown
Blacksmith
Artist

# From a Little Different Viewpoint

## An Island Blacksmith's Childhood on Chappaquiddick

I was born on Chappaquiddick. My mother was Bertha Belain. My father was Lawrence Jeffers. My mother was a Belain from Gay Head. She was John Belain's daughter. There was six girls and four boys and my mother was the third oldest. There was a woman down Lower Main Street in Edgartown. She was a great-aunt to my mother, name of Webquish, and she had a restaurant down there. I guess she got kind of old, and she was still running the restaurant, and it was quite a chore for her. So she told my mother's father if he would let one of his daughters come down and work with her in the restaurant, she would leave him the property. So my mother went down and my father used to come in there to eat. And that's how they met.

Anyway, shortly after that, the old lady, instead of leaving the property to my mother's family like she'd promised, she sold it to somebody else and moved to New Bedford. And my mother never got any money for all that work. She never paid her any wages or anything, so it was just like slave labor, you know?

My father was a woodworker by trade. Very talented with tools. Give him a piece of wood and some tools and he'd make something that would almost talk back to you. Very talented. His mother was a Gay Header, too. She was William Jeffers' daughter. She had these two children and she died quite young. And then his Aunt Lydia Jeffers Webquish of Chappaquiddick brought him up.

My mother's great-uncle, Joe Belain, was a whale man all his life from the time he was, I guess, twelve or fourteen years old. He died in New Bedford in 1926. He had been retired for years. He was an old, old man. And when they brought him to Gay Head and took the body into the church for the services, this pigeon flew in from the sea and landed on the hearse. Sat there all during the funeral services. When they brought the body out it flew out to sea again. They thought it was a very singular thing and there has been a lot of theories on

what caused it. They wrote about it in *Ripley's Believe It or Not*. I don't think we'll ever know, but it was a very singular thing.

When I was young, Chappaquiddick was far different from today. There was very few people even in the summer. I think there was only about fifteen or twenty families that came down in the summer, and in the winter we were the only family of children that went to school from Chappaquiddick. God, acres and acres when I was a kid was wide open, and now it's all grown up into woodlands. There wasn't any houses, and there was more roads than there is now because the old-timers had rode their horses and oxen all through the woods and swamps. You would take shortcuts and go all over the place. A lot of them I still remember. But you could go anywhere you wanted around the fields and pick beach plums and grapes and blueberries. Nobody ever bothered you. You'd go down the shore and dig a bucket of clams and quahogs and go swimming, and nobody ever bothered you. Today, you can't go off the road three minutes without somebody screaming at you. One of them told me one day — we were out trying to pick some beach plums — says, "This is private property. We pay big taxes and we don't like to be disturbed."

There were only two farms when I lived over there. There was Tom's Neck Farm. They had a big herd of sheep and quite a good-sized herd of cattle, and they used to have a big vegetable garden in the summer. They used to butcher the sheep and sell lamb and eggs and vegetables and milk. Then Jerry Jeffers' grandmother, Sally Jeffers, she had a farm. She raised her own vegetables and she had cattle for milk, and she used to put on clambakes and dinners. There were certain summer families that used to eat there a lot, suppers and things. My mother used to cook some for her in the summer, pies and stuff. My father built a building down on the shore for her, a big roof with a kitchen building and then all tables in under there. And you could sit right there on the edge of the pond and eat. Very pleasant. And down on the beach they had a big cement slab. We'd build a big fire on it and get it smoking hot, and then clean off the ashes and put rockweed on there and put clams and lobsters in there, and cook them right on top of that. And they served right down there. She always put on good food, boy. I never heard anybody complain. She did pretty well there, I guess. I think she was somewhere around one hundred when she died. She told me herself that her parents were slaves.

All they had for a ferry when I first remember was a rowboat. You would ring a bell and the old fellow would come over on a rowboat and pick you up, bring you across, and bring you back; a nickel each way. A fellow name of Jimmy Yates. Nice little guy. When I first remember, he used to bring the cows across. One guy would sit in the stern of the rowboat and they put a rope around the cow's neck and Jimmy would row across and the guy would hold the rope to keep the cow's head out of the water. And they would swim them across, cattle and horses. Lead them up on the other side and drive them up the road.

My sister and I, we'd walk home from there after school night after night. About three, three and a quarter miles. Quite a hike. I still remember it. It was all open, that wind blowing across. It was cold. And we'd be hungry and tired, and it seemed like if you lived to get home, you'd live forever.

When I first started school, I didn't know a single kid in the first grade. None of them. I never came to Edgartown except with my mother to go shopping. The first couple of days I might just as well have been up on Mars. The whole thing with school was a total new thing. I didn't know what school was all about. And because I was dark-complexioned and didn't know anybody, they used to gang up on me and make fun of me and push me around. And I'm a pretty easy-going sort of guy. I used to look at them and think, "What gives with these guys? What's the matter with them? I got no hard feelings toward them." But they used to keep it up.

So I told my mother about it and she had the same problem when she came down from Gay Head. So she says — she called me Miller — she says, "Miller, you're going to have to fight, that's all, or they're never going to stop it." Well, it went on and on, and I didn't fight. And one day I came home and my shirt or something was ripped. My mother says, "All right," she said, "when you go to school Monday morning, and those kids start picking on you again, which I'm sure they're going to do, and you don't fight back, when you come home Monday night I'm going to give you another beating." My father was sitting over behind the stove in the rocking chair, he leaned right around and he looked and he says, "That's right." He says, "That's just what's going to happen."

I had all weekend to think about that one. So, I went to school Monday morning and I pretty well set my mind what was going to happen. We used to have recess from ten-thirty to quarter of eleven. We would go out and run around and play tag. And I was standing in the building all by myself and up comes four of them. Well, they took one of the kids and gave him a push and says, "Hit him, he never fights." So he hauled off and he smacked me on the arm. And then it was over. I let fly and hit him in the face, hard as I could, and knocked him down, bloodied his nose. He got up and ran off squalling and bawling. I turned around and looked at the other three, you know, and off they went. I never got any more trouble.

In the summer my mother used to cook and clean for summer people and my father used to do carpentry work and things like that. And then he'd go scalloping. Sometimes he'd go swordfishing. He did mostly shellfishing, clamming and quahogging, and some bluefishing and bass fishing. Of course, in those days, there wasn't any rods and reels. You used to heave and haul. You used to buy this, what they called beach line. It came in long skeins, you know? You had to rig it up, and they used to use these big, long lead jigs. I guess they weighed, some of them, six to eight ounces. He always made all his own jigs. They used to take and wind the thing overhead and throw it out. And they'd coil the line down like that on a stake, and then they'd walk it in along the beach. He used to do quite a bit of that.

Most of my fishing was in the harbor for mackerels because I wasn't big enough and strong enough at that time to heave and haul it down at the beach, but I used to do a lot of mackerel fishing around the point of Chappaquiddick. Same thing, only we used a much smaller jig, but it was the same principle. Heave and haul, yep. We used to get them, though.

Before they opened it up where that Kennedy bridge is now, the water in Poucha Pond was brackish. It wasn't salted. It was chocked full of white perch. God, tons of them in there! We used to go down there when the tide was running in, and I guess they used to come up in there and get the bait. And almost as fast as you'd drop your line down, *wham!* You'd haul out a perch. In the spring there was a nice herring run there. Used to go down there in the spring and get herring and eat the roe and things.

But they said there wasn't salt enough to grow clams and quahogs, so they opened it up. And they killed all that. The perch all went off. It was a great pond for duck hunting because a lot of brackish water plants used to grow in there. And the ducks used to come in and the geese — killed all that. And the cranberry bogs all around it, the saltwater killed them. Full of blue crabs and flounders, all gone, when they opened it up. It has just never been the same. It wasn't all that good a move, I don't think.

We always had a big vegetable garden because my mother used to can dozens and dozens of jars of string beans and tomatoes and piccalilli and even used to can chickens. We had a lot of chickens in the fall, so we'd kill them and pick them and everything, and she'd can those in jars. And she used to put up these blueberries and blackberries in big quart jars. She'd make pie out of them, or dumplings, or we'd eat them just plain with our dessert, you know. So it didn't really cost us that much to live because we had chickens to eat and we went clamming and quahogging. We had rabbits and wild ducks. So, we always had plenty of good food to eat, but money, forget it.

It used to get cold in those days, bitter cold. My father used to sit up to one or two o'clock in the morning and keep the wood fires going, because it was a big house and, boy, it cooled down fast. A lot of times I'd get up and there'd be that much ice in the pee pots in the morning. I was fifteen years old before I ever took a bath in a bathtub. It was real life. We just thought nothing of it, you know?

There wasn't much to do at night. That's how I started drawing. I used to do a lot of drawing. I'd walk around and look at things in the fields and woods and I'd draw them.

When I graduated from high school, I won a scholarship. I'd been drawing for years, and my art teacher in high school was quite hopeful that I would pursue it. But even with the scholarship I just didn't have the money. And so, these friends who used to come summers to Chappaquiddick, I asked them how I could use the scholarship. They're the ones that suggested I take up the metal work because at that time there was only one blacksmith in Edgartown, Orin Norton. He must have been in his sixties then, and they said, "Somebody's got to take his place." And they got me into Wentworth in the welding course. So I've been the blacksmith here in Edgartown for many years now.

I've been kind of thankful that I was born on Chappaquiddick. It gave me an outlook on life I don't think I would have ever had if I'd been born over here in town. Used to go out in the fields and do a lot of thinking, and I've always been kind of glad I did.

And my father was a lot that way, too. He had a lot of ideas and I used to spend a lot of time weekends walking with him. We used to go walk around the beaches and fields, and he taught me a lot about the history of Chappaquiddick and things. It gave me an outlook on life that's different from most people. I had a chance to sit back and draw my own conclusions, you know. I've always been very interested in philosophy and metaphysics, and having lived that way gave me a chance to kind of step aside from the orthodox things and look at something from a little different viewpoint.

*Interviewed 1998*

## SIDNEY HARRIS
b. 1911 · Chilmark
Engineer, Farmer
Inventor, Stonewall Builder

# I Knew All the Paths

## *Growing Up at the Chilmark Brickworks*

I was born here on the place in 1911, in the old farmhouse. It was an active farm then, but it used to be a brickyard. It was a local venture. William Mitchell had a small yard, then the Boston Fire Brick and Clay Retort Manufacturing Company bought it and expanded it. It was about five hundred and some odd acres that they owned outright, and they bought maybe a thousand acres of mineral rights. And they made bricks and they shipped clay. They had a wharf off there and they used to dig kaolin clay and ship it to Boston. The kaolin fires at thirty-six hundred degrees and the wood wasn't hot enough to fire it so they used to bag it up and ship it. But they made red brick down here. The red brick is made out of the blue clay. They call it gardener's clay. The red bricks they shipped to Providence and Fall River and New Bedford. Most of the mills were built from the bricks here.

My grandfather bought this place right after the Civil War. That's when the Boston Fire Brick and Clay Retort Manufacturing Company failed. The economy was bad. My grandfather was the president of the Atlantic Bank in Boston. They took the mortgage on all this property. But the economic conditions were such that the bank couldn't sell it for what the mortgage was. So he finally took it over. He paid about twenty-five dollars an acre for all the land and the mineral rights. The brickyard had kind of run down, so he hired people to restore it. He wasn't in the brick and clay business, but he rebuilt the brickyards. So he got it going again, to give people employment around here. He built a bigger chimney — maybe too elaborate a chimney. He spent quite a lot of money on it.

My grandfather used it as a summer place, the old farmhouse. And they had a house in Chilmark, up near the Town Hall. My father as a boy used to come down, but for only a few years after the Civil War. Then he went west.

On his way west, he spent some time down in Florida. He was a botanist and did a lot of research on how they used plants down there. He found that the Seminole Indians used the root of this plant and made starch out of it. And he sent it up here, and the Sunshine Biscuit Company used it for starch in their cookies and crackers.

He went to Texas and was in Texas from 1870 to 1898, I guess. He was deputy for Judge Roy Bean. He had a general store out in Pecos. And the cowboys would ride in town, fire guns and like that. They used to get drunk, you know, and get wild. My father used to get out there with a broom and scare the horses away. And they used to round up people robbing stagecoaches and things like that, ride out and catch them. There were trials there. I guess they hung some of them. They didn't have too many laws to follow. The judge made up his own rules. But I guess he was fair.

Then my father left Judge Roy Bean and worked at the Howard Ranch in Texas running sheep. He bought sheep up just east of Little Rock and drove them down to Pecos. Then the sheep that they wanted to get rid of he drove from Pecos to San Francisco. Sold them to the whaling fleet.

It was around 1900 that he came back. He never said why. And he came down here to take care of the place. He started raising sheep first. And then he started the clay works, the China Clay Company. It was an experimental company. He went over to Cornwall, England, and learned how they processed the clay. He did that because the brickyard didn't have any fuel at that time. There were no trees left on-Island. They cut all the chestnut trees that were on the Plains. Of course, a lot of them died because of the blight, but they used the wood off the Plains.

So he processed clay. He took the sand and mica out of the clay. And it was finer than talcum powder. They just washed it and bagged it. He had buildings and tanks, and he used to get water out of Roaring Brook and wash it. And he had a building that had a furnace — put steam through to dry the clay out. They shipped it off-Island. They put another dock down there on the Sound. Zeb Tilton used to take a lot of the clay to Boston. They used it in chocolate creams until the FDA prohibited the use of it. He ran it up to about the First World War, and then shipping got bad because of the U-boats around here and all that. Then there was the labor shortages. So they just stopped.

After Dad got through with the clay he raised wheat and stuff. And sugar beets, because in the First World War there was no sugar. It was hard to get food, so we raised our own. We had three cows, a pair of oxen, a horse and the sheep. He had five hundred sheep on the place at one time, and turkeys. My father used to hatch eggs in an incubator, raise them for Thanksgiving. Some of the Indians in Gay Head used to come down and pluck them.

Dad was very friendly with the Indians. A lot of the Indians worked at the brickyard, and they lived down here. All this land was Indian land. They had a mid-line from Waskosims Rock to Menemsha Pond. All the land in Chilmark north of the midline was once Indian land. It was all bought from the Indians. Most of them moved to Gay Head, but in my father's time they used to come down through here to go to Lambert's Cove for the winter.

Some of the Gay Headers helped with the ice harvest. There's a pond up here on the hill. It was a kettle hole. When I was a youngster, I used to run the oxen and pull the mud out of the pond so the ice would be clean. They had a drag, a scoop that they pulled in the pond with the horses, and then the oxen pulled the mud out. They used to do it in the summer, just put in a few days and pull all of the mud out. Anyway, they would cut a hole in the ice and saw it out into blocks. The ice was just for the family.

And there was a room in the ice house where we kept all the milk. Most of the food was either kept in the ice house or in the spring. I had to run down to the spring to get a lot of stuff. And I used to fish, go down before breakfast and throw a line

in and catch a flounder. And we would dig clams and catch lobsters. I used to take the rim of an old wagon wheel and put a net into it. Put bait in the middle and drop it down in the bottom. Let the lobster crawl into the middle of it, and then you lift it up slowly and pick him out. You'd put down two or three of them, and go from one to the other. If it's a calm day you could see the bottom. If it was a rough day, you had a box with a piece of glass on it. Then you could look down and see.

Yeah, we'd find all sorts of strange things along these beaches. When the *Port Hunter* was sunk off Vineyard Haven we had a lot of leather vests that used to come ashore, and candles for the soldiers in France, and soap. I picked up a lot of that.

And there was rum running along here. It was usually miserable nights that they would bring it to shore. They used to come right down through this road here. They had these bamboo poles, about twenty feet long, with a flashlight bulb on top and a battery on the bottom, and they used to signal with them. They would have people stationed from where they would land the boat all the way up through the woods, so they knew where they were.

I knew all the paths. I didn't have to have any light to travel around. I used to go out there with a .22 rifle and shoot at the lights. And they started shooting back at me! I had to crawl through the swamp there. I wasn't particularly scared. They were only shooting at me when they heard the gun go off. My mother was worried about what they were doing.

When I graduated from high school, one night I came home late and I met a couple of these men in the road here. I had a Model T Ford with the headlights set up on the fenders. They went up to me and they said, "Put your lights out." And I said, "Why?" They took out a gun and shot out both my headlights!

I went to high school in Vineyard Haven. I used to ride down on a bicycle. I had to start, maybe, at seven o'clock and get there at eight. Earlier, I went to school down here on the North Road, to the Cape Higgon school, and I used to walk down there. On the way there, I'd stop at

Rebecca Manter's. She lived over where Cagney bought. She was getting old. I used to get her a pail of water, then I'd walk out back here to the North Road and down to school. At school, the boys used to start the stove, and the School Committee cut the wood. My father was on the School Committee for a while. And Gil Hammett and Ernest Flanders. I guess they all donated wood for the school. There was a girls' door on one side of the room and the boys' on the other. And the only time they met was when they came down to recite in the front to the teacher. We studied while the other grades were reciting. You learned what the older people were taught, so when you got in that grade you had the answers.

After this school closed I went to the Chilmark School, and most of the Chilmarkers used deaf and dumb language. They were all conversing by hand signs during exams and I didn't know what it was all about. Everybody was giving information to everybody else and the teacher didn't know it. She didn't know the sign language because she was from away.

We used to go to the store at noontime, and some of the people who were deaf and dumb would be sitting there playing checkers. We wouldn't hear a sound. And people who came in the store would make all the signals and get their groceries and pay for them, and not a word spoken. When a fishing boat was coming into Creekville – Menemsha was known as Creekville then – they'd go out on the dock and watch it come in. A man with a spyglass told everyone on the dock just how much fish the boat had caught, and what they had caught long before the boat got into the Creek. The summer people couldn't understand how he knew. No radio then. But they had all the information before they got ashore!

*Interviewed 1995*

## Dorothy West

b. 1910 • Oak Bluffs
Writer
*Gazette* Columnist
Active in Harlem Renaissance

# I Think Writing Is a Compulsion

## *Writing on the Vineyard and New York*

My father was born a slave; he was freed when he was seven. His mother had been a cook in the "big house." And my grandmother — I never saw her, she died before I was born — my grandmother went to be a cook in a boarding house. She sent my father to what they call the open market to get fruit and vegetables. And then it was that he began to be interested in buying and selling. He would do errands for the boarders and do many errands for this particular man who stayed there. And this man taught him how to read and how to write and so forth, you see.

Well, then my father, as I told you, fell in love with buying and selling. When he was ten years old at Christmas they had got their presents and he said to his mother, "I have so much money" — I'm very sentimental about cigar boxes because my father saved his money, when he was a boy, he saved his money in a cigar box — "and how much have you?" And she told him. And he said, "Let's have our own boarding house." So then they rented a building and then my father, he had to go to the market and buy all the supplies and foodstuffs.

Then he came north to Springfield, Massachusetts and he set up an ice cream parlor. It was rather extravagant to go to an ice cream parlor. Only ladies went, I mean, well-to-do people. You dressed up that particular day and so forth. So my father had that store and then he had a fruit store. He was always a fruit man.

My father loved horses. When he was maybe thirty-odd years old, now he's got a little money, and there was a race horse that was retired; he was old. My father bought that race horse and named the horse Ned. To this day I love horses, because my father would tell us about Ned. He didn't race it, of course. He hitched it to a buggy. My mother was fourteen years old. She was at the ice cream parlor with her aunt, and saw this man — she didn't even know who he was, of course. And he didn't

even notice her because she was a young girl and so on and so forth. But she saw this man with a race horse. And she used to say that he went around the corner on two wheels. Well, they eventually got married and moved to Boston.

He became a very successful businessman. When I was growing up, he had a big fruit business in Boston, buying and selling fruit. And my family would come here every summer. I had my first birthday in Boston, and then the next day I came to the Island. I have only one summer that I did not come here — I was in London or Russia, I think, or someplace. But that's the only summer that I missed. And now, of course, I live here year-round. I write for the *Gazette*, you know, my Oak Bluffs column; I was the cashier at the Harborside, and I do my own writing. This is where I can write.

I had a very good mother and father. The point of my saying that is because my mother and father were supportive of me. Everyone said I had my father's brains, whatever that means. But because my father was a businessman, some of my family were very disappointed with me. I'll never forget an aunt of mine said to me, "This is the only thing I'll never forgive your mother for, because she let you be a writer." Of course, she meant, she let me be a poor writer; if I had only been a businessman!

I remember the biggest quarrel my mother and father ever had. Well, not the biggest, but I remember this quarrel very well because I remember my mother and my father, their mouths fell open. I'd never seen mouths fall open.

They had decided I was smart, and my father said I was going to be a little businesswoman. And my mother said I was going to be a pianist. Then they argued back and forth. My father said, "She's my child." And my mother said, "She's my child." And I'll never forget — I was five years old and I looked at my father and I said, "I don't belong to you." And I looked at my mother and I said, "I

## LEONARD VANDERHOOP
1896 – 1989 · Aquinnah
Patriarch Gay Head Wampanoag Tribe (Aquinnah)
Deacon, Gay Head Community Baptist Church
Selectman; Fisherman; Caretaker for Squibnocket Farm

# The Old Ways

## *Gay Head Life, Neighbors and Ways*

In my father's day, he used to tell, when Gay Head was a district, before it was a town, everyone lived down on the south part of Gay Head. The main highway — Old South Road — was down, down below where the road runs now. And the Old South Road always had a gate. When you came up to Gay Head you always had to open and shut gates.

They had a pasture where everyone could turn their animals out. At a later date, they had a North and South Pasture. And they had wild horses and animals they kept. At a certain time, after it got warm from the winter, they would say, "Turn out your animals to pasture." They kept a fence up which everyone worked to maintain and kept the cattle in one large group.

Then there was another pasture they called East Pasture. When it was a district — I've heard my father tell about it — down in the east above Menemsha Pond on the west side. They had a pasture they would tend, plant and plow in community. Well, they didn't call it community then, but everyone planted together large acres and acres of Indian corn. Everyone joined in, and if you didn't join in and help and cultivate the corn, well, you wouldn't be able to harvest any. But everyone worked together.

They used to have a mill up here where the parsonage is, but that was gone before my time. They used to take the corn down to Manter Mill, down on the Roaring Brook in Chilmark. And I remember the boys who used to ride the ponies down, said that Mrs. Manter, Rebecca Manter, "Oh," they said, "she is a lovely woman." She'd always have some goodies, cookies or something made to give to the ones who came down with the corn. They'd put corn in bags and sling it across the horse's back to carry it down. The mill would take a percentage out for grinding it, and give them back the rest. And then they'd bring back the meal in their bags.

There were Indian ponies, wild ponies here. If you went out and lassoed a pony you could have it. They had the Indian ponies here for years that they claimed were the toughest horses you could get. I remember the last three or four Indian ponies. My Uncle William had one named Bess, and Aunt Pia Diamond, she had one named Major. Deacon Jeffers had one named Hornet. Old man Aaron Cooper, he had one named Nancy. And I remember when my sister Polly and I used to want to go down to play, down to Cooper's or down to Belain's. He had that old Nancy out there in the pasture. You know, that crazy thing wouldn't let us go by — blooming thing would bite! If she was there, we always had to go way out around the wall, you know. Seemed to know we was afraid of her. I guess, the last one I remember was down on Tuckernuck Island. And Bart Mayhew down Chilmark, I know he bought him off of someone. They went down to Tuckernuck Island and he had a terrible time, but they finally caught him. He used to drive the stage from Chilmark to Vineyard Haven, and he claimed that he was one of the toughest horses he ever had. He named him Tuckernuck.

Now Pilot's Landing, when I was young, that's what we called the steamboat dock over north. The boat came in around nine-thirty or ten and stayed 'til about two, two-thirty. The Pavilion was down there where the boat landing was. That was for the people, if it was bad, rainy weather, or if they wanted to rest there, they could. And the ox carts would be backed up to get anyone who wanted a ride up to the north gate of the lighthouse. The ox carts had two wheels with a seat on this side and a seat on that side with backs on them and all cushioned, you know. It would take two, four, eight, about ten people, I guess. They would charge them ten cents for the ride.

They'd get a big kick out of going over the stones, you know. And, of course, the great wheels would go this high and then bump down and the

**LEONARD ATHEARN**
b. 1918 • West Tisbury
Farmer
Antique Car Enthusiast
Raised and trained oxen

# They Lived Off of the Pond to Quite an Extent

## Tisbury Great Pond People

I grew up in this house. This is my mother's family's property. It's been in the Look family for, I think — I'm the ninth generation on the Island — I think it's about five or six generations we've been right here. It never was a big place, particularly. I own about twenty-five acres. It's grown up a lot — the woods down this way was all open as far as you could see. The Spaulding place was always right in plain sight until just a few years ago, you know. And down that way is Arnie Fischer — James Look lived down there, was my mother's uncle — and you could see that house very plainly. So, it was all much more open until, oh, twenty years ago. It's kind of depressing now, the way things have grown up so. I've kept my land open, but the rest is all grown up.

The Look bunch that lived around here on the Tisbury Great Pond, they called them "Pond People." They would go fishing in the winter, seining herring and perch and catching eels in the winter, and shooting ducks. In those days when my mother was young, you could shoot ducks and geese commercially and sell them for meat, you know. And they would ship off barrels of ducks. A lot of them went to Boston to hotels and such places. And then they would get shellfish out of the pond. They lived off of the pond to quite an extent.

And then my grandfather did some farming, he had sheep, and he did a lot of teaming too. Teaming was like trucking now, but in the days that they did it with horses, they called it "teaming." The Teamsters Union started in the days when they had horses, of course. Anyway, he would do jobs for people, go to Vineyard Haven and bring freight up.

My grandmother was from the Nickerson family. They didn't go way back, but I think she was the third generation that lived here in West Tisbury. She grew up at the corner of County Road, where that bungalow with the hip roof is. It was a post office when it was first built. There was another old-fashioned building there that burned and they replaced it with that building. Originally it was my grandmother's father and mother that had the post office, and after they died, Phoebe Cleveland took it over. She was the postmistress when I was a boy.

Diagonally across the street was Gifford's Store, and that was a grocery store, a general store. So right in that area was the main center of West Tisbury for a number of years. Up at the Alley's Store, that was kind of at the outskirts of town. We always told about "going over the brook" that "so-and-so lives down over the brook." Like being on the wrong side of the tracks, depending on which side of the brook you were on!

By this house we had a well. There's no water in it anymore, but it was quite cool down there. We'd hang things in buckets to keep them cool, eggs and milk, a few things like that. But there were so many things that you keep in a refrigerator today that you'd never think of putting in and out of storage in those days. You'd just eat it and use it.

Now, my father wasn't a farmer. He worked as a plumber. We had cattle for milk, mostly, but once in a while we would butcher one for meat. But not often, it didn't pay to process your own meat that much. My parents bought it mostly from the market. They got it from the down-Island stores, Bangs' Market in Vineyard Haven. When I was a boy, they used to run what they'd call a "meat cart" up-Island. You know, a car would come up maybe twice a week and go from door to door with meat and some groceries and stuff. Howard Downs, Connie Leonard's father, drove, and he was a good friend of my father's. They were about the same age and grew up together in West Tisbury. He would come in here and talk with my father. They were both very interested in sports, and they would read the paper about baseball and prize fighters and talk back and forth for quite a while, and people were waiting for him on the route while he was sitting and talking about sports!

Of course we'd get fish. One thing we used to have was eels. That's one thing I miss terribly, you can't get eels around here anymore. My mother usually cut them up in pieces, and fried them up and we'd eat them like playing the harmonica. There's other ways to cook them — in a chowder — but she didn't seem to branch out much from that.

When I was young, my father and I used to go some, but by that time the eels had begun to get more scarce. They used to be able to go for a day, or, you know, several hours, maybe a day's work, and get a barrel full in the old days. There were certain parts of the pond that you'd be more apt to catch them than you would other places. Usually up in the coves is where they were, not in the big part of the Pond so much. We went down to Town Cove a lot, that was a pretty good spot. Used to get enough to eat there whenever the ice was good and we wanted to go.

We used spears, cut holes through the ice. They would go into the mud, you know, in the winter and sort of hibernate there, and that's why you would get them with a spear, spear into the mud and come up with them. You jab around through the hole in circles, trying to cover as large an area as you can. If the eels were thick, you'd get an eel almost every jab. If they weren't, it might take ten or fifteen minutes to get one. They get caught between the tines of the spear — you can feel them wiggling. You haul them up, then lay them out on the ice. They wouldn't wiggle away, they get kind of frozen up on the ice. Of course, you've got to have enough ice to walk on. Sometimes people would go when it wasn't all that safe, and it was nip and tuck whether they made it or not.

It is kind of a vicious sport. I never cared much for fishing, but I did enjoy eeling. You had to suffer to catch those eels — it was cold and windy out there. My mother had a drawer of woolen mittens we would use when we went out eeling. Those woolen ones would get wet and freeze up good and keep your hands warm.

Other people would fish for eels in the fall with what they called beach pots. They had these fences — weirs they called them — that guided the eels to the pots. I never did this, so I don't know all the particulars, but they'd set them in the fall, when the eels were looking for a way to get out of the Pond. And if the beach wasn't open, there was no way out, so there would be these accumulations of them there waiting to get out. So that was when they would catch them. Always at night, it seemed.

Daniel Manter's father and some of the others, years back, owned shacks down at the beach. They would go down and live there for a few days and nights while this eel fishing was going on. It was a little camp, right on the beach around Quansoo, down near Crab Creek. They call it Crab Creek now, used to call it Black Point Creek. There was a bridge over that creek, you could go over it with a horse and wagon. There were two or three of these shacks or camps, and they all got washed away in the '38 hurricane.

Gunning and sport fishing in those days was a big thing. My great-uncle Jim Look built his house — the one that Arnie Fischer lives in now — and he took in hunters. He raised and trained tame decoys, Canadian geese, that they'd send out, and they'd lure in the wild ones. They'd shoot the wild ones and keep their own. His yard was always filled with these tame geese. They called them "flyers." They'd nest along the marsh there, and when we'd walk down to visit my uncle, all along the road the males would come after you, hissing. They were patrolling to protect their nests.

Course, I always had access to the Pond. Most of the people that lived in this area were all relatives of each other. There was no problem getting permission. But, you know, you hear people talking nowadays, they say, "Oh, when I was a boy you could go anywhere you wanted to." Well, that isn't so. Everything was private property, always was, but the owners just didn't care so much about people walking across their land. And as I say, most of us had relatives that had Pond property, so we had no problem. But the people from down-Island that wanted to go to the Pond had to get permission same as they do now.

But the big thing when I was young was the eels and fish and gunning waterfowl. The Pond was used for food. They'd seine perch and herring in the spring and winter, and put them up in barrels — barrels and barrels and barrels of them. And they would truck them all the way to Edgartown and Vineyard Haven to ship. The herring went to the fishermen who would buy them for bait for the Georges Banks, fishing for halibut and stuff. White perch, they were seined for food, great eating fish. They'd ship those to Boston and New York and places where there were fish markets and stuff.

The herring and perch would come in certain times, if the beach was opened up at the right time. The herring, when I was in grade school, used to come up all the way to the Mill Pond, by the Garden Club there. There was a pool there which they've let all grow in again, you don't even see it anymore. But down just below the dam, just below the bridge, there's a pool there, and it would be full of herring in the spring. And we kids would go in there, take our shoes off and go in there and drive them up under the road where it was shallow and catch them by hand. I don't know why they don't come anymore. But I have an idea, too, that it's because the Pond isn't regulated as carefully as it used to be, opened at the proper time, you know, when the herring want to come in. They used to make a kind of business of it, regulate the salinity and open it in time for the fish to come in.

But I remember when I was big enough to work down there, it had gotten to the point where the only reason they opened it was to satisfy the people that had camps around the Pond, so they wouldn't get flooded, you know. And we'd go down and open it by hand with shovels, which seems like an impossible job, but it can be done all right. But before, years back, they used to open it with horses and oxen with scrapers.

When I was a kid there were very few pairs of oxen around. There was always a few, two or three pair up in Gay Head, but they were rare. Mostly horses in those days. What I remember was tractors for farming and horses. Even horses were going out, with a great deal of tractor work being done. But for certain kinds of work that they needed done, they

did use oxen. Around here the trap fishermen used them quite a lot, in Menemsha and over to Lambert's Cove, to pull out the nets. My Dad worked for a trap fisherman up in Menemsha and he brought the oxen home and kept them for the winter. He used to plow snow with them. He had a big wooden V plow. I remember he took us to school with it one winter, over my pasture and up by where George Manter lives and up that way to school.

My Dad was through using oxen by the time I was big enough to know anything about it. But I was always interested and wanted to have some. I think I had seven or eight pairs all together. I never used my oxen for anything that was useful, really. I kept them for the fun of it.

I'd begin to work them as small animals. Try to teach them what "Whoa" means for the first thing, and go on from there! And I taught them to be tied up in the barn, and halter-broke so you could lead them around. Then very soon, I'd put a yoke on them because, really, they're easier to handle, two together, than they are one at a time. When they're real small, they wanna play and jump around, and if they are together they kind of hold each other down to some extent. And you start in a very small area, fenced hopefully, and start gradually, that's all. It takes a year or so to get them what they call handy, but you can always train them some more, no matter how long you have them.

I only had one pair run away and they were probably a year old or better, when I hitched the cart to them for the first time. They didn't like those rattling wheels behind them and their heads went up in the air and they started going faster and faster. Well, it was quite a thing, but they finally got fetched up on a tree and I got them calmed down and put them away for the day. The best way I found to deal with anything as drastic as that is just to ignore it. There's no way to reason with them so you just start the next day as if it didn't happen, that's all.

*Interviewed 1995*

# NANCY WHITING

b. 1925 • West Tisbury
West Tisbury Librarian
Founding Member of Martha's Vineyard Community Services

# We Had a Chance to Influence People

### *Five Vineyard Women and the Civil Rights Movement*

Kennedy was assassinated in '63, November. Well, that was when we voted into existence a branch of the NAACP here. We went ahead and did it that day, even though he'd been assassinated, thinking that was an appropriate thing to do on that day. And that had been in the works for a year. Henry Bird, of course, is the name that comes to mind right away. He was then Rector at Grace Church. Henry Bird was involved in the Southern Christian Leadership Movement with Paul Chapman, Harvey Cox and others.

The person who really helped us start the local branch was Kivi Kaplan. He was the Chairman of the Board of the National NAACP, and very active and helpful telling us how to go about it. The original cast was an odd mix, us good liberal kids, a few blacks — the Tankards were very involved — the clergy and some people from the Jewish community.

At that time, some of the people I knew here on the Vineyard were following Martin Luther King's course closely, and enormously interested and hopeful about it. His relationship to politics and religion and non-violence was really terribly exciting. Henry and Paul started going down to Williamston, North Carolina — the place that we wound up — joining with the civil rights activists to protest conditions there. These were people we knew, we saw them here on the Vineyard. It was so real. We wanted to do something to help from here.

Well, I guess when I say we, I mean Virginia Mazer, because she's my closest, oldest friend here. She had come to the Vineyard with her husband, Milton Mazer, who had just started the mental health clinic. And Polly Murphy and Nancy Smith. They're sisters. Peggy Lilienthal was the other person that was so heavily involved. And she was really the wildest of all of us. She was very dramatic, and that was her mode of being. Certainly Virginia and I were on the shy side, and tended to be understated and oblique in our natural states, but we were also passionate about fairness and peace.

Virginia and I always talked about what was happening to the world. Virginia had been active in protests in New York against bomb shelters. With the formation of the NAACP and our thoughts about what we could do, a momentum grew. It just built up. It's almost like a saturated solution. You know that process in chemistry? You use a vehicle of liquid and you begin to drop a substance in drop by drop, and when it holds all it can, one more drop and the whole thing crystallizes. It was like that. So that it was no one thing. It was the gathering sense that we could be of influence. And that's what led to the trip to Williamston.

For a whole year before we actually went, and certainly for a year after, our relationship to these people in Williamston kept growing. They came to visit us. We raised a lot of money, and they came on a bus and they stayed in our houses, and we had a prayer meeting in the Old Whaling Church. There was a man named Golden Frinks, he was here. One of King's organization leaders. He was funny, a marvelous salesman, very attractive, jazzy kind of guy. He urged us to come, told us how they were having boycotts for unfair labor practices, so people were not working, and they had no money for food and clothing. He said how much help it would be.

I'm sure it was Peg who said, "Hey, let's go for it." And I think each of us by then knew that we might. And then there's the challenge, the excitement of it. As someone said, "You will drive them absolutely wild. Five women from the North. You must wear white gloves and get dressed up, and it will just drive them wild." We didn't quite do the hats and gloves, but we were very clear to wear dresses and not be slouchy.

I can remember packing my suitcase. It was supposed to be that we weren't going to jail. We were just going to take the food and the clothes and the might do it. I remembered about Pleasure Highway 13. I remember being in the car and being aware of wanting to get as far away as fast as we could.

Afterwards, I think we felt we'd been empowered, we'd been strengthened. That's one of the great pleasures of it, because you really lose your sense of self-consciousness. You are a part of something. That changes your own boundaries. And then within the group itself we were all so terribly different. We were temperamentally very different. There were all these interactions going on. I think that's the miracle of it all. We pulled it off as a group, to be absolutely true to each other, and that each of us knew independently absolutely not to speak for the whole group.

I know that when we came back — I was at that time the tax collector in West Tisbury — and I thought, "I don't know if this one's going to fly." Of course, I'd been elected, duly elected, but I thought, "Well, there is such a thing as impeachment." And the first time I walked into the office, which was then the old police station, after we got back, there was Nelson Bryant, the chief selectman, and Charlie Tucker. "Listen, tell us about it. What was it like?" They were all excited. I was just stunned.

We were prepared for the worst. It was a radical thing for us to have done this at that time, from here, a sort of apolitical, insular sort of place.

That summer, the Williamston people were back here — that was the Mississippi summer when they killed the young civil rights workers. And the whole New York and Boston intellectual community was right there with our NAACP efforts. By this time there were a lot of people involved, certainly the liberal summer community was totally into it. There was a concentration of power and money for this effort. It was just when the movement itself was snowballing, too. So it was an exciting time.

And the Civil Rights Bill passed into law. I remember finding myself astonished to be sitting up there in the Tabernacle in chairs alongside of Roy Wilkins, Kingman Brewster, Kivi Kaplan, all these important people. There we were in this wild, larger-than-life kind of thing — the feeling that a person or group of people can have a real influence and effect on the course of events.

*Interviewed 1993*

# Land a Big Swordfish

My boat, the *Venture*, a lovely wooden sloop, I used to skipper her for her owner, Davenport Pogue. When he bought a big new power yacht, why, I bought the *Venture* from him. He gave me easy terms. No interest. And I was taking out fishing charters to help pay for it.

I had quite a few charters out of Menemsha for swordfishing by hook and line. Not harpooning. The Holy Grail of a sport fisherman is to land a big swordfish, rod and reel. And they had big heavy rods and reels. And I fixed up a chair in the middle of the cockpit that would swivel around. And we would sew up a big hook inside a mackerel. When we'd see a fin, we'd maneuver around so that the mackerel we were towing would pass in front of the fish, and sometimes the fish was suspicious and wouldn't be a bit interested in the dead fish. But others would. Several times we hooked a fish, but they were able to get away by pulling the hook out of their throat. They're very powerful, strong swimmers. Well, they're just one big bunch of meat, all muscle.

I remember one guy. He was so disappointed that he wasn't able to use his very expensive rod and reel. He wanted to show what a good fisherman he was. So he said, "You a good swimmer?" I said, "Yes." He said, " I could bring you in alongside with this rod and reel in five minutes." And I said, "I'll bet you ten dollars you can't." So, he tied the line onto my belt, and I went overboard and got a good distance away from the boat. And then, he yelled out, "Okay, that's far enough. That's all you can have. Now, I'm gonna bring you in."

See, one thing he hadn't figured on, was the swordfish, if he's hooked, it's attached to his head. Whereas I was only attached to my waist. So I could maneuver. And secondly, I could watch him, you know. When you're reeling in a fish you pull the rod up until you figure you've got some slack and then you lower the rod quickly, and take up the slack of the line, as you're lowering it. Well, I could watch him. The minute he lowered that rod, I lunged away from him, so he didn't gain very much. He tried and tried to reel me in, but he couldn't do it in five minutes. I won the ten dollars.

*Pat West*

and my brother and I went occasionally with him when he hauled his traps there and at Tarpaulin Cove. And then we walked across Naushon to Kettle Cove and he hauled them in there. And that was a great deal of fun.

My first awareness of the Island was these summers of lonely and delightful paradise out in the open country. And the neighborhood was very open and green and sunny and beautiful.

And we reached the Island then, leaving New Bedford on one of the old sidewheelers. I'm not sure whether I ever came on the *Monahansett* or not. I could have, but I know I came on the earliest *Martha's Vineyard*. Those sidewheelers were interesting. The older ones, the *Monahansett* and the *Nantucket* and, I think, the *Gay Head*, had a shaft going crossways from one paddle to the other across the main deck, and it was that shaft that turned the paddles. All the passengers had to get out by way of the freight deck, so you'd have to walk and duck under the shaft. But when the *Uncatena* came, she had it so that you could walk over the shaft. It was lower.

I remember Charlie Osborne, who was the ferryman here at Edgartown, one of the old-timers, and he was on his wedding trip. And he had a tall silk hat, plug hat, and he didn't duck far enough. He was a little nearsighted anyway. The trip was sort of crippled because he bashed in his hat, not ducking far enough to get under the shaft.

It took about two hours to get to Woods Hole, and half an hour from Woods Hole to Vineyard Haven or Oak Bluffs. Oak Bluffs was then called Cottage City; the name was changed in 1907. Then, to drive up-Island we usually got a horse from my uncle, Captain Cromwell, who had married my mother's youngest sister, my Aunt Emma, and we drove up on the State Road, which was very recently built. And it was constructed of what they called water-bound macadam. It was a white surface. Didn't know anything about the blacktop then. Except that I think in Cottage City they did have tar roads, because I remember that on a very hot day you could pluck some of the tar out with your fingers and make a little ball of it. We enjoyed doing that.

But, anyway, there was this drive up-Island. It took an hour and a quarter behind this old farm horse, a retired farm horse, to get from Vineyard Haven to our house, which was soon named Fish Hook. My father always explained it by saying it was the end of the line, which, of course, it was. Gradually, we gave up driving up-Island behind a horse. Walter H. Renear, who was also the sheriff — he had kept a livery stable and that evolved into a garage — we went up in the Ford cars with him.

The nearest post office was at North Tisbury, in the building that was until recently the Red Cat Bookstore. On summer nights we would walk over the hills — it was about two miles over through the woods to the post office — and sit there on the stoop in front, waiting for the mail stage to arrive. In my earliest memory it was driven by two horses, a two-horse team. It was driven first by Fred Mayhew and then Bart Mayhew, and they would take the two horses off at North Tisbury, cross the road to the barn, which was the Mayhew barn, and replace them with fresh horses to drive on towards Gay Head. And they'd bring the mail in, and Lillian Adams, the postmistress, would sort the mail and we would wait there until she sorted the mail. Then we'd walk home again in the twilight, the gloaming.

There was a well-worn path, something of a path, all the way. After dark we could find our way by the feel of the ground on our feet. You could feel the path. We didn't have any lantern or anything of that kind. We didn't need it.

I don't know whether it was warmer in those days, but we could go swimming all through October. We went swimming on a beach just west of Cedar Tree Neck, and it's just east of the present Seven Gates Farm, which was owned then by Professor Shaler. I remember seeing him once on West Chop wharf, a very tall man with white hair and a white beard, and my mother told me that if he spoke to me I must be sure to call him sir. But he didn't speak, so I was not put to that trouble.

We would go to Vineyard Haven perhaps once during the summer to get a haircut and we'd get ready to go the night before. Have everything ready, we'd be bathed and dressed in our good clothes, and the horse would be ready. Then we'd lock the house and we'd drive down to Vineyard Haven to visit my aunts and get a haircut. And often we would go to Cottage City on the trolley, which was still running. It ran until 1914, and then they took up the tracks for metal for the war. But that was quite a thing.

They were open cars, and they went rocking along merrily from Vineyard Haven, across the Lagoon bridge into Cottage City, where my grandmother had a cottage — on the Camp Ground, Number Seven, County Park. She was a very religious, delightful old lady, but very religious. I'll never forget one Sunday we spent there. We couldn't do anything, because it was Sunday. All we could do was take a walk. Couldn't even read a book unless it was a Bible.

So that was the paradise in which we grew up. I still have it, through all that has happened since. That's what remains most vividly, is the Island of my boyhood and my youth. I'll never lose it.

We came to Edgartown to live in 1920, took over the *Gazette,* and it was on the second story of a building which then stood where the Harborside Liquor Store was until later. And it was pretty primitive. All the type was hand-set and had to be distributed, and the press was bound together by wire where it was broken. It was shimmed up by pieces of wood and so on, and it was turned by hand.

That whole staff consisted of Mr. Marchant, who was our predecessor as editor, an older girl, Leona St. Pierre, and Mr. Marchant's daughter, Elizabeth, who was somewhat younger. And then we soon added a pressman or compositor, whose name was Ezekiel Matthews, and he was a Lancashireman, came from England. And he came into the office, I remember, and he saw the two girls working at the type cases, and he said, "Ah, so you have female comps here!" So we did. We had female comps. And that was rock bottom. And we went on from there.

Because it was everything. And nothing. There was nothing that we could continue with. We had to plan to replace everything. So we bought a linotype the first year, and a year later moved to a build-

ing next to where the *Gazette* is now, but that building was very small and has since been torn down. It was years of struggle. But the *Gazette* was old, established, so we were stepping into a routine, and we had to carry on from there.

The thing to do would be to discover the needs, to discover the characteristics and what the local newspaper should represent. And I did have some general ideas as to that. This all sounds so pompous and deliberate, and it wasn't that way. It was all just from day to day and spontaneous. The whole thing was very flexible and dynamic. And we worked such long hours that we had little time to think about theories. It was mostly practical decisions from week to week. But we soon got the idea of following the seasons of the year.

The Vineyard was so uncrowded, and there was a rhythm, and the round of the seasons illustrates that. It was not one of these clamoring, intensely competitive places, as it has become with all the excursion lines and all that sort of thing.

There would be the period of summer when the summer people came, and so many of the men who owned boats would become boatmen and take parties out, or lease their boats to summer people for the summer. Then would come the fall. It would be the harvest of such agriculture as there was, and the Agricultural Fair. Some of the exhibits were marvelous, the vegetables that were grown, and the livestock.

It was quite a period. Then as the fall came on there'd be the cranberries and the wild grapes. And then in winter the fishermen would go out maybe hand-lining for cod or on the Island fishing for eels, spearing eels through the ice, if there was ice. And they would harvest ice from the ponds to store in the ice houses to be used in the summer. Then with the spring would come the planting again. Then the boats which had been hand-lining in the winter were fit for swordfishing, and so on into the summer.

But other than that it was just the application of such principles of newspaper work as one would know after growing up in a newspaper family, and after being graduated from the Columbia School of Journalism.

## LORRAINE ARMITAGE
b. 1916 • Tisbury
Printer and Photographic Technician,
Mosher Photo, Tisbury

# We Moved to Indian Hill

## The Farm, Locust Grove School, and Fifty Years at Mosher Photo

I was born in Vineyard Haven. My father was Benjamin Norton, and my mother was Anita Smith.

My Grandfather Norton owned that property that was Hillside Farm on the Vineyard Haven–Edgartown Road. He sold it to Mrs. Burke from Edgartown, who had a turkey farm there. And then it was sold for the seniors' places.

He did a lot of stonework down to West Chop, and he had horses with those big drays, they called them, and he'd go to work with that dray every day. And they used to say that his horses — he had two horses — had been back and forth so many times that he'd sit down and go to sleep and hang the reins over the edge, and the horses would take him where he was going and bring him back home. He'd sleep all the way, both ways. But he'd start out early in the morning, of course. His whole life was work, and he'd go early in the morning, come home late at night, and, I guess, go to bed and do the same thing over again the next day.

My mother was an only child. Her mother was from the Chilmark Cottles. Her father's name was Louis Smith, and he was always around the water. He was a pilot for many years and piloted boats over the shoal, they used to call it. There were boats that would come from foreign countries and didn't know the waters around here. He'd take the boat into Boston or wherever they wanted to go. That's what the pilots did.

My father worked for Seven Gates, and we moved up to West Tisbury — Indian Hill Road. We lived at what is now Arrowhead Farm. Seven Gates provided all their help with homes. That was part of their salary, I guess. Their salary wasn't so big, but other than food and clothes, that's about all you had to have because they delivered wood for your heat. Seven Gates' men cut the wood and delivered it, horse and wagon. And you had your own gardens and everything, you know. You grew vegeta-

bles. We had cows and we sold milk to the half dozen neighbors around, especially summer people.

My father milked the cows before he went to work. I'm sure my brothers probably helped him, but I don't remember any of them getting up that early, because by seven o'clock he was gone. When he'd come home at night I'd watch for him, and he'd come through the fields. There was an opening, like an arch of trees, and then when I'd see him come through there, I'd run and meet him. Because he always would save us something in his lunch pail, so that the first one who got there got whatever it was.

My father did most everything over at Seven Gates. He did a lot of masonry work, stone walls and like that. And I remember that one of the people that lived there, owned there, had an English garden built. They had somebody from England come, and my father worked with him all the time he was here. And he worked in the dairy, and I know they all worked come haying time. Some of my brothers worked there when they got old enough to work, too, in the summertime.

At our house, everything was cooked on the woodstove. Mother was spoiled. My father always got up and got the fires going and he'd go out and milk the cows while the house was getting warm. And come in and make the coffee and then he'd call her. My father always raised hogs, pigs, and the young beef, too. They'd always be cut up and put away, and we'd have that in the wintertime. We had our hearty meal at night. We'd always have meat with it. We'd have vegetables of all kinds with it, and there was always a big pitcher of milk sat on the table. And I never drank any of it. It's just that I didn't care for it, that's all. The only thing I ever drank milk with, that was when I'd be down to my grandmother's. I used to stay down there weekends quite often, especially after I got into high school, because there was no social life up on the Indian

# ERFORD BURT

1898 – 1994 • Tisbury
Boatbuilder, Owner, Burt's Boatyard, Tisbury
Marrried to Alice Burt

# I Started Building My First Boats

## An Island Boatbuilder and Designer

I started building my first boats in the attic of the Seven Gates Farm dairy, where they processed the milk. The great big attic up there was doing nothing, sitting idle. My father was the manager there, so he let me. I'd buy lumber and put it up there. And I started in when I was very young, building rowboats, skiffs.

I had been in and out of boats, working in them, the bigger ones. Working around the fish pounds and so on with my uncle, Obed Daggett, on the North Shore. I spent at least four years working for him there — when I was between, I suppose, fifteen and nineteen, maybe. He had his fish traps over in Buzzard's Bay and we went back and forth every day in a boat. That's where I got a lot of my boating, in all kinds of weather.

We went in a boat built over on the Cape somewhere. It was lapstrake and she was thirty feet. She was a big one, and we had a ten-horsepower motor, one of those two-cycle jobs that you have a pin you pull out of the fly wheel. You grab hold of that and you pull it up and you try to get it to start. If it ever backfired, it could break your arm. And, I mean, this pin sticks right out and it has a spring to pull it back. I used to run the engine entirely all the time. I worked for him because he wouldn't have anything to do with motors. So I was the engineer. I've had a lot of experience on that job, believe me.

We'd go almost regardless of weather, during the summer season, you know. I can remember a storm we had. My father had a fish trap up at Robinson's Hole right alongside of the opening into the bay, under that high bluff. We had a little trap you call a bass trap. It was one of the smaller type. I went over with my father and I was a little youngster. I was just five or six years old, I suppose, at the time. And Mr. Daggett had traps down by the French Watering Place, which is just above Tarpaulin Cove and the lighthouse. And then Otis

Luce had traps over there somewhere, I can't remember where his were.

I remember we'd all pulled our traps in the morning, and this hurricane came. They didn't call them hurricanes then, the way they have since, for some reason or other, but it was a dilly, and we all took off for Woods Hole. We tried to keep track of each other going down. We had to go slow. It was awful rough and my father's boat was the smallest of the lot. His was only, I think, it was sixteen foot. It was a yawl boat, same as on the back of the sailing schooners. It was converted from that use and had a motor put in it, and it was my job as a kid to try to keep it bailed out. He had a lot of fish loose in the bottom of the boat, so it made it hard to bail because it was full of flounders in there. But I'd be bailing and my father, of course, was watching like a hawk to keep it under control so we wouldn't get knocked over or something.

We got into Woods Hole and I guess it was getting worse all the time. That night, of course, we didn't try to come home. And I remember sleeping all night in Sam Cahoon's Fish Market, up in the loft upstairs, with all the empty barrels and boxes, you know. And the rats were running around like crazy. Had me half scared to death.

My father had a friend over there somewhere, and he got invited to stay for the night, but he left me there. Mr. Cahoon's father, I think, had a room near the office. So he was in the building, and I slept on some boards laid across some barrels. I suppose that was to keep me off the rats. I remember he went up to town and he bought me some candy and I remember what kind it was. It was the little chocolate-covered nuts. Chocolate almonds, I guess. So I had those to munch on. I could sit there and I could hear the foghorn going down at the point, Nobska Lighthouse, banging away all night. Some things you don't forget.

When I first got married, I went to work with

## ELISHA SMITH

b. 1923 • Oak Bluffs

Farmer

Chairman, Conservation District of Dukes County

President, M.V. Agricultural Society; Member and Director, Rotary Club

# I Guess I Knew Just About Everybody Who Lived on This Island

## Farm Life at the Head of the Lagoon and Thereabouts

I was born in the town of Oak Bluffs, up at the head of Lagoon Pond at the old homestead. It's been in my family since John Smith built the house and had the land. He was one of the first settlers here, from the Mayflower, around 1620. So, I was born in the old house there and I was the seventh generation named Elisha in that house. The house right now is over three hundred years old. My grandfather and grandmother brought me up because my father died when I was a little over three years old. They adopted me because my mother was going to leave the Island. George Smith was his name — he was my adopted grandfather, actually. He was my father's uncle, but I always called him my grandfather.

He was a farmer, and he and my grandmother taught me everything about animals. I had my own pigs and chickens from the time I was six years old. I learned how to milk a cow then, too, and they gave me a heifer calf when I was about seven. So I worked, and I had my own horse since I was about ten or eleven. Actually, I bought the horse from a fellow in Edgartown named Mike Cleveland when he got old and blind. Two buggies and two harnesses and he sold everything to me for twenty dollars.

I was up five o'clock every morning, whether I went to school or not. Get out and milk cows — we had forty, fifty cows. Feed the chickens, the pigs, whatever had to be done and eat your breakfast, change your clothes and run like hell to catch the school bus.

I used to have to take a basket of eggs to school every day, five or six dozen. My grandmother would pack them in a wicker basket. At noon time we had an hour lunchtime, so I'd walk down through the Camp Grounds and had customers everywheres there. Quite a few people would live there winters those days. Then I would go up Circuit Avenue,

Kennebec Avenue. I had all the stores: Old Mr. Studley that had the hardware store, Mr. Pearson had the drugstore — the Arcade Drug Store — and he always bought two or three dozen, Mr. Rogers, he was a photographer that lived in the Camp Grounds and Mrs. Barney. She was Ethel Barney, I'll never forget her. A tall, skinny woman and she was real nice to me. Her husband had the coal yard right at the foot of School Street as you go into the Camp Grounds. That was a coal company that he had. Right next to it was the laundry. Old Mr. Nichols had the laundry there. Ernest Nichols. He was another one of my egg customers, too. Eggs were fifteen cents a dozen in those days. This is in the early '30s.

So, then, some of the boys at school would want to come to the farm and stay over the weekend. They couldn't ride on the school bus that I used to ride on. So I would take the horse down in the morning and the buggy. With grain and hay, if there was cold weather, and a blanket to put over him. I'd tie him in the woods behind the Oak Bluffs School. And then, when we get out of school, four or five boys would jump in the buggy and come home. They'd help me around the farm on the weekend, you know, cleaning pig pens, chicken houses, whatever we had to do. And cutting wood and all that stuff. Then we'd play or go down to the Lagoon with a canoe. We'd race across the Lagoon, the upper Lagoon Pond there, and swim, or whatever we wanted to do, after we got all of my chores done. The boys loved it, too, to get out of town.

So, anyway, when I got to about thirteen and a half, my grandfather died, and I've been on my own ever since. I took care of the farm for my grandmother. She lived another ten years after my grandfather died.

Originally, he had around six hundred acres

here. But then the judge in Edgartown was the administrator of the estate — my grandfather's best friend — he says, "I'll take care of the boy," he says. Well, sure did, he sold everything he could. He stole everything he could from me. I had one farm that was still in my name and some of the other property I have right now. The rest of it he sold off for peanuts. And when I got to be twenty-one years old, he called me to his office in the courthouse and he had ninety-eight plus dollars for me, out of all the land he sold off.

It was most of the land all around the head of the Lagoon Pond there, where now the Featherstone Farm is. That was one of the farms that my grandfather on my father's side owned. We have our own cemetery up on the hill near there.

It took in all that land coming up through to the highway, up where I am now and then where ComElectric is, that whole area there, where Goodale has all the trees. Where the Windfarm is, that was part of it, and then where the strawberry farm is, Thimble Farm. That was actually my farm. When my grandfather died, it was already in my name, see. He tried to sell it, the lawyer did, but the court wouldn't let him because it was already mine.

Then the two houses where Tilton Rental is, at the blinker light, that whole area there is part of it. Effie Tilton's house, that's been there way back in the late 1880s. That was my grandfather's Clambake House. That's what he called it. My grandfather put clambakes on all summer, see, and that white house across the street was the clubhouse for the racetrack he had, at what is now Deer Run. He had a racetrack there and people used to bring their horses in and used to sulky race them. A sulky's a two-wheel wagon, you know. The driver sits right behind the horse there and the horse has a harness on it. There's trotters and pacers and they have these harnesses, so they can only pace. They can't put their legs way out because the harnesses control them. They're trained that way, you see, and the driver just has to make them go a little faster, quicker steps, to try and win the race.

At the clubhouse there they sold peanuts and soda pop. That's what they called soda in those days, soda pop. The old steamboats used to come in through the bridge and come up to the head of Lagoon Pond, and there was a dock right there at the dike. That dike was built in 1850 across there to hold the water back at the upper end there, see. And they'd bring the horses up and go to the track. Some of the foundation is still there for the grandstand and the stalls under it for the horses to go into.

I'm not sure when they stopped racing. I found some tickets when I was cleaning out the old farm house. "Girdlestone Park, 1904," it said. "Bicycle Races, Horse Races, Baseball Games!" That was all open land, there was not a tree in sight. There was hay fields there. But the track was there, all laid out. As I got bigger, I used to ride my horse around or my bicycle around it. So many trees growing in there now, and they've chopped the land up so much with houses and everything in there.

Then he had a lot of land in Vineyard Haven across from the cemetery where Trippy Barnes's junkyard is. That whole area back up through there and that house. Then, where the grapevines are, Chicama, up in there and all across the street there. That whole area. And then, going up the Airport Road, where Deer Run is, up there. You know, Barnes Road Extension. That road wasn't there until '43. The Navy built that road from Oak Bluffs through, cut our land in half there. There was only a dirt road that came up to the pumping station from Oak Bluffs.

The pumping station at the head of the Lagoon, and all the places down below, where the waterworks is, that too. My grandfather built the waterworks, put in the pumping station. Before that, he used to pump water in a big tank and haul it to Oak Bluffs to sell fresh water to the people in the Camp Grounds. They had no fresh water. He had a big five hundred gallon wood tank on a wagon. He had four horses to haul it to Oak Bluffs. He used to tell me about it.

The waterworks was built about 1890. My grandfather had worked in Texas for seven years for the Union Pacific Railroad. He was their chief engineer. So he formed a company with his brother-in-law and they built the pumping station. They built everything — the standpipe, run waterlines into Oak Bluffs, the trenches all dug by hand. They hired Portuguese or Italian or Irishmen. They come over by the hundreds to work and they would start, say, seventy-five guys when they start digging the trench. The first guy would take the first scoop out and just keep working forward. There'd be another guy behind the first one and this guy behind him and another behind him. And by, say, the seventy-fifth, they had the trench four feet deep.

Eventually, they sold the company to the Town of Oak Bluffs. It's a nice big stone building, right up to the head of the Lagoon Pond. It's still there, they still use it, too. There was all steam pumps they had, and they used to use soft coal to fire them up to get the pressure up, so they could pump water.

I remember an old fellow from Oak Bluffs, he used to truck in the soft coal in an old Model T dump truck. He could back up, and then it would dump it and it'd go down a chute. Shovel it in wheelbarrows and take it over to furnaces and shovel it in. I remember seeing my father do that. My father was engineer there, starting when he was sixteen years old. They got all electric pumps in there now. I don't know what they ever did with the old steam pumps they had. They took them out, I guess, when they got electricity down through there. That was, I think, in 1934 or '36 electricity got down there.

My father used to deliver milk with the horse and milk wagon, and we'd have the milk in ten-quart cans. We'd start maybe six o'clock at night, maybe seven, after the afternoon milking. Because you'd take it right fresh to the customers. We had hotels and the drugstores, we had two or three of those. They made their own ice cream at the drugstores. And I remember Yates Drug Store, it was Tilton's before then, that would be the last stop at night. I remember going in there with my father when I was only three years old and I'd drag out the empty milk cans and he'd take in the full ones. We'd be eleven o'clock at night delivering milk. They had a regular little ice cream parlor they set up one side, back end of the drug store. I remember the two fellows that worked there, Fat Hutch and Skinny Hutch. The name was Hutchinson, so one guy was a big fat guy and the other a little tiny skinny guy. I'll never forget them. I remember my father'd have a big dish of ice cream and they give me a little dish of ice cream.

As a boy, I guess I knew just about everybody who lived on this Island. There was only about four thousand people here and, later on, my grandfather and I used to do the milk between the three towns. We had all the houses, for darn sake. He'd drive his old Model T and I'd run in, I was this size, running in with the milk. Really helped him, you know. It was glass bottles, quart bottles. And later I did Edgartown, so I guess I know just about everybody around.

*Interviewed 1997*

## MILDRED WADSWORTH
b. 1899 • Oak Bluffs
Homemaker
Teacher, Oak Bluffs

# There Were Hundreds and Hundreds and Hundreds of Lanterns

### One Hundred Years on the Camp Meeting Grounds

I was born April 6, 1899 in what was then Cottage City and is now Oak Bluffs. The name was changed in 1907. I was born in Cottage City in that circle that goes around the Tabernacle. I lived in the Camp Meeting Grounds until I moved in 1925. I'm the oldest of ten children, and I'm the only one left.

My mother died when I was fifteen. It was difficult, much more difficult for my father than I realized until I got older. Because he didn't have money to hire a housekeeper. And we sort of, with what he could do and what the family could do, we sort of just grew, and the older ones took care of the younger ones.

My father was born in Maine and my great, grandfather was a shipbuilder and he had his own schooner. And when my Grandfather Bunker moved his family to the Island here, my great-grandfather brought the family and all their goods and belongings on his schooner and landed over here in Eastville. There used to be an inn where the hospital is now, the Eastville Inn, and there was a pier down in front, on the waterfront there.

On the Camp Meeting Grounds, it used to be much more beautiful than it is now, the grounds were. And all the cottages, so many of the cottages, had wooden washtubs in front of the houses with great big hydrangeas in them. And in the fall they went around with this great big dray and a horse, the Camp Ground people, and picked them up. They painted the name on the side of the tub and put them in the cellar of the Camp Ground building. And then they brought them out in the spring and returned them. So all over, especially the inner part of the Camp Ground, everybody had a tub or two or three of hydrangeas out in front. And I don't know why they took them in, because now you plant them outdoors and they grow. But they did. That's what they used to do. I've seen them, many times, with the dray loaded with hydrangeas, taking them in and out. And then, of course, they had flower beds on the Grounds. Beautiful flower beds.

I loathe the colored houses that are there now. To me they don't belong at all. They belong someplace like Revere Beach. Because in my childhood — they claim that they've gone through coats of paint and have found colors underneath — but I never remember any colors when I was small. And now there's blue houses and pink houses and lavender houses. When I was growing up, the houses that were painted would be white. The trim would be dark green or brown or something of that sort, the trim of the house. But never any colors. It was very, very conservative. You know the pink house? Oh! To me that's an anathema. I hate it. And there were no shingles. Everything would be clapboard. And every house on the Camp Meeting Ground had some scrollwork.

And then the Camp Meeting Ground, when I was very young, they had a lamp-lighter. And he lived next door to us for some years, and he had his little ladder. And every day he'd go out with his little ladder, and his can of kerosene, and rags, and he'd clean the globes. Like the welcome lights you have now, in front of your house, on the post? And he'd go around and clean the lights, put fresh kerosene in. Those were the Camp Ground lights at night.

They had hand pumps in the Camp Ground for water. Today, I could take you around to six or seven places where they had the street pumps. I remember them that well. And they had, you know, a pit, with wooden boards over it, and the pump. People would take their pails, their buckets, whatever, and pump water. They were near the cottages, you know, so people would come and fill up pails of water for their cooking and things. We had water in our house. There was water into the Camp Grounds when I was young, but the pumps were still used.

In the summertime, it was a day wasted if you didn't get to the beach. You just about lived there. You could spend the whole day at the beach. You know, if we went in the morning we wouldn't bother to come home for lunch. I suppose my mother used to worry. She couldn't do anything else but let us go. There was no such thing as babysitters. She had little babies at home and always was having another one. And I, looking back now, I think she must have worried. I think she must have been glad when she saw us come trudging home, you know, to know that we were all right.

The Oak Bluffs beach was very different than it is now, you know. There were rows and rows and rows of wooden bath houses up high, you know, along the shore. And there was a boardwalk the whole length of that. I've had many a splinter from that, too. If you were a tourist and wanted, you could get it just to use for that day or you could rent it for the summer. I think it was seven or eight dollars or something like that. And then each one had a shower that you could use when you came up from the beach. To get down onto the beach you went down through a building. There was a store in there that sold popcorn and ice cream and later on sandwiches, much later on. And there were hot salt water baths. To come up from the water you came up a long flight of steps to the bathhouse level, because they were up on big high pilings. You could walk under them to go into the water from the beach part, you know. And then, of course, it was open beach from there to the wharf and from there on down.

In my day, no one went down on the Edgartown Road to swim. There were big, high dunes. I can remember, after I was married, and three or four of our friends, we used to go down there swimming. We'd leave our stuff on the beach, and go in the water up to our necks and take our suits off. Oh, the wonderful feeling of the water against your body! Taking off those big, heavy bathing suits. Nobody was around, so no one would see us.

One of the pastimes, the summer pastimes, was watching the boat come in and watching the people come off. There was a bandstand up at the head of the wharf when the boat came in in the morning. And for the first boat, the first important boat of the morning, they played while people were coming off the boat. And they'd take a little rest, and they went down to the beach. And down at the beach there was a high platform there; they'd play for the bathers in the morning. There was also the bandstand that still is there in Ocean Park. One of my pet peeves is that they call the bandstand nowadays a gazebo, and it is not.

People walked. That was the thing people did. They took a walk in the evening after dinner. All the ladies with their long skirts and their hats. And there were so many things going on downtown.

We had Darling's popcorn store, taffy and candy and all that sort of thing. Across the street was a hotel, where that corner store is now. Downstairs was a drugstore, an old-fashioned drugstore, with a marble floor and marble counters. Big colored glass jars in the windows.

Next to Darling's was the Pawnee House and next to it was a big fruit stand. It belonged to an Italian man, Mr. Romero — we called him Mr. Romeo. And he had a big fancy cart, horse and wagon, that he'd take around and sell fruits and vegetables from. Very good.

Rausch's Ice Cream Parlor was quite exclusive, very fancy. You could get a dish of ice cream and cookies. It was on the corner where you cut through from Circuit Avenue to Kennebec Avenue.

We had two Japanese stores. One was Ishikawa's and the other was Miyanaga's. And they sold all sorts of Japanese things. Dishes and knickknacks and things. And Japanese lanterns. And Japanese dishes and kimonos and little Japanese dolls. All sorts of little things.

The owners were just here in the summer, but sometimes the boys stayed here and went to school in the winter. And then, of course, the war came and you know what happened to the Japanese people. It was devastating for them because they had been brought up in this country, all the children. The store wasn't opened for two or three years and when they tried to open it again, it just didn't work. But I know they were grieved over — how they were treated. When they were here on the Island they were accepted just like anybody else.

And the Tivoli! Oh, Lord, yes! We danced! It was where the town offices are now. It was a big building. At one end there was a stairway that went up, and it was a great big hall upstairs, with a big, wide porch with a railing around one end and in the front. So after you finished dancing, you could go out onto the porch and cool off, you know. At one time, there were seats around the edge of the dance floor, but they took those away. It was a very popular place. Very popular place. A perfectly respectable, nice place. And they always had a good orchestra there, the same orchestra all summer. I think it cost a quarter. And then you'd dance all evening for that. You didn't have to have a boyfriend to go. You'd go with friends. You'd always meet somebody you knew; you always had plenty of people to dance with. And then every year to open the season, the Rebecca Lodge used to have a very formal ball, and decorate it beautifully. They called it the May Ball. Everyone came from all over the Island.

We went to the merry-go-round, the Flying Horses we called it. And the old man who ran it had a summer home next to the Camp Grounds. And he was a lovely old man, Mr. Turnell. And, of course, he knew our family; he went right by our house going home. It was five cents a ride. When we went we had enough for only one ride. Unless you caught the gold ring, and then you got another ride. And, of course, everybody tried to make up to the young boy who worked for Mr. Turnell. Help him fill the wooden thing, hoping he'd give you the gold ring, because he could. As Mr. Turnell was collecting tickets, he'd let you keep the ticket for another ride. And he'd turn and whisper, "Keep the ticket." He did it all the time.

And then across the street was the skating rink. If you skated, it was about a quarter. And you went in and you skated as long as you wanted to. You didn't have your own skates then. The skate boy was in the skate room. And after a while they got to know you, and they'd save your skates for you. And there again, you didn't have to pay every time that you went. Sometimes you'd go and they'd say, "Go ahead in." So we'd go in and skate for free. But we never, to the best of my knowledge, nobody ever tried to take advantage of it. Nobody ever went unless they had the money to pay, hoping that they would say it. Because they didn't always, but sometimes they would.

The first ice cream cone that I ever saw or had was when I was a child on Circuit Avenue, where that arcade goes through. This man had a little stall there. And he had a big thing of batter. And he had some sort of an electric thing shaped like an ice cream cone. And he used to stick this hot, hot iron thing into the batter. And it would cook it. And he would take the ice cream cone off and fill it with ice cream, five cents. Those were the first cones I ever saw, or heard of. Now they wouldn't let you through the door for five cents!

And the road where you cross over from New York Avenue, between the harbor and the pond, we'd call that Jordan. That was the original name, because the first Camp Ground people who came here came to attend religious revival meetings and they stayed in tents. Then, you know, the tents were gradually built into houses. There was just one house that was still a tent that I remember when I was young. They came on excursion boats, steamers, which landed, you know where the beach club is? There was a wharf there called Highland Wharf. And the boats used to come in there, and in the summer when they had the religious gatherings they used to come from there and walk to where the Camp Meeting Grounds are now. And when they crossed where the two joined down there, they called it "Crossing Jordan." We never thought of saying anything else but crossing Jordan.

*Interviewed 1995*

## JANE NEWHALL
b. 1913 • West Tisbury
Fair Entry Clerk
Church Choir Member
Active in Church and Community Affairs

# Handing Out the Ribbons

## *The Family and the Fair*

I was born in San Francisco in 1913 and have lived there all my life, and on the Vineyard in the summers since 1947. My grandmother, Virginia Whiting, lived in what is now the Old Parsonage Bed and Breakfast here in West Tisbury. She grew up there and loved it, and when she married my grandfather, who was from California, she brought her children back here whenever she could. All their vacations and summers, and so on. She came back once or twice a year. And in those days, it was a long and arduous trip.

This house was built in 1837 by her grandparents, Asa Johnson and his wife, Anna Frances Adams Johnson. He hoped to have a store here, thus the doors onto the street. The basement was to be a store. But that was not successful because what was the precursor of Alley's Store was there next door and used more than Asa Johnson's store. So this house became what they called an ordinary. And the stage that went to Gay Head used to stop here for lunches and things like that. Daniel Webster was supposed to have been one of the people that ate here, at our dining room table. The table is still here, and we tell people to be careful because Daniel Webster ate there.

In the late 1840s, Henry Lawrence Whiting, my great-grandfather, was with Coastal and Geodetic Survey, and he was sent to the Island to do a topographical map of the Island and survey it. He lodged here while he was doing that and fell in love with the Island, and with one of the daughters of Asa Johnson, Anna Frances Johnson. And so they were married and acquired the farm next door, the Old Parsonage Farm. And he had great plans of having orchards and grain and animals and so on. When he was home he enjoyed fixing, arranging for the farm. His son, Johnson Whiting, carried on the farm, my grandmother's younger brother. He and his family lived there afterwards. My father enjoyed working on the farm with his uncle.

Judge Davis, Judge Everett Allen Davis, was brother-in-law to my grandmother and they lived in the house where Allen Whiting now lives and has his studio. It was interesting, we found a little notebook that told about that house being built. I think it was 1879 and the cost was four thousand dollars. Quite a difference from prices of houses today! Because it's a big house, ten rooms or so in it.

My grandmother's greatest regret was that she couldn't be considered a native. Her mother was visiting in Philadelphia, and didn't get back to the Vineyard in time for my grandmother to be born here. She was born in Philadelphia. She said she never forgave her mother for that. Even though she got here at about six weeks of age, she could be an Islander, but not a native.

West Tisbury was a smaller, closer-knit community then. When my grandmother was away at boarding school, they got to talking one night and saying, "Well, now, where are you from and where are you from?" and so on. Some would be from New York City, and some were from here and there. Then they came to her, and they said, "Well, now, tell us about West Tisbury. How big is West Tisbury?" And grandmother said, "Well, just a minute. Now let's see. There's so many so-and-sos, and so many ... Athearns, and so many Manters and so ..." She said, "I guess about seventy-five." So, you did know more of the people.

She met my Grandfather Newhall when she was in school in Brooklyn. He was visiting her roommate, whom he later married. And when their child was about to be born, she said to him, "If anything should happen to me when our child is born, Virginia Whiting would make a good mother for our child." And I guess she had a premonition that she might not make it, and she didn't. And so my grandfather, Edwin Newhall, came east from California and married Virginia Whiting.

The ties between California and the Island are

## ALFRED K. WILDE

b. 1908 • Edgartown

Postmaster and Clerk, Edgartown Post Office

Involved with Masons

# Edgartown Was My Town

## *The Edgartown Postmaster*

I was born August 12, 1908 in Fall River, Massachusetts, and I grew up in New Bedford. It was a cotton mill city, one of the biggest cotton manufacturing cities in the country at that time. I went to grade school in New Bedford. I did not go to high school. It was Depression times. When I got through grade school, I went to work in one of the cotton mills. I put wires on a loom. They called us wire boys. I lasted one week. It was too noisy! And then I went to work in the Pierpont Glass and Silver Shop. That was quite a famous glass and silver company. I worked there six years. But then when the Depression really got going there was no work. People were not buying glass and silver in the Depression.

So I went for the Civil Service. I took Civil Service examinations at different places. Then I came to Edgartown, and about twelve people took the examination. I was number one on the list, so they took the first one. Mr. Alfred Averill was the postmaster. And he took me over to Mrs. Teller's house on Summer Street. And there I stayed for several years, until I got married and got my own house.

I started as a post office clerk. Which meant waiting on the window, sorting mail, things like that. You didn't have the electronic things you have now. You cancelled mail by hand, and you had to sort the mail by hand. You read everybody's handwriting. If you couldn't read the words, you'd recognize the letters. Everybody got their mail, and they got it in their own box. Because there were no deliveries, everybody came to the post office. No matter who they were. The rich people and all came to the post office. Or their chauffeurs came. In those days people had chauffeurs. They came in June. They left in September.

In the little post office on Main Street, you had to stand on Sears Roebuck catalogs to put mail in the boxes. It was a little cramped when a lot of mail came in in the summer time, and especially when the Sears Roebuck catalogs came, thirty or forty sacks full of them. Piles of Sears Roebuck catalogs on the floor, on the walls. Everybody had one.

There would be complaints. But I had no problems when I was postmaster. I had a man come in and he was pounding his fist and giving me this and that. And I just listened to him. And then when he got all through I said, "Mister, I agree with you, absolutely." His jaw dropped and he looked at me, and his eyes widened, and he turned on his heel and went out. The mail was late, it couldn't be helped. He had legitimate complaints and I listened to him. It apparently threw him. He didn't expect that.

I loved the Santa Claus letters at Christmas. I answered all those, when I was postmaster. Previous to that they weren't answered. But when I was postmaster, I taught them, "You see any Santa Claus letters, you put them on my desk." And I answered every one of them. Maybe they weren't too well received on the other end, but I answered them. "I'll see what I have in my bag for you," and "Maybe we can get that." You know, vague promises. Oh, I loved Christmas. I retired two days after Christmas so I wouldn't miss the Christmas rush.

After work I used to play cards, go play poker. And, of course, I used to like to fish. I fished at Squibnocket. I fished at the bridge. I fished at Chappaquiddick, at Wasque. I'm sure I've fished every beach on the Island at some time or other. I never went boat fishing, always on the beach. And I always joined the Derby. I never got a really big fish. A thirty-pounder is the biggest I ever got. I caught that at Gay Head. And my wife loved to go fishing. She entered into the Derby as well.

And I belonged to the Masons. We used to have cribbage every Monday night. The Masons do a lot of charity work and it's a fraternity — a place to be together with friends. I was Master of the Lodge back in 1951. You're Master just for one year.

## JOHN WHITING
b. 1908 • West Tisbury
Anthropologist
Professor, Harvard University
Writer, Fisherman

# I Had to Turn It Upside Down

## An Anthropologist's Early Life on a West Tisbury Farm

I was born in the farmhouse in Quenames. It was one of the original Mayhew houses, built in about 1680. Jonathan Mayhew, who got his degree at Harvard in 1740, lived there 'til it burned down. I was born in the rebuilt version of that house.

I lived on the farm with my parents, and when I was sixteen or seventeen, I went away to Andover, then to Yale, and then to teaching. But I've spent every summer here, but one.

My grandfather, Henry Whiting, was a surveyor with the Coastal and Geodetic Survey and was sent to the Island to do a topographical map of the islands. He fell in love with the daughter of the innkeeper where he was lodging — the building next to Alley's. They got married and bought the farm next door.

My grandfather loved the land, but he didn't know anything about farming. He got a job teaching at MIT. And he would go from the Vineyard to Cambridge and take Father with him. So Father started going to school in Cambridge. They lived in Cambridge for the fall term. But Father hated the school and said, "I'm not going back there." So he only went for that one term.

Father thought farming was great, so he built up the farm. He bought horses. And he kept up — although he was not an academic — he kept up with all the latest innovations. He was really an innovator. He got a lot of information from farm journals.

He was very, very modern. He rotated crops, and he planted crops that would put nitrogen in the soil, like clover. So the rotation was to plow up the field and plant oats and barley, and then hay and clover. Then harvest the hay and then you'd turn the sheep on it. So, it was sort of a ten-year rotation.

He had the first mowing machine that was used on the Island. Before that, everyone used a scythe. And then he had a binder and thresher. He had a one-cylinder boat motor, and he had it tied up to pulleys which ran a corn grinder, a sawmill and a threshing machine.

He would order the equipment from Iowa, that's where they were built. And they would come into the dock. We'd get a pair of horses — we always had a pair of draft horses — and usually we'd go down in the hay wagon, because we'd use that when there was something heavy to haul. It would take all day to go down there, load up the wagon with these boxes of equipment, and come back.

Then I would get out the directions. And Father said, "Put those away. If you're not smart enough to put a machine together, you're not my son." So we put them away. And we put it together by figuring it out. I learned a lot by having to make this decision of how to put these together. He'd say, "Hold the parts upside down and turn them over." We'd figure out how it worked.

Very early on, about 1915, I guess, we got a generator run by kerosene motor. One-ten volts, and then we rigged up wires to the Davis house and going across the Parsonage Pond to the Newhall house and to our house and to the barn. Big wires on poles that went across the field and across the pond. So we had the whole thing wired. First electricity in West Tisbury, I think.

My father had practically a thousand acres of land. Some of it was in the center of West Tisbury, maybe two to three hundred acres there. There were five hundred acres in Quenames. And then there were three hundred acres up at Peaked Hill, which was not farmed. But he would take sheep up there in the summer. He probably had between one and two hundred sheep. They always kept getting out, so that didn't work very well.

We shipped the wool off-Island, and Mother had a project of making blankets, of having blankets made. She found some place in Maine that would make blankets, and then she sold them from the house. "Vineyard Blankets," she said. They were nice. They were good, heavy blankets, monocolored, but with a trim on the end.

And cows — that varied — usually three or four. Sometimes Father would think that selling milk was the thing to do. Then he got a butter-making machine. So then the cows might come up to a dozen. And then he'd decide that's no good, and he'd go back to just one or two, enough for the family. Then chickens were the thing. He built a dozen chicken houses, and had — who knows? Two or three hundred? More, probably. And then I had to go pick the eggs. I didn't like that. For some reason I found that demeaning.

Then we went into pigs. We had a dozen pigs. And those we'd keep in the cellar. Then he thought that the pigs would root out scrub oaks, and that would clear land. So he took them all down, took maybe a dozen pigs, and put a fence around the scrub oaks and put them in. Didn't work.

Oh, he did all sorts of experiments like that. He was very inventive. He read that lime was good for the soil. So he said, "Well, look, there are great mounds of scallop shells. And I look in the garage, and there are all piles of rubber tires that have been abandoned. So," he said, "tires, I understand, burn pretty well." So he made a great heap of tires and then went up and got piles of scallop shells and put them on top and put some kerosene on and lit a match to it. He got great complaints from townspeople for the smoke. But he had a good home-made lime that he put on the field. Sure, there were rubber ashes mixed in with it, but anyway, it worked pretty well.

Another thing that Father did, he decided, "Well, there's a nice field here" — the field in the Panhandle — "let's have trotting horse races." So he built a race course. He built a big tower with a bell on top of it, and the bell would ring to start the races. And people would be up there with megaphones and spyglasses. My uncle, Everett Davis, had a fancy trotting horse that would usually win all the races. And everyone would try to get a horse to beat him. George Fred Tilton would be one of the ones who would race, and I think Uncle Everett's horse would always beat him. George Fred wouldn't like that very much.

Myself and all my age-mates after school would go to our big barn, and go to the hay mow, and we'd play what we called beam tag. It was a big barn and they had beams. And the beams were running all over the place. And we'd play tag. You'd run and jump from one beam to another. Fred Woodaman, his father bought Sam Mayhew's store, and Charlie Turner, Tony Campbell, Frank Schultz and Hollis Fairchild, they were part of the gang.

We would move to the Pond in the summer. Down to Quansoo. We had a camp that we built down on Black Point Pond. We'd always go down and live there in the summer, and come back as soon as school started. And I would hate it because all my friends were back in West Tisbury, and I was all by myself down there.

On an anthropological note, Wampanoags lived up Indian Hill in the winter and also would come down to the Pond in the summer and get the shellfish and catch the herring, and one thing and another. The Mill Brook and another stream came down to the Great Pond. And, clearly, that was an advantage. It gave you water before you had pumps. And so we moved to the Pond in the summer, too. The animals would move down, and we would. And most of the fields, hay fields, were down at Quenames. And the sheep were moved down there, and the horses moved down there. So the whole farm was moved down.

The marshes were wonderful for the sheep to graze on. And the grass that grows — bluegrass, marsh-grass — is what the French use to fatten their lambs. They get a higher price for lambs that are brought up "*près du sel*," near the salt, and they're especially good. And so we raised our lambs "*près du sel*."

So anyway, it was good pasture. And another thing was the marsh hay, a little bit further toward the marsh, was exceptionally good for bedding for the horses and cattle. Because it wouldn't grow in the garden, being marsh hay, the seeds wouldn't germinate. We used old bedding for garden mulch and manure from the barn for fertilizer in the garden. So marsh hay was very good for bedding. And as a matter of fact, I still use it.

Mother had an old bill, from 1696, for charging for a pair of horses and three men's labor to open the Pond. There were all sorts of reasons for open-

103

ing the beach. You had to let the herring in who come to spawn, and if the beach isn't open, they can't get in. And the next thing is, the eels have to go out to spawn. And so they had to be let out. So the herring had to be let in in the spring, and the eels let out in the fall, and the marshes drained so that the hay can be cut in the summer. And Daniel Look, I think it was, went and bought several barrels of white perch, which had never grown in the Pond, and they did beautifully, and they harvested two hundred barrels a year. And from 1876 until 1935, the sale of perch was more than enough to pay for opening the beach. So regulating the opening of the Pond was very important.

After the war, Johnny Mayhew, Willie Huntington, my brother Everett and I worked on a few experiments on the Pond. We set up the Quansoo Shellfish Farm for growing and harvesting oysters, and we invented a machine — a pump and a rake of pipes — that would flush up steamers out of the mud on the bottom. That was very successful. In fact, everyone uses it. Now it's called the "traditional" way to clam — traditional since 1946.

In the summer when I was young, I had to help with the hay. My main job was running the hay rake. It was one of these dump rakes, and you had a horse that you'd drive. Picking up the leavings of the hay that was left after they'd put the first load in the wagon. And that was a very important bit of training for me. Because I'd look, and I'd say, "How can I get the most hay with the fewest turns?" And I'd look at what was left, and I'd figure it out. And that was very important training for my work as an anthropologist. How to solve problems.

When we got two loads of hay, we'd take it up to West Tisbury to put it in the barn up there to feed the animals in the winter. So somebody had to drive, take the hay back. When I was about seven years old, I remember I was driving up the Quenames Road, and somebody with a car came towards me, and I stopped, and they pulled out, and they said, "Hey, look at that little boy up there. That little native." And they said, "Wait a minute, let me take your picture." And so they got out their camera and took a picture. I was very embarrassed and angry.

Father had a rig from the barn that would take the hay from the wagon, lift it up and run it along the top and dump it in the hayloft in the right place. You had a horse that would pull a pulley that lifted the thing. That was a job that I had. I'd take the horse, and they'd pull out the hay and they'd say, "Whoa!" And then I'd have to stop the horse, and then they'd dump the hay, and I'd bring the horse back, turn it around. Then wait until they'd hooked another. I loved that job.

I got interested in anthropology because Mother was very interested in old logbooks. And she got me to go up into people's attics and lofts and help her find them. And then she'd tell me about them. So I learned about the Pacific Isles and Fiji and Samoa from Mother's logbooks. And so anthropology came naturally.

My experience on the Vineyard gave me insight, so that I was able to look at what was going on in New Guinea and in Kenya when I was there on work. They were farmers. I had to figure out how the farmers solved their problems. When the farmer went out to look at his orchard and crops, I watched them, and I said, "Well, that's the way they do it on the Vineyard." That's just what my father would do. Go look at the orchard, see how it was. And you'd look, look at the garden. And I still do it. When I come back here, the first thing I do is go down and take a look at the garden.

If I wanted to find out how clams or oysters reproduce themselves, or how do you plant and grow potatoes, that's a problem of sequence. So, when I got to Kenya, I had to figure out how they were growing their yams, their crops. And it was somewhat different. But the same general principle. And how about bananas? That's something, again, different. And then I had to figure out how the farmers solved their problems.

It had to make sense. I had to turn it upside down. So I'd have to understand the culture that I was studying; the way that I understood the farm. And the Pond. So the farm and the Pond — my life here on the Vineyard — were a very important part of my education.

*Interviewed 1995*

104

## LOIS MAILOU JONES
1905 – 1998 • Edgartown
Artist, Exhibited World-wide
Active During Harlem Renaissance
Art Professor, Howard University

# My Career Was Really Formed on This Island

*A Painter's Love for the Vineyard*

I was born in Boston. My mother and father were from Paterson, New Jersey. My mother's mother was one of the first settlers on this Island; her name was Phoebe Ann Ballou. She lived in Vineyard Haven, and she worked for rich people named Hatch. She was like a member of the family. That is, she ate at the same table and they loved her, really. I am named for one of them — Lois, Lois Hatch. She was with them for many years. And she had much foresight because she bought a lot of land here in Edgartown. It was very unusual in those early days for a woman of color to do that.

Every summer of our childhood we were here. My mother was a beautician. In Boston she had a beauty shop with a French friend. For summers she had private customers, like Mrs. Gibson, in Vineyard Haven. Then there was another wealthy family, the Wares, who lived on West Chop. She would do their nails and shampoo and massage and things like that. It was strictly private and she always would dress very lovely in the morning to go to her clients. I can always see her with her fancy hats. My mother loved to make hats. The hats were very, very stunning. They were straw and they sometimes would have a ribbon in a certain way or a sort of a flower arranged — beautiful hats. Her customers used to love her hats. Anyway, she would leave early in the morning for her appointments and then she would come back to our house in Oak Bluffs. Around half past four o'clock she would be finished for the day.

Mrs. Gibson discovered that I was talented and she said I must come and paint in her garden. That is very important in my career because she said, "Let Lois come over and paint in my garden. Then she can borrow these books." She had a wonderful set of Japanese books of handpainted flowers. I used those flowers for my cretonne designs and those cretonne designs were printed and sold all over the country, as far as California. It was all going back to Mrs. Gibson who lived in Vineyard Haven.

I think I was one of the first members of the Martha's Vineyard Artist Association. This Ruth Mead, I think was at that time the director. We worked together at the Sculpin Gallery. I exhibited there and with her. However, my first exhibit was in Vineyard Haven when I was seventeen. And that was held in the garden of Mrs. Henry A. Ritter's home, in Vineyard Haven.

We had on this Island quite a settlement of very distinguished Negroes during the summer. Like Harry T. Burleigh, the arranger of Negro spirituals, and Meta Warwick Fuller, the sculptress. Harry Burleigh used to say, "When I can't go to Switzerland, where the lakes are so blue, so beautiful, I go to Martha's Vineyard Island because there the water is blue like the lakes of Switzerland." Then there was Madame Lillian Evanti, the internationally acclaimed mezzosoprano, who had sung in the opera at Cannes in France. She was the leading singer in Milan, where she was the prima donna. She was a very beautiful-looking woman and she stayed at the Shearer Cottage. So did Ethel Waters, who was internationally known for her singing, and the Adam Clayton Powell family. All of those distinguished Negroes stayed at the Shearer Cottage. That was the one place where these distinguished people of color could stay because they couldn't stay at the hotels because of the color situation.

My career was really formed on this Island when I was about seventeen. We used to swim at the Highland Beach, which is over there near where we lived. One day I was on the beach with Harry T. Burleigh and Meta Warwick Fuller talking about my career, and Meta's career in France. They both said, "Lois, you know you're not going to make it in this country. It's true you are very talented, but because of the situation, you're not going to have any success with your career. You are going to have to go abroad."

Of course, Meta suggested that I go to France

## ANNE CRONIG
b. 1917 • Tisbury
Childrens' Librarian, Tisbury
Manager/Bookkeeper for Cronig's Market, Tisbury

# They're Hard-Working Young Men;
# They'll Make a Go of It

### The Cronig Family

My father was brought up in Lithuania — at that time it was all Russia. He lived in a small town in a farming area. It was a difficult time in Russian history. It was a very cruel time. The Russian Czar was God Almighty. His word was law. If a country has problems, you have to have someone to blame it on. So he blamed it on the Jews, a minority.

So life was very difficult. My father was the oldest in the family. And he was a student. And by student, I mean he was the oldest and his parents expected him to become a rabbi. But there were no schools where he lived so he had to go to the city and live with strangers to get an education. He slept with other young men in what seemed like an attic from his description. Because he had to support himself, he used to get up very early in the morning to go and help a baker. He'd gone to bed early, and did not know that everybody had been ordered off the streets. And these Cossacks on horseback were going through the streets, and if anybody was on the street they had a whip. And this Cossack took a whip to my father, and my father was fifteen years old. He made up his mind right then and there — evidently it had been in the back of his mind — "I'm leaving this country just as soon as I can." He stopped school immediately. He worked full time. It took him two years to save the two hundred dollars to come steerage to America.

He had to sneak out of the country because I don't think the young people that were with him had papers to leave the country. But they would bribe the border guards, and the border guards were glad to have a little bribe. He made his way to Germany, and from there he took a ship to the United States. Well, in those days they welcomed young people who were able to put in a good day's work. All they had to do was pass a physical when they got to Ellis Island. So he had no problem.

So, when he got to New York, he worked for a while in the city. But he hated the city. He was a country boy. And it was affecting his health. He knew he had a relative in New Bedford. So he got to New Bedford and they looked in the newspaper for a job for him. There was an ad saying something to the effect of, "If you're interested in working on Martha's Vineyard for the summer, on a farm, go down to the steamship and ask for a ticket." So the relative went down with him, because he could speak a little English, but not very much. He hadn't been here very long. So they got a ticket for him, and he got on the boat. He landed here in Vineyard Haven, and he asked for the direction to Captain Daggett's farm, which was located where the hospital is now. So he walked over there and Captain Daggett made him very welcome. They had no children. He was a retired sea captain. And he worked there for them. He was about seventeen at that time. And Captain Daggett used to teach him English.

My father worked for Captain Daggett for a number of years and then went to work in a grocery store which was where the Patisserie is now — Washburn and Call, I think it was. There was a picture of him for a long time, up at the store, driving the horse and wagon. He was a delivery boy. He did whatever, you know — stock boy, delivery boy, deliver orders or whatever.

One at a time, he brought his brothers over. Some worked in New Bedford and wherever they could find work. And then in 1917 they got together and pooled their resources, such as they had. I think it was Helen Hart's father who backed them financially. As I remember, he got in touch with the wholesale company in New Bedford, and he said that he knows that they're hard-working young men, and that they would make a go of it.

Things were quite different then. Things were not packaged individually the way they are now.

## PEG KNOWLES
b. 1910 • Edgartown
Artist
Active with Historic Cherry Hill, Albany, NY
and Martha's Vineyard Historical Society

# We Decided We Would Bushwhack

### Edgartown Summers and a Walk Around the Island

The first summer we came to the Vineyard was in 1917. And we came to Mrs. Goell's Boarding House. Mrs. Goell had three houses in Edgartown, off Dunham Road, on the water. And it was a perfectly lovely place. If we were awake, we could see the *Uncatena* come in at night. It came in to the Memorial Wharf, Steamboat Wharf. You could stand in Mother's window and look out and see the *Uncatena* searchlight looking for the spit at Chappaquiddick and the lighthouse, as it came in the channel. And wonderful food. The dining room was family style, and big tables. We had corn on the cob, and we had the clams that you dip in butter — steamers. We had lobster, and home-made rolls and muffins. Good, wholesome meals. Nothing fancy, nothing foreign. The people were very congenial.

Edgartown then was very different from what it is now. People came for the whole season, and they brought maids. Everybody went to the bathing beach in the morning, which was run by Mr. Chadwick. He had a sign up which said, "Barelegged Women Will Not Be Tolerated." When you were twelve years old, you had to wear black stockings. People came over either in the bathing beach launch or sailed over in their cat-boats. We went in our rowboat. We rowed across Katama Bay and left the boat on the beach and walked across. And the bathing beach was very simple then. There were little wooden bathhouses that had a bench and pail for water to wash your feet, and a broom to sweep the sand out. And Popcorn Harry came. He was one of the Collins family, who lived on the corner of the road that goes down to the Reading Room. He always said he was the wayward son of a respectable family. He could recite the books of the Bible backwards. He sold Darling's Popcorn, five cents a bar. It was delicious. He was one of the colorful characters, and he was there. And the ladies sat on the benches there and knitted,

or watched the crowd. When I was a child, in 1917 and 1918, along there, the ladies had long white skirts to their ankles and white blouses with, I think, high necks, and hats.

I was seven when I first came to the Vineyard. And I was terribly lucky because I was the bottom of a heap of a group of children who played all the time. We played kick the can in the evening, and hide-and-seek, and we went off in rowboats by ourselves. It was considered too debilitating to go in swimming more than once a day. And the maids also were allowed to go to the bathing beach in the afternoon. So you never went there then. But we used to go down in our rowboats to a place we called the rocks. It was under what was Billy Dinsmore's house. It was a long breakwater with jumbled rocks. And we all made little houses. You'd find a formation and you could move some of the rocks a bit. Somebody gave me a pink knitting bag, and I used to take it to lunch, and put the rolls in it. We'd carry them down there and make little fires, and toast them in the afternoon. We picked sea lavender, which, of course, we shouldn't have been doing, and decorated our houses with that.

We walked across what we called the Moors — they call them the Plains — to South Beach, but nobody swam at South Beach. The undertow was considered very dangerous. And there were no ticks. When we came back here in the '30s was the first time we ever found any ticks.

Once a summer we would go in Chester Pease's coach, which was an automobile, it had seats cross-wise, and we'd go to Gay Head. It was an all-day expedition. We would stop on the way back at the Spinning Wheel House, where the Adams sisters served tea. And, of course, we were fascinated to see those little ladies and hear their stories about their travels with Tom Thumb's Circus.

The road from Edgartown to West Tisbury was dirt, very sandy, and — even in the '30s — the roads

## EDWIN NEWHALL WOODS

b. 1917 · West Tisbury

Farmer, Rancher

Wine Grower, Conservationist

# This Was Home

## Family, Farm and Fair in West Tisbury

The reason for my being back here in Massachusetts at all is because of my mother's mother, my grandmother, who was Virginia Whiting. She married a Newhall who was from the West Coast, and that started her sojourning back and forth cross-country. My first visit to the Vineyard was in 1920. My mother motored overland with my grandmother and my brother and sister and me in two automobiles. At that time they had twenty miles of paved road between San Francisco and Boston.

This was home. This was tradition. And this was family. This was it. It was here, on the Island, in West Tisbury in particular, because that's where the home was. I attended school in West Tisbury. I believe I started there when I was either in the third or fourth grade. We would ride horseback over the hills from our house on the North Road to West Tisbury to go to school through the wintertime. We rode to school, or we'd drive with a wagon, depending on the weather. Or we'd take a sleigh. Whatever. I knew there were three ways. Over to Grannie's barn. Then we'd put the horse or the pony in that barn while we went to school. Go to school and come back here and do our homework. Kerosene lamps, that sort of thing. All the good stuff.

We'd get together hanging May baskets on each other and that sort of thing. In the evening time, you'd go over to the store, which is Alley's Store today. Ray Woodaman was running it in those days, and Charlie Turner took it over from him. We'd go over there with our nickels and dimes, and buy little candies, penny candies, put them in a paper bag. And we'd decide who we were going to hang it on, and we'd run up and rap on the door and scream, "May basket!" in a loud voice, and disappear into the moonlit night.

The object was to have them come out and run us down over the snowy fields, or whatever it was, depending on the kind of spring you had. And we'd just hang around there, pretty close by, where we were easily encountered, and then they'd bring you on in to the fireplace, and you'd sit around and have a little hot chocolate, or you'd roast marshmallows, and eat candy, and play games, and whatever. Just a way to pass the evening. The usual community type of thing that, you know, you don't see these days. It's a changed world.

Our family had three houses, right in a row. It was family. I remember distinctly going over in the evenings and having a family gathering — with my aunt and her husband, Judge Davis, coming over to Johnson Whiting's home with Aunt Emma, and my grandmother coming over with three children, and visiting. Just sitting around the fireplace and telling stories and anecdotes, laughing and roaring. Uncle Everett would tell a story, and Aunt Emma would remember something and chuckle and chuckle, and laugh, and have just a good time. We'd roast marshmallows and maybe a little popcorn to go along with it. But the family would gather in the evening in the living room. That's why it was a living room. We sat around the fireplace. We had these get-togethers. Had a gam.

Johnson Whiting, Uncle John, was farming. He had his sheep, and had corn and hay down at Quenames, down by Black Point Pond. And we'd go along, and I think we helped him. Antoine Campbell was his hired hand at the time, and he'd actually do most of the work, but we kids liked to pitch in and help him. We'd stow hay or we'd help him drive team. Antoine would cut the hay with a mowing machine and a team of horses. Then raking the hay was with a single horse and a little dump rake, just walk through the fields. Got to drive the horse quite frequently doing that. That was something a kid could do. We'd leave the hay in windrows and then come along, pick up the hay with a pitchfork, and load it onto the wagon. We'd the cows. The pond over here froze up the day after Christmas, and the ice didn't go out 'til April that first winter we were up here. Of course we still had the milk route in Vineyard Haven which we had to do. I had a Model A touring car that I drove the milk in, and eventually I got a truck. Peddled to probably twenty-five houses.

You'd get up in the morning and milk the cows and bottle the milk and then go to Vineyard Haven peddling it. Sometimes in the winter it might freeze and the cream would be sticking up above – push the cap up. But people never thought much of it then, because they were used to it. Spring of the year, when the grass was good, you'd get about fifteen quarts from each cow. When the warm weather came along, we only peddled every other day. We had to ice it down. We had to get ice in Vineyard Haven, bring it up so to keep things cold because we didn't get electricity here on the farm until 1948.

There might be three of us peddling on the same street. Like Robert Norton and Orlin Davis, or a Mr. Chase, he'd come from Oak Bluffs. And that's why we eventually got the Co-op Dairy going. Some of us met together and decided, "Why are we all peddling down the same street?" So we made a deal to get the dairy that was owned by Mr. Dutton. We had twenty-eight members at one time and we had trucks that went around, picked it up in the morning and peddled it around. We got paid by the Co-op.

Of course I peddled ice, too, down there to Tashmoo, and water, because the drinking water wasn't good there. I'd buy the ice from Harry Peakes, used to cut it on the Old House Pond, then I'd bill the people myself. Right behind where the M.V. *Times* office is now, he had a place there and you'd pull in there and he'd say, "What size pieces?" So he'd cut them to about the size that I wanted. I had tongs and put it right in the back of the Model A Ford.

When John Bassett died, my brother and I got his sheep. Then eventually we got a flock of our own going. Harry West come in with the hand clippers and clip and shear them, before we butchered them. Then we'd sell them to people with freezers back during the war. Then we'd send the wool away to somewhere in Maine. Every twenty-two pounds of wool, we'd get a blanket back. It took eleven pounds of wool to make a blanket.

I used to raise chickens. And that could be a chore, because the Cedars — when I had them for a customer, down to West Chop — Tony the Chef would order a dozen chickens, and then you'd get them ready Friday night, so you could deliver them Saturday morning, so he'd have them for Sunday. Might be picking them by lantern light.

During the war, when I was peddling them out to the Cedars down there, of course there was a shortage of sugar and butter. We delivered in ten-quart cans. Sometimes when I picked up the empty can, it might weigh quite a lot more because there might be some sugar in there, might be a couple of pounds of butter in there, because I was in good with the chef. Bartering. So I'd take him to Oak Bluffs — Thursday nights was his night off. So we might go bowling or something, you know.

People used to help each other. If I didn't have a hay rake, I'd borrow Mr. Keith's, and bring it down on the hay trailer, and then back and forth. We'd go up and help put hay in up there, and Ozzie and a couple of guys would come down and help put hay in down here. No money exchanged hands.

Another thing that helped the farmers was the Ag Society. It used to be very active. I was president of the Ag Society for, what — four or five years. Priscilla and I joined in 1946. As life members. Back then, we used to have speakers down about once a month on poultry, dairying, different phases of farming. And new machinery they'd talk about, you know, so you could be more efficient. We'd get about fifty people out to a meeting.

But to bring it up to date, Eleanor, who's our oldest girl, she's interested in the farm and the sheep, and my son Arnie is, and so a few years ago we got incorporated. So, I'm the president of the corporation, my wife Priscilla's vice-president and Arnie's the secretary and Eleanor's the treasurer. So hopefully we've got it set up so that we skip an inheritance generation and the kids won't lose the place.

*Interviewed 1996*

155

## ARNOLD FISCHER
b. 1915 • West Tisbury
Farmer

## PRISCILLA FISCHER
b. 1917 • West Tisbury
Teacher, School Principal, West Tisbury School
Homemaker

## DEAN K. DENNISTON, SR.
b. 1913 • Oak Bluffs
School Principal, Railroad Worker
Active with the Church of the Covenant, Boston, MA, and
Union Chapel, Oak Bluffs

# Thank God for the Change

### *The Bradley Memorial Church*

My father, Oscar Denniston, came to Martha's Vineyard from the British West Indies in the year 1901. There was a sea captain in Vineyard Haven, his name was Madison Edwards. He was the chaplain from the Seaman's Bethel. And Madison Edwards used to sail between the Vineyard and Jamaica. On one of his trips he became ill over there and my father was a chaplain in a seaport area there, comparable to the work that Mr. Edwards also did. And when Captain Edwards became ill my father assisted him, so they became very good friends. So whenever he went to Kingston, Jamaica, he and my father would have a reunion. So it was that Captain Madison Edwards of Vineyard Haven invited, or more or less convinced, my father that Martha's Vineyard would be a good place for him to come and live. So it was in 1901 that my father came to Martha's Vineyard. Captain Madison Edwards provided work for my father at the Seaman's Bethel in Vineyard Haven.

In days gone by there was a lot of travel from Europe and other countries. And you would have to pass by Martha's Vineyard up until the time that they built the Cape Cod Canal. And if there were a storm, then the boats would have to come into the harbor and throw anchor. Madison Edwards would take his little boat, his launch it was, and go out to the various vessels, bring the sailors into the Bethel, give them a religious service and some hot cocoa. And they would always provide them with what we called a "ditty bag." Now, in this ditty bag was the New Testament, needle and thread ... I believe that was it. And each sailor would get a ditty bag. When they came in from a storm, there would be a religious service, some recreation, a chance to read, and at the end of the service we'd put them in the launch and take them back to their ships. So my father, when he first came — he was a great speaker — he assisted Madison Edwards in the services at the Bethel.

Then after a while my father became — they called him an evangelist, at a mission called the Oakland Mission, in Oak Bluffs on Masonic Avenue. And that particular mission was run by a Susan Bradley. What Miss Bradley did was to help all the Portuguese people that had come from Portugal and from the Azores to the Island. They assisted them in becoming naturalized citizens. The Oakland Mission assisted them in learning to speak English and do simple math, because they came directly from their homes and they brought their native tongue with them. So this Oakland Mission taught them many of the essential things that they would have to know to get along on Martha's Vineyard.

Susan Bradley was the founder of the Oakland Mission, and my father went from the Bethel to the Oakland Mission as her assistant. Then after Susan Bradley died in 1907, my father at the same location founded Bradley Memorial Church. And he led that congregation, or that church, for forty-six years. My father was a Baptist minister, but he did not wear a label. In the summertime we had people of all religious faiths joining in the service. When I say all — Methodist, Baptist, Episcopal. It was a church. And they came.

The chapel was on Masonic Avenue. We would have church meetings in the chapel attached to the house we lived in. It was a space set aside for the particular purpose of worship, with benches and hymnals and our organ. It was not a space that we lived in. The organ was played mostly by my two sisters, Amy and Olive. And there was a lady called Sarah Wentworth. She played mostly by ear. I don't think she ever had any training, but she did a fairly good job. But it was my two sisters that were in charge of the organ with bellows. You had to pump that baby to make her go.

There were perhaps fifteen or sixteen benches, and we called them pews. I guess that was the cor-

## TOM TILTON
1887 – 1984 • Tisbury
Fisherman
First mate on Zeb Tilton's *Alice S. Wentworth*, the last
coastal schooner on the eastern seaboard
Zeb's Nephew

# You Might See Some Rum Floating

### *Rum Running*

**W**ell, I never got into that, only a little. We was loaded with oysters once and there come a summer sou'easter, blowed hard. We had the buyer with us — sometimes the buyer would sail with us. I says, "You want to keep your eye out, you might see some rum floating." We went into Stonington that night for harbor. Because it was so rough out, we didn't come through to the Vineyard.

The next day there was a heavy swell. I said, "Keep your eye out. You might pick some rum up."

He took it as a joke, finally, and he says, "What's the matter with you? You're always talking about picking up rum." We went about a mile or two and I saw a box floating.

I said, "That looks pretty good out there, but there's only one." We went along, and we see two or three more. I said, "You launch the dory; I'm going to find out what they are."

We picked up thirteen cases of liquor. Under the cabin floor we had a place where we kept our coal. It was empty with a carpet over it. We stowed it away in there. When we got home we thought it better to get it out of the vessel. We didn't want to keep it there.

So it was Saturday night, we laid in here, in Vineyard Haven, and went out in the dory about nine o'clock. They had a meeting at the Bethel and everything was quiet when we landed. We took half the liquor in the dory, brought it ashore, and put it in a wheelbarrow, four cases to a time, and wheeled it up and put it in my house.

I had a big fireplace. I had a big piano in front of it. Stowed it away in there. We got the whole business stowed away.

Well, my wife and I were pretty nervous with it in the house, didn't know what the landlord would say if we had liquor stored in there, if he ever found it. So I said, "Well, I'll get rid of it."

I went up to Phil Marks; I knew he used to handle it. I told Phil, "I've got some liquor. Can you handle it?"

"By God!" he says, "I had to quit. My wife gave me the devil." So he says, "I had to get out of it, but I'll tell you who can handle it. Go over and see Brownings at the Bluffs. He runs the hotel; I think he'd buy it off you."

So over I goes to see Brownings, because he belongs to the Red Men and I belong to the Red Men. So that was all right. So he said he'd buy it. He give me fifty dollars a case for it.

He says, "I'll send a truck over for it. You get it on the truck and then it'll be up to me."

I said, "Okay." I got the liquor out from behind the piano, stowed it away in the barn. The truck came, and we loaded the truck. Brownings came in the house and paid me. "Now it's up to me," he says. So, well, I got rid of that.

Afterwards I found out that the lady of the house was looking for a case. She came up to Phil and wanted to know where she could buy a case of liquor.

"My God," I said, "that's going some." Her tongue was hanging out for liquor. If I'd knowed it, I could have sold her a case and got more money for it.

*Interviewed 1982*

My grandfather and my uncle, they had cranberry bogs. There were bogs down there on the Menemsha Pond. And up and down the whole North Shore, that was cranberry bogs also. So at night, I'd go right over to the North Shore. They had oxen down there. When they picked the cranberries they used to put them in big bags. The men would load up the ox cart with the bags. And I would bring that ox cart up here to my uncle's place and dump it, and then take the oxen and the cart back down there for another load of cranberries.

Then, also, my uncle Arthur Herbert — he had the inn up there to the Cliffs — and he had a fish trap. When I was a little kid, I used to drive the oxen when the men would be doing the work on the traps. And then I used to go down there, take and bring the nets home, and spread them out to dry. Then, in the spring of the year, when you're getting ready to set your traps out, you'd load the nets in the back of the ox cart, then you'd stretch them way out and all on the beach. Or we used to, when you brought the net in, you'd take and drive the oxen right along over the net, and then load the wagon right up with the nets.

I used to take and go down and get those oxen from John Bassett's farm and bring them up to Gay Head, here, when I was getting ready to use them for fish traps and all like that. I think they used to give me twenty-five cents to go down and get the oxen and bring them home. That was my pay, but that twenty-five cents was big money for me then. In those times.

When I was young, we got a pair of oxen. I was just a young kid, but, still, I wanted to take and break them and train them and be able to use them and everything else.

These were calves. Little calves. And I started in bringing them up right from the very beginning, in just my spare time. I had been with other people that owned oxen ever since I was a little kid. And so I was kind of used to knowing, seeing how they controlled the oxen. I would take them out, and then I'd start walking them around, and getting them used to going around, and trying to give them commands, so that they'd understand you and all.

"Gee" and "haw." Haw is to the left, and gee is right. You'd stand right up close to them. Control them right there, close to the head. The nigh ox is the nearest, and the off ox, the other one. When you start off training them, you have a rope on their horns, so that when you say, "Haw" you pull on that, and make them so they come to you. And then to gee, you go ahead and hold your whip out in front of the off ox to make him slow down — gee off — and make your nigh ox come around more.

The whip, it's a director, and it's kind of making them do your commands. Sometimes just a little tap. The whip is not to really beat them or anything else. Just make them follow your command. Say, you want him to haw to you. You'd slap the off one, and he'd have to come around, because he knows he's liable to get it stronger.

To train them, took probably three years' time. And a lot of patience. Matter of fact, I had them trained pretty well even when they were too small to hook onto an ox cart. So, I made a small trailer out of automobile wheels, the axle front end of an automobile, and put a long tongue onto that, go up between them. And, so, it would pull easily, and yet get them used to it, to a wagon and all.

The ox carts, oh, they were big. I don't know as if you ever seen ox cart wheels. They're about five foot tall. And just two sides, most of them. Open in the front and in the back. I remember when I first started breaking mine, trying to get them used to a wagon and all. I came right out on the highway, right up here. And the oxen kind of looked back and they see this wagon coming right behind them. And they started in getting afraid. First thing they did, of course, they tried to separate apart because they was looking back at this wagon coming right up behind them all the time. Then they started in running. I was trying to get them to stop; I had a rope on them then. But they would not stop with me. Because they started really running up the road, trying to get away from that wagon. So, anyway, it's a good thing that the pin of the wagon come unhitched. They was going up the road, and, of course, I still had hold the rope — I was young; I could run and do everything active. So I got behind that ox and when I got off to one side a little bit, I took that rope and give it a pull — like this — and it kind of tripped him. And that ox went down. Fell down. When he did, of course, the other ox swung right around and went right into the sand bank. So that stopped them right there. They didn't know what it was, a wagon coming on like that behind them. So, I got them up, did it right away, and got them straightened out again, immediately. So, I was up in front of them and stayed right there, so I wouldn't allow them to look back and think about what's coming behind them. Lucky there were very few cars on the road in those days.

I used to take other people's oxen down to the Fair. It took about two, three hours to get down there. They had pulls pretty much the same as what they are today. But I never took mine down. Mine weren't a well-matched pair. We used to use those oxen for plowing. Plowing the gardens.

One thing I used to do a lot with them was go down along the beaches. At that time, a lot of lumber used to wash ashore. It used to come ashore because when there were ships coming from over across, they'd have everything battened down with all of these boards. So, when they get off the Vineyard, they'd be just getting ready to go into New York and places west of us here, and they used to start taking them crates apart, and throw the lumber overboard. So I'd go along the beaches with the oxen and pick up lumber and bring it home. And I brought a lot home and built a big extension onto the back side of our barn, so that we could store more hay. And also keep the cattle in. No cost of lumber. It was good lumber.

I remember one time I was taking a fish trap net out of the back of a wagon, down at Lobsterville. And I come to the end, and wanted the wagon to turn around and go back again the other way. So I says, "Haw, to!" And I was standing way back, quite well back on them. They took and started in turning, coming around. And the off ox, he swung right around towards me, I don't know why, he just really sharp turned. And that wagon tongue pushed the nigh ox right over. And the off ox was kind of stepping sideways, because the other ox was pushing him. And he stepped right on my foot and held me right down! And there he was — right there. And the other ox was coming around. I went down in the sand, like that. And these oxen come right over top of me. I looked up and that's all I could see, was oxen bellies going over top of my head! First thing I thought about was that other ox. He's going to step right on me or something, you know, like that. And those were big oxen. So I let out a big yell and scream. Cripes, men all run down there and see. They thought I must have been hurt. I was fine. It just scared me so, to see them oxen going right over. And I couldn't even move because he stepped right on my foot in the soft beach sand, you know. Didn't hurt my foot any.

*Interviewed 1995*

## GALE HUNTINGTON
1902 – 1993 • Tisbury
Historian, Teacher, Farmer,
Fisherman, Musician, Author
Married to Mildred Huntington

# Right Fal Da Da Diddle Day

## Music, Fishing and Farming in Chilmark

Mildred and I got married in 1933. I'd known Mildred for quite a few years. Her family was known as the "singing Tiltons." They sang at night. They sang when they got together. They would sing if you wanted a song. "Say, Willard, will you sing a song?" or "Welcome, will you sing a song?" They would sing unaccompanied. Just sing. "Round Cape Horn, The young men go, When the young men go away, Then the young girls dress up neat, And they go cruisin' down the street. Right fal day, Faddle diddle day, Right fal da da, Oh, faddle diddle day." And so on and so on. That's one I got from the Tiltons. You see, they were deep-sea sailors. And singing was very, very important on ships in the fo'c'sle and in the cabin and in steerage. They just learned the songs and brought them home. I've still got a lot of Welcome's songs. I should have gotten more for my book. Most of the songs in the book are from whalemen's journals, back pages. And I should have gotten a lot more than I did, but I wasn't collecting songs then. I just liked singing them.

And I used to play fiddle. I played fiddle for the dances we had. There was a hotel in Gay Head and I played there. There was Artie Look, he played the accordion, I played the fiddle, and Willard Martin played the piano. Sometimes we'd get three dollars a night. Sometimes we'd get five dollars a night.

Mildred liked to go to the dances. She loved to dance. She was good. I can remember one dance we played. Mildred was there and she danced all night with Jimmy Cagney, and I thought that was a little overdoing it. But there was nothing I could do about it because I had to play fiddle. But one time, she was dancing with somebody and she fell down and broke a bone and she was laid up in bed on a board for a long while. I'd go up and talk to her and try to keep her amused and tell her what was going on. One day out of a clear sky she said, "Gale, you've got an education, when are you going to use

it?" I thought I was using it. I thought that was very funny. I said, "What would I do?" She said, "Well, you might teach school." I thought that was even funnier, but she meant it and kept after me. So I eventually became a schoolteacher. But that's another story.

Anyway, we played quite often at the Town Hall in Chilmark. Not the present Town Hall, but a little room over the town offices. It was small, but that was where you'd have the dances. We'd play waltzes and foxtrots and the figure dances. The Virginia reel, always had one Virginia reel. Sometimes we'd play the *chamarita*, which was the Portuguese dance. Quite often the Portuguese from down the Middle Road would come up.

And a lot of the deaf and dumb went to the dances. They could sense the rhythm through the floor and they danced to that rhythm. Chilmark had a tremendously large deaf and dumb population. And that was supposed to have been caused by intermarriage over two or three hundred years. But they were valuable members of the society. There was no discrimination. They were treated just like anybody else. They went to church and to town meeting. And almost everybody in Chilmark could speak the language with their hands. I couldn't talk very well, but I could understand everything they were saying. I knew them all. There was Katie West and Eva Look and Josie West. Now, Josie West was the one that Thomas Hart Benton did the portrait of. Josie's business was wood, firewood. He had a big woodlot and he'd bring it to you all sawed and split or in cordwood lengths. We were neighbors for a long time on what they called Rumpus Ridge. That's the hill that goes up towards Gay Head from the Chilmark school and post office.

And that's where the deaf and dumb community was centered. And when we were first married, that's where we lived.

In those years, we lived two inches ahead of

starvation. We were poverty-stricken. I went fishing, I went scalloping, I went quahogging, and I worked on the road with Bill Smith. And finally I said, "Mildred, we gotta stop this." So we bought the Polander's house. It was beautiful land and I had a big market garden. And I ran the market garden for quite a few years. And grew vegetables and peddled them. And we did pretty well that way.

I had a boat. She was a power dory. There's a story connected here. It was a good set of scallops that year. And I was going to use her, of course. I had her all rigged and I was over at Menemsha one day getting my culling board in place and fixing things up to go scalloping, and Roy Cottle came along. He was another fisherman. We talked and he said, "Gale, you want to sell this boat?" I said, "No, I won't sell it, but I'll trade it for that violin of yours." I already had about six fiddles. But that was a beautiful fiddle. And he said, "Okay." So I went home with the fiddle. And Mil said, "Where'd you get that?" I said, "I traded the power boat for her." She burst into tears. She knew me. But I had to row my scallops out that winter and I did all right. Course, my day was longer than the power boats', but we got enough scallops. I've still got that fiddle.

I used to go dory fishing off Squibnocket in the 1920s. That was a famous fishing place. It had been an Indian and a colonial fishing place. The dory was a typical fisherman's dory. Flat-bottomed so you could haul it up the beach. They used the same boat on the Grand Banks. They had them stacked on the deck of the vessel. The size we used off Squibnocket mostly was sixteen foot. I found my boat on the beach. It evidently had gone overboard from a vessel, a schooner, and it was on the beach, no oars, no thole pins. So I went home and got a pair of oars and some thole pins and rowed it around to Squibnocket. And that was my dory.

And they had a dory sail, which was a little spritsail. Almost none of the dories had a centerboard. So the sail was only good going downwind or across the wind. They were good rowers. They were heavy, but if you had a good pair of oars, you could row. It was tippy, you had to know how to handle it. Fortunately, I went with a good dory

man, Linus Jeffers. He was an Indian from Gay Head. He taught me a lot about fishing and boat handling, too.

We caught our fish off Squibnocket or off Gay Head. I would take the fish and peddle them. I'd stop at people's houses. Sometimes I'd get as far as Vineyard Haven before all my fish were gone. I'd go to Lagoon Pond Road, Chicken Alley, and I'd finish selling my fish there because they were crazy about *bacalhau*. That's the Portuguese word for codfish. So I'd always get rid of them.

We'd mostly fish for cod, some fluke, but mostly cod. We used a handline. It was a regular cod line. That is, a strong cotton line, twisted, you know. And you'd use a heavy sinker and let it down and keep doing this, up and down. The cod would knock against the sinker and you'd feel that, and then pretty soon they'd take the bait. And they come up hard. The cod is not a game fish, but they fought. When we did get them in the boat we hit them on the head so they didn't suffer. And then clean them when we got to the beach.

We'd try to fish on the slack water. We'd go out half a day, depending on the tide. We had ranges where we knew the bottom was good. One was Squibnocket Point. Sail or row up until you could see the lighthouse and anchor there. That was one range.

At one time there were a lot of fish houses at Squibnocket. Jerry Look had a fish house there. When I was a small boy I used to go down there and pester him. I learned a lot from when he was working around his fish house. The fish house is just a shack to keep your gear in, oars, lines and everything. Sometimes there'd be barrels of pickle, if you wanted to pickle your fish. It was just a shack to keep stuff in.

At Lobsterville, some of the fishermen used to live in their fish houses, and sometimes their families would come and live with them in the summer. And that was a real house, you know. That was a regular village. When I was a boy it was very strong. There were two streets, Front Street and Back Street. Then when power engines came, everybody moved to Menemsha. Lobsterville became a ghost village.

And at Squibnocket, I think Linus and I were the last two to ever go off there. When engines came you couldn't haul 'em up on the beach. Most of them put engines in their boats, which ruined them from my point of view.

But I enjoyed my days of dory fishing. I certainly did. You were out by yourself and nobody was bothering you. And you could look at everything there was to look at, the birds and the water, and the sky and the clouds, and everything else.

*Interviewed 1982*

## MILDRED HUNTINGTON
b. 1912 • Tisbury
Trust Officer, M.V. National Bank
Town Auditor, Chilmark
Homemaker, Married to Gale Huntington

# The Harbor Was Full of Boats

## *The Seaman's Bethel and Sailing with Zeb Tilton*

My best friend was Austin Tower's daughter, Miriam. Mr. Tower was chaplain of the Bethel, you know. All the time I was in high school, I think from seventh grade, I spent a lot of time at the Bethel.

And time after time Mr. Tower would take us out on the Bethel boat. Either the *Madison Edwards*, which he had first, or the *Helen May*. Either one of those boats. We would go out in early evening and get the sailors, bring them ashore to the Bethel.

Almost always, Mr. Tower would have something arranged whereby there would be a program. And sometimes Miriam and I used to sing duets when he couldn't find anyone else to do anything, you know. It was a lot of fun.

The Bethel had a big long room with a door on the north side. And another door on the south. There was a — I guess they'd call it a podium today — where Mr. Tower used to stand and give a little sermon. And there was a small pump organ there, which Mrs. Tower used to play whenever we had meetings there. After Mr. Tower's sermon and the hymns that we sang from the Bethel hymn book, if there was no other entertainment, the sailors were invited to stay there and play dominoes, or checkers, or Flinch. Down on the other side of the room there were tables that had magazines, books, checkers, dominoes and Flinch cards. Never any playing cards, never. Because playing cards signified poker. And playing poker was a sin.

The Towers were very, very strict, and very strong Methodists. They had a lot of ideas about what things were sin and what weren't. Buying a newspaper or a stick of gum, buying anything on Sunday, was breaking the Sabbath. Sewing a dress, sewing a button on a dress, on Sunday, that was breaking the Sabbath. Ballroom dancing — I don't know why that was a sin. Maybe because it was suggestive? Perhaps. I don't know. All those things were sins. Ballroom dancing, never!

After the meeting, we would have another ride when we took the sailors back out to all the vessels. And there'd be a lot of boats in the harbor if there was a storm coming. I never went on the boats. No. The fun that Miriam and I had was tossing the newspapers and magazines — which were always rolled up in bundles — so that they would have reading material. Mr. Tower had them all rolled up. And we would be delegated to throw those on board, and see that they didn't go into the water before they hit the deck.

Then, if it were a weekend, we could stay the night down at the Bethel. And it was great fun because we always slept in the fo'c'sle — the upstairs room, overlooking the harbor.

But it was, to me, a beautiful sight. Really beautiful. The harbor was full of boats. All sail. They were beautiful. We had two-masters, three-masters, once in a while a four-master. Maybe — I don't know, I wish I had counted them — a dozen? Dozen and a half? At least that many, usually. They were there waiting for good weather, you know. That's why they were there. And then, when they all set sail, it was a beautiful sight. Just beautiful.

This business of going to the Bethel, it meant something to me. I don't like to go along Water Street now, I'm miserable by the time I get to the new steamship terminal, where the Bethel used to be, because the Bethel means so much to me. When they took that, they took a lot.

Well, on to better things. When I was about, maybe four years old, I was thin and puny, and they tried giving me Scott's Emulsion and Father John's Medicine. As I recall, terrible stuff, fishy-tasting oil, terrible stuff. I know I didn't like either one of them. They couldn't do anything with me.

My great-uncle, Zeb, had the *Alice Wentworth* and my father was his first mate. So, finally, my father asked the doctor if he thought it would help me if he took me on the vessel with my mother.

And the doctor said he guessed it wouldn't do me any harm. So, they took me on the vessel with my mother. I spent all one summer on that boat.

And every good night I slept outside, on a mattress, and loved it. And one thing I remember is the stars, the sky. If you're out in the middle of the ocean, and look up, and you just see those stars, sometimes the moon. It's a wonderful sensation. I'll never forget it. Those were good nights.

Sometimes the weather was bad. And I loved it. I loved that it was rough. I loved it. The one thing I remember is, you know, they had the dishes on the shelf. But in front of the dishes there's a ledge that sticks up. Like this, see. That's so if it's rough the dishes won't go on the floor. And here were those things clattering, you know, making all this noise, I remember that. That was beautiful. I loved every bit of it.

I broke my arm while I was on the boat. There was this bad storm. And the meal was ready, so we were about to partake of our food. But the storm was coming, and so Zeb was up on deck. And my father was down eating with my mother and me.

Then all of a sudden — they had me on a stool, I remember I sat on a stool, and my mother and father sat on chairs — all of a sudden, Zeb let out this awful yell. And I guess that to my father meant that there was something terribly wrong upstairs. My father had his foot on my stool so it wouldn't tip over, because it was so rough, you know. But when he heard Zeb, he forgot all about Mildred and the stool. He dashed up on deck, and Mildred went on the floor, off the stool, and broke her arm. I remember that.

And of course, we were out there, and no way of getting to a doctor at that point. We were headed for Perth Amboy, or, I don't know, Greenport. But I don't remember anything about it, whether it was painful. I suppose it was. All I remember is getting off that stool, watching those dishes and the stool going. That's all. Only a few things, like the sky, the stool, the dishes, I loved those dishes. You know, a kid would. Jiggle, jiggle — you think they're going to go any minute. That was fun!

And then every day I had Zeb's baking powder biscuits. Only I think his were Saleratus biscuits. I think that's what he called them. Delicious. And sometimes they were gray, and sometimes they were maroon, all depended on what the cargo was. If they were maroon, it was brick; and if they're gray, it's coal. But anyway, they agreed with me, whatever they were. And I really blossomed.

Zeb was a good cook. Yes, he was. He'd make those biscuits, always had those biscuits, seems to me. And then, "Tilton's Glory." It's made out of sliced potatoes, and salt pork, and onions. Had a lot of that. He'd cook up a pot of beans. Or make a stew. He was a good cook. And there was a big stove. Down at one end, a beautiful stove. It threw a lot of heat.

By the end of the summer I was in bloom. I had blossomed. I'd put on weight. I was a different kid.

Zeb was so great with me. I always thought a lot about Zeb, I really did. He always told me I had to eat raisins. Lots of raisins. And the only kind I should eat were the sticky ones. I believe those are the seeded raisins — sticky. Not these dried things. Because, you know, they had had all the goodness taken out of them. But those sticky raisins were going to make you strong; a big, strong girl. But you have to eat the raisins.

So it got to be graduation time from high school, here I am, eighteen, he came to me with this present all wrapped up. I opened it; it was a beautiful pocketbook. I can see it now. A pink and tan purse. Beautiful.

I opened it, and inside was a crisp $20 bill. Now, a $20 bill back in 1930 meant something. It really went a long way. I was delighted. I thanked him profusely. Then he pulls out his hand from behind his back. He said, "Milly, this is your real present." And he hands me a naked box of sticky raisins. I'll never forget it. He was so cute. He really was.

He was very generous, you know. And he looked like a rough man, you know. He had the reputation of being the homeliest man on the East Coast. But he could be very compassionate, very. He was always friendly, always welcoming people onto his boat.

187

I met my husband Gale because of Zeb and his brothers; my grandfather, Welcome, George Fred, William and Willard and John R. They could all sing, most of them beautifully. Gale used to go around, when he was collecting songs, and get them to sing him some of their songs. He'd come by and get songs from my grandfather Welcome. And William would sings songs but he wouldn't sing a shanty. Gale was very disappointed. But shanties were never sung onshore. They're work songs. They're only to be sung on board ship during work.

But he learned some songs from Zeb. "Grannie's Old Arm Chair," and "The Parlor." "The Parlor" is a soft, delicate song. When Zeb was singing that, he would really go into a trance. He was cross-eyed, very cross-eyed. But when he sang that song he became more so.

*Interviewed 1995*

## DAVID WELCH
b. 1926 • Tisbury
Tisbury Police Department
Oak Bluffs Water Department
Custodian, M.V. Regional High School

# You Help Me — I Help You

## Pig Slaughtering and Farms in Oak Bluffs

I was brought up by my grandmother in Oak Bluffs. She was born in the Azores. She arrived here in 1902. She came into New York and then she had to wait two weeks for people from New Bedford to come pick her up. And I can remember, she said she cried for the whole two weeks. Because she thought people were — you know, they had forgotten her. But it took time to get money and take the train down and get her.

And then she came over here and married my Grandfather Phillips. Well, their name wasn't always Phillips. The name was Silvia. I think it was her father-in-law worked for a man by the name of Phillips. And this man convinced him to change his name to Phillips. Well, at that time they said there was too many Silvias. I mean, almost all Portuguese on the Island here was named Silvia. I guess in those days they could change their name without having to go to court or something.

She spoke Portuguese with her children. But with the grandchildren she wouldn't. Because I often asked her to teach me how to speak Portuguese. "I came to America. I'm an American," she said, "this is my country, I'm never going back to Portugal, so I'm not going to speak Portuguese." But she would talk Portuguese if someone of her generation came to the house. They talked Portuguese for hours.

The Portuguese community in Oak Bluffs was close-knit — I mean, it seemed like everybody pitched in, you know? One family would help another. You knew everybody in the whole neighborhood. So, you couldn't do anything wrong without somebody knowing about it. They didn't have telephones then, either. But news got around pretty fast.

From Vineyard Avenue over to Wing Road and from — well, Main Street goes all the way up and goes into Wing Road — so up to the Lagoon Heights was all Portuguese people. And there was some along the Ball Park.

Everyone had gardens and they had their animals. Well, most everybody at least had chickens. Some had chickens and pigs. Some had pigs and horses. But pigs were a staple for the people. Those who could afford a cow, would have a cow, and those who could afford horses, they had horses. A lot of work was done with horses. Tilling the soil was done with a horse. And a plow behind it, to make the furrows and turn the soil.

Well, my grandmother had an acre of land in Oak Bluffs. On the back end was what they called the woods because the wood line started right there. So they put the pig pen down there, and the cow barn was down there. They had a cow. Sometimes they had a couple, usually they only had one. My grandmother had a garden right behind the house. In fact, everything that could be planted was planted. Potatoes, and corn, and peas, and string beans, and kale, some cabbage.

She pickled stuff for the wintertime. That's the term they used. Well, you call it preserves today, but they had glass jars, with a rubber ring and a cap, and they preserved stuff that way. And we used to have kale soup. And then she used to make fried dough.

But pork was a big thing. Because they used to raise their own pork. Everyone did. They used to raise pigs and then slaughter them. Slaughter them in late fall. Carry you through the winter.

Slaughtering would be in the morning. Sometimes it would be in the afternoon, depending on what time they got there. Because they'd go from one place to the other. If my uncle was slaughtering a pig at my grandmother's house, then they were slaughtering a pig someplace else after that. But they probably would do about two a day, maybe. You help me slaughter my pig, I go help you slaughter your pig. It was like a circle. You know, one neighbor helped another slaughter their pigs.

They slaughtered right in the backyard. They'd run two poles up and then they'd put one across the top. Then they'd hang a pulley from the middle of it, in between. And they'd get the pig and tie it by its hind legs and hang it up, and somebody would stab it in the throat. But first they bathed the pig in good hot water because when they slaughtered the pig, then they'd catch the blood in a large pan they had in the kitchen. And they'd make blood pudding with it. Oh, yeah, a lot of them wanted blood for blood pudding. Other ones wanted the feet. Other people wanted — you know. So by the time you ended up, you didn't have a whole pig. You ended up with part of a pig.

There was a sort of a salt brine that they would put the pork in, in one of those big crocks. Maybe two or three of them, depending on how much. The walls on them were about three quarters of an inch thick. They were made out of clay. Some of them were white on the outside. That's what they'd use, and then they'd cover them over with all the old clothes and stuff, to keep stuff from getting into it. There'd be a cover, but they'd still cover it over with a cloth.

They always kept the intestines of the pig for the blood pudding. They'd wash it, you know, and then pull it inside out and wash it again, then put it back. And I think they sewed one end and then they just — I don't know whether they added anything to the blood or not. Except spices and stuff. And then they'd put it inside the piece of intestine. And when it got so far, then they'd tie it in a knot, and then just cut the rest of it off. They used to fry it. When it was cooked it was black. I didn't like it, so I never ate it. But a lot of the people did.

My uncle would take the bladder and make a football out of it. That they would turn inside out, make a cover over it. Well, the one I had didn't have a cover. It was white. I don't know how long that lasted, but it lasted for a while. If I can remember correctly, it was like a round ball, that's all. But it was a pig's bladder. That's why they call it a pigskin. He just says, "Here, here's a football for you."

*Interviewed 1994*

# They Don't Let Go 'Til Thunder

We'd see some pretty strange things in the fish traps when I was trapping with my father, Norman. Lot of sharks. We seen whales. I've had a lot of stuff come in the herring nets, too. Had a two-cylinder outboard motor come in once, in the net.

The other day — I'm cutting herring roe now — I was pulling in on a net and I was pulling in an awful lot of mud and moss and slime. And I take my hands and pick it out and throw it away. Because the net wants to go back in the boat clean as I can get it. And I kept pulling for quite a little ways, and all of a sudden, I see this big wad of slime, you know, coming like that. Well, I didn't pay much attention to it. I thought, "Gee, that must be a stump." You know, a tree stump or a bucket with slime all over it. Well, I ordinarily would take my hand and gone down and cleaned that slime, like that. But, lucky, I didn't do that this time, I just pulled it up on the beach there. Then, the biggest loggerhead turtle come out you ever see. He was that big if he was an inch!

And do they bite? Bite? They don't let go 'til thunder! He'd have taken my hand right off. He would have. And he looked on the beach there like he was going to jump at me. He backed up, went up over the top of the net and went out. He'd been in a net before. He knew what to do. But I've been awful careful since. I could have been in a lot of trouble. Never had that happen before.

*Franklin Benson*

## ROBERT NORTON
1904 – 1990 • West Tisbury
Farmer
Founding Member of M.V. Cooperative Dairy,
Member of M.V. Agricultural Society

# There Were a Lot of People Peddling Milk

## Buttonwood Farm Milk Run

We sold milk in Vineyard Haven. I guess there was milk going away from that farm into Vineyard Haven for forty years. My father did it first. He used to have a milk route in Vineyard Haven, sold it from house to house.

In those days we had milk in cans. Didn't have milk bottles. Didn't know what a milk bottle was until he was growing up, 'til later years. You had a tin quart can. Fill it with milk, a quart measure with a handle on it. And he'd pour out a quart of milk. You had to furnish the utensils to put it in — the pitcher. Then they got milk bottles.

The first milk bottle that I remember had a metal top, with a push-down clamp that held it on. Then they came out with the paper milk bottle caps. Now, of course, they have paper bottles.

My father had a horse and wagon at first. Then finally he got a truck.

There were a lot of people peddling milk. Alice Merry lived above us; she was the first in line. Then there was the Tashmoo Farm. There was Joe Merry, Lloyd Merry's father, over here; then Orlin Davis and Virginia Silva, and Alton Tilton in Vineyard Haven, and the Fischers, Arnold Fischer's father. I'd go to this house, somebody else would go to that one. One person would buy milk from me, but they wouldn't buy it from somebody else. They had their pet milkman.

One funny thing. I don't know as I ought to tell these things. One morning one man came to us and wanted to buy milk. My father says, "You have your own milkman, I don't want to take any trade away from him."

"Well," the man says, "when I put fifteen cents in the bottle for a bottle of milk and I get a bottle of milk the next day with fifteen cents in the bottle of milk, I think it's time to change. I wouldn't care if I knew it was my own fifteen cents, but I'm not sure that it's my own."

As long as I can remember, there was a milk inspector came down sometime every year. You'd never know when he was coming. You'd be peddling milk, you'd go into the house with a quart of milk and come out and find this man standing by your wagon with a bag, taking samples of milk. More for butterfat content than anything else. Then, eventually, they took samples and took it away and tested it for bacteria.

They didn't bother with that in the beginning.

*Interviewed 1982*

## ALICE PURDY RAY

1911 – 1998 • Tisbury

Homemaker

Manager of Boarding Houses, Oak Bluffs

# My Father Was a Lighthouse Keeper

## Childhood at the East Chop Light

I was born in Nantucket in 1911 at Sankaty Light. My father was a lighthouse keeper. Dad's name was George Walter Purdy. My mother's name was Mary Jane Purdy. Her name was Ganz before she got married. They both came from Newfoundland. My mother came here and was working for a minister in Brockton. And my father came on and they were married.

My father was a lobster fisherman. And when he came down here, I think it was in New Bedford, he got on a lighthouse boat, the *Azalea*. He was the chief engineer. A lighthouse boat brings supplies to the lighthouses. At that time they used to bring coal and all kinds of supplies.

Pop had only one arm. He lost his arm on the *Azalea*. He was down in the engine room showing somebody how to run the motor. In those days the motors didn't have any guards around them at all. They were open and his sleeve caught, and before he could get it, it took it off about here. And before they could get into New Bedford, to the hospital, gangrene had set it, and they had to take it off.

And that's why they put him on the lighthouses. They put him at Nantucket first, then at Gay Head. My brother Walter was the only one that wasn't born in a lighthouse. Charley was born at Gay Head, I was born at Nantucket, and Luther was born up here at East Chop.

Anyway, I was born in the fall, and we moved to Martha's Vineyard in the spring. They moved my father up to Gay Head, then into East Chop. That was heaven up there in East Chop then. There weren't any trees across the way. It was just plain meadows. The girls — there was three of us that used to be together in the summertime, all the time. Just go across the big open field down to Crystal Lake and around. We used to go skating there. The boys used to say, "Come on, Pop, let's go skating down on the pond." And we'd all go down there and ice skate at night. I'd say, "Dad, it's nine o'clock."

"Yes, I think Ma's got the chocolate on the back of the stove. Let's go." Maybe about ten, twenty kids go up there. She'd have a big pot of chocolate. But there was always a note: "Wash the dishes when you get through." Well, I don't blame her. I don't think I'd like to get up and have a big sink full of dishes in the morning. Now I can see it, but then I couldn't!

The house there, they don't build them like that anymore. The cellar went right straight up to the roof. It was brick all the way up. And the roof was slate. In the wintertime it was beautiful. You would never know what the weather was outside if you were in the house. You wouldn't know whether it was raining, blowing, sleet. You'd stick your head out the door, you'd say, "Hey, oh, look at it!" But you'd never know it in the house because the house was so solid that it wouldn't show anything. It was just as warm and nice as could be. In the summertime it was cool. The oil house was down there in back — where they stored the oil for the lighthouse in barrels. And then at one time down here there was a wharf, and the boats from New York used to stop there, we called it the New York Wharf. And the government used to land there and bring stuff up.

There was another building they called a tool shed, and there was the barn across the street. You see, Dad decided he had to have a cow. So he asked the town if he could put a cow across the street. There wasn't anybody there. It was just open field. They said, "Go ahead," so he went out and bought himself a cow. Every time I think of that cow I see a cat. I think of when Mom used to milk it, the cat used to sit there and she'd squirt milk in the cat's mouth. You know, that foolish cat knew when it was four o'clock in the afternoon, and he'd come in the barn and sit there.

And we used to have a vegetable garden. You should have seen the gardens my father used to have in there. Oh, those rambling roses. They're still growing wild along the fence in front.

In the summer my father was up at five because the sun would be up. And that light had to be out. Because the lens — see, the lenses were powerful. They were 62,000 watts. So you had to get a covering on them before the sun got up. You couldn't go up there without it being covered because you were afraid of the sun burning your eyes. So he used to get up early and put the covering on it, and so that when it did come up it wouldn't shine in the little place upstairs. It was like a black window shade. It would go around, you know, and he'd pull it, walk around with it. Like curtains. And, especially in nor'easters, they'd put them on and kind of tie them down so they wouldn't fly around. My father washed the windows every day, especially on your lights upstairs. They had to be done every day.

Every spring he painted the lighthouse. It was maroon. They used to send down paint, and my father didn't like it. It was dark, almost like a dark red. And he said, "I don't want that stuff on there." So he used to go into Phillips' and get a gallon of oil and mix it all up in it. And he said, "Now that's better." He'd say "Hey, Alice, slap some on. Slap some on!" He used to put the ladder up on the tower, and I'd tie it up on the railing up above. I used to get up on that little round thing up on top, where all the railings were, and I'd scrape it. I used to help Pop up there. Now, I happened to be up there one day recently, and the Coast Guard was up there. They were scraping the lighthouse. They put up a smaller one now. And they were scraping it with an electric scraper. And I'm sitting there, and I'm watching them. Finally one of the fellows says to me "Lady, what are you doing?" I said "I'm watching you. I know a one-armed man used to scrape that all by himself." He said, "How long did it take him?" "Two days." He said, "You're kidding me!"

It was a hundred and twenty stairs to the first landing. Then there was about ten stairs from there up to where the lights were. You'd light the light up

there. But you always made sure that you got it lit before dusk. He'd have his lamps all ready, so all he had to do is just put them into their foundations, on a tray, like, and then put them up. Then you had to crank up the weights which turned the light. You had to make sure that the weights went right up to the top to keep the light turning through the night. And the light would turn. It flashed red. It flashed two reds and a white. And West Chop was two whites and a red.

And there was the storm warning tower. It was all made out of metal. It was seventy-five feet up, four sections. And it had a rod that was up in the air. In all, it was about one hundred and twenty-five feet. And you'd put lights up, and if you were having a nor'easter, you'd put two reds and a white. If it was a windstorm, you'd put the flags up. And they were funny-shaped. Of course your flags would go up higher than your lights.

When the government automated the light they asked my father if he wanted to stay on. He asked us at the dinner table, "Would you like to stay here?" And I looked at him, I said, "Pop, what's the rent going to be?" "Oh," he says, "a hundred dollars a month." "Oh. Naw, I don't want to. It's too lonesome up here." There wasn't anybody up there in the wintertime.

So the house was taken down. The men came down from the government. And they told my father they'd have the house down by the afternoon. My father didn't say anything. He says, "Hey, Alice, let's you and I sit over here and we'll watch them take the house down." We did. We sat there. So finally one of them said "Hey, Captain Purdy, how's this house built?" "I don't know. You said you could take it down. Take it down. Take that big ball you've got up there and hit it." It didn't even budge. So they looked at him. He said, "You said you'd have it all down by the afternoon." And we sat there and watched them. I said, "Pop, don't you dare laugh." Finally he said, "Boys, take the siding off it and see what's underneath it." "Well, I'll be go-to-hell," one of them says, "it's brick." Anyway, the government just took it down. I could never understand why the government pulled it down. Why didn't they sell it to somebody? It was pretty nice up there.

*Interviewed 1995*

## JOHN COUTINHO
b. 1914 • Oak Bluffs
Carpenter, Fisherman
Contractor
Married to Alice Coutinho

# I Worked Right from the Beginning

## *A Workingman's Life*

I was born on — they called it Chicken Alley at that time — but it was Lagoon Pond Road in Vineyard Haven. Down from the post office, the road that goes down towards Burt's Boatyard. Chicken Alley. Everybody had a garden in back. Chickens and pigs, and everything else. There used to be a big pond there. On the left, where that bicycle shop is at Five Corners, used to be a stream came up there. There was a pond from there all the way down to the shipyard. The pond was almost up to Hinckley's Lumber Yard. In fact, Hinckley's Lumber Yard was part of the pond. And Tisbury Market Place, that was the Vineyard Haven dump. I used to go down there and kick stuff around and look for stuff, you know. As kids you'd do that. Now that's all landfill in there, they dug the harbor out and filled that all up. All the way down to the Shipyard, all landfill.

They used to have a little stretch of land going right across by that little shack there, below the Marine Hospital. That was the only way to get across from Burt's Boatyard to Beach Road. They used to have planks going across there. We used to call that Three Board Bridge.

The Marine Hospital was on the hill. They had a lot of old-time marine men there. There was a guy who used to live there, an old-timer. He was always hunched over, with two canes. You'd go down there and he'd put these ships in bottles. You ever see these schooners and stuff, in a bottle? He used to put them in there, and sell them.

The Marine Hospital used to burn coal. All the ashes they used to dump on that road, to make the road solid. My father bought us a little red cart. We used to go and get leaves for the pigs, and do this and that. We used to go on the road, pick up all the coal that wasn't burned, and cart it home to burn. There was a lot of coal there. That's a fact. We used to go and get the coal off the road.

And then, for some reason or other, we moved.

My father sold the house and we moved three or four different places. Down on Causeway Road, then up to Pine Road. We had a garden there and we had grapes — my father made wine, everybody did. Everything they could with what they had, you know. A lot of the Portuguese families had stills down cellar. They made their own booze.

We'd buy flour by the barrel — you had to get a lot. People didn't go to the store unless they had to. You tried to do what you could. We could only afford a pair of shoes once in a while. We never wore shoes in the summertime. The minute school let out, we never put on a pair of shoes except to go to church. And, boy, don't you think the bottom of your feet didn't get tough after a while. Like leather, you know. We used to go down and pick over the dump, running barefoot all through that dump. Of course, my father, when his shoes wore out, used to take an old tire. He used to cut a piece out of it, make his own soles for shoes, and they wore like iron.

Our house had two bedrooms. My mother and father had their own bedroom, but the five of us stayed in the other big room that we divided with a partition. There were five kids, three of us boys in one bed, the girls in the other.

I don't know much about the history of my family. But they came from Madeira. I don't know why they came to the Island. But they landed here anyway, and they stayed here all their lives. Of course, my father had an idea he wanted to go back to Portugal. So he took some of his money and shipped it to Portugal. Put it in the bank so he'd have money when he gets there. Well, we didn't want to leave the Island. We didn't want to go to any Portugal. Why the hell would we want to go to Portugal? I wasn't very old then, but I can remember it like it was yesterday. And finally, you know what happened? He lost everything he had over there — the banks went bankrupt. So that saved us. He was discouraged, but he got over it.

My father went into the fishing business. He had a small catboat and had a mooring in the Vineyard Haven harbor. My father used to barrel his fish and ship it to New York. He did pretty good fishing. He worked for it, but he did well.

But these guys come down here from the old country, they worked like dogs, you know, they worked hard. When they first came here they were digging — making stone walls. Some guys, two or three Portuguese, built that stone wall around the cemetery in Vineyard Haven. And they used to dig a whole cesspool, years ago, for two or three dollars! You know, they did stuff like that to make a living.

I worked right from the beginning. I used to run errands for people. I had four or five customers I'd run errands for. Go downtown and get groceries for them, mow the lawns, weed their gardens, for twenty-five cents. If I made any money mowing lawns, I used to go home and give my mother everything I made. Except, maybe, keep something for myself to go to a show or something. We used to go to the show for fifteen cents. And we used to go blueberrying. All the land we used to go blueberrying on, there's houses there now. But I used to get a lot of blueberries. We used to sell them for twenty-five cents a quart. And mayflowers. We'd go mayflowering. Bunch of mayflowers, go and ask fifteen to twenty cents, you know, to different houses. We had to make money somewhere.

They had that six-hole golf course up in Tashmoo, where the Lookout is, that field there looking down and part of Tashmoo Farm fields, that was a golf course at one time. A nice six-hole golf course, beautiful. Just right for someone starting to learn. And I went up there to caddy, because I was a young fellow then — had to make money somewhere. I used to caddy two big bags for these old women. Two great big bags. They only needed two golf clubs, but I had to lug these two great big bags. For thirty-five cents. Local people and summer people used to play there. We had some good golfers on this Island. We'd go up there whenever we could, when nobody was around, and go and play and practice, you know.

I quit school at seventeen to work at Paul Bangs' grocery store. And I worked for seventeen dollars a week, sixty or seventy hours a week. A week! Not an hour, a week! I started in the grocery department and I learned the meat business there. They used to run a meat truck. It used to go up-Island loaded down with groceries. A store on wheels — groceries, meat, vegetables, bread and everything. Used to load it right down, so you could hardly see out of the windshield. Go all the way to Gay Head on Monday. The rest of the week it'd go to Chilmark, West Tisbury, Menemsha, and stop at these houses. And they used to have another truck that came to Oak Bluffs three or four days a week. And I got stuck with both routes. Three days up-Island, and three days down here. I used to leave at seven o'clock in the morning, and come back at five or six at night. So finally I told Paul, "I can't stand this anymore, I need some more money. I can't live like this."

So the First National, where the Bunch of Grapes bookstore is now, they offered me a job, only forty hours a week, twenty dollars a week. So I went with them and stayed for nine years. I managed the meat department in the Oak Bluffs store for three or four years. Then the Depression got to be so bad they finally decided that they were going to cut out the meat department and just keep groceries because there was no business. It was terrible. Nobody had any money.

But the Tivoli — that used to be some place! I paid for half of it, I swear I paid for half of it! I used to go there Saturday night. I'd come home and dress up, and go back to the store and then get the store closed and be down over there to the Tivoli Dance Hall, ten o'clock at night.

I was lucky. I went from one job to another. I went back to the First National in Vineyard Haven and worked there for a while. Then everybody was working at Otis Air Base getting a hundred and fifteen to a hundred and twenty dollars a week. I was making twenty dollars a week, and it didn't sound too good. So I got a job at Miles Standish in Taunton. They were building Army barracks there. It was a war thing. I worked there for quite a while. Then I came back here and went up to Peaked Hill.

We built a lot of barracks up there. You know, they kept moving us from one place to another. Then they were building this base where the airport is now, that was a Navy base. They had a big gang working there. We put up a great big hangar, and those other buildings. Then toward the end, I went down to the Dunes. Down in Edgartown. They built bases down there. Right by the beach, where the restaurant is now. All government stuff at that time.

And I was in the fishing business for twenty years. Going all over – Georges Bank and Noman's and Sandwich down to Boston Bay. I made some trips with my dad. Then I went fishing with another fellow and I learned the business through him. Finally I said, "Well, I'll get my own boat." I figured if I'm going to fish with somebody else, I might as well run my own boat. So I went to Point Judith and saw a boat that I'd wanted for a long time. I had it for fifteen years. It was a commercial dragger, forty-foot dragger. It was a small boat.

But I did go on the big boats, the heavy big boats that would go as far as the hundred-fathom measure. They call it the Northern Edge. We used to go down there in the wintertime, fishing for fluke. And lobster, too. One time we hit a nor'wester, and everything froze – froze up the gear solid. You see, coming in, everything's spraying. Every time it hit the rigging it would freeze. And then the scuppers would freeze up, and the water wouldn't run out. Everything gets heavy. It could roll over very easily, you know. We finally got to New Bedford and used a steam hose to steam it all off.

We were swordfishing one summer. I was cook on that boat. And I worked on deck just like the rest of them. But my extra chore was cooking. I got a percentage for that. They wanted three meals a day – which is wrong. You know, when you swordfish, you're not supposed to have three meals a day. You get breakfast and supper. Sandwiches during the day. Because the day is when you're doing your fishing. So they'd all pile down the fo'c'sle and have lunch, and about that time somebody'd yell, "Swordfish!" and everybody'd be trying to get out the same time. These guys, I don't know.

After a while, I went on the *Viking* with Joe Ferocious. I learned a lot from him. When I got through with him I could build a net right on deck. Took a bobbin of twine, maybe five or six missions, they call it. And cut that net right down, like somebody was doing a sweater, or something. Put it together, you know, used a shuttle.

Anyway, when I didn't go fishing in the wintertime, I did carpentry work. I couldn't just depend on fishing and raise a family. So it got to a point I was doing more carpentry than fishing. So I said, "I'd better quit one thing or the other." So I went into building houses. I put up seventeen on the Island.

So I worked. Oh, Christ, I'm telling you, I never stopped! You know, it's all water under the bridge now. When I stop to think of all the things we did when we was young, it's unbelievable. It was one thing after the other. I can't remember ever having had a vacation between jobs. Of course, I got married, but I kept working and working, doing this and that. But I did accomplish quite a lot, if I do say so myself.

*Interviewed 1994*

teaching them English. And that was kind of a mistake, you should keep your language in the house. Because if you have the Portuguese, you know, you will always have it. But my mother wanted to learn, and my mother did, finally, get her citizenship. Very proud of it. But I did get so I could understand Portuguese quite well. Because they got letters from Portugal, and I'd read along with my mother.

I enjoyed playing the piano and I played all I could. I took lessons from nine years old until fifteen, I guess. And I taught piano. In my married years, I taught piano for a long time.

Anyway, after I got out of high school, I went to work at Paul Bangs' market, and I was there until I got married. My husband, John, worked there. He used to go door-to-door selling vegetables, and we got together. He wooed me there. He would bring me back the roses that his customers gave him from their gardens. We got married in '36, at the Catholic church in Vineyard Haven.

Church was a big part of our lives. The first church on Martha's Vineyard was in Oak Bluffs — the Sacred Heart Hall, where they have bingo, up there by the ball park. Well, that was the first Catholic church on Martha's Vineyard. And my mother lived in Vineyard Haven and she'd walk to this church and back on Sunday. Maybe not every Sunday, but lots of Sundays.

In Madeira and, I imagine, Fayal too, all those Portuguese islands, everything was for the church. Flowers were grown for the church. John's sister grew flowers for the church. She never wanted to see the altar without flowers. They didn't have anything, but they grew flowers and gave them to the church. And it was the most beautiful sight to go to church and see all the flowers everywhere.

And, oh, Portuguese holidays! Christmas is the biggest one. At Christmas time they'd go around singing and playing guitars and violins. On Christmas Eve they'd go around knocking at the doors and waking people up. And they'd stamp on the porch and play, singing a song in Portuguese,

and say, "Owner of the house, please open the door to us." And they'd come in, and inside they'd have an altar to Jesus and wheat growing and all these decorations. We had beautiful figurines brought from the old country, statues, you know. The Baby Jesus and everything. And embroidered skirts around the altar. They would have some food and some wine. And they would sing all night, going door to door. The last thing they would sing "A Bom Natal," which meant a good Christmas, a good Nativity.

One time it was snowing. They came here and the lady next door woke up in the night and she told me the next day, "I woke up and I thought I was in heaven! I heard these violins playing." And it was them walking up the street singing and playing along.

John's family had a big part in it. John played the guitar, his father played violin very well, and his cousin Siggy sang and played the guitar. And his cousin played the dancing dolls. They went out Christmas and New Year. They kept going for a long time. At the end of the evening they would come by here and the children would rush out of bed and sit at the top of the stairs and listen. They'd sing all the religious songs and then they'd branch out to other songs and roll back the rugs and dance. I went one night, and I didn't get home until morning! But it got so after a while it kind of fell away.

I remember we used to go see *chamaritas* at the PA Club, the Portuguese–American Club. The *chamarita* is sort of like a square dance. They wear costumes; the girls had the blouses and velvet skirts and kerchiefs. When you dance you stamp your foot in the middle. No matter what you do, that's the step your feet are doing. And then they do-si-do.

The *chamarita* was done at Feast time. The Feast was started in Portugal. They did it to feed the hungry. And it was all free. They gave out beef, which they roasted on an open fire, and they made a lot of soup with cabbage and potatoes and linguica and mint. The mint is the secret. If you don't put mint in it, forget it. This is Holy Ghost soup. It's *Spirito Santo* soup. At Feast time they really made it a wonderful time. A band would come from New Bedford. There were many, many flowers decorating everything. They danced and sang a lot. We don't do enough of it here anymore. The *chamarita* is a wonderful, wonderful Portuguese dance that should not be forgotten.

*Interviewed 1997*

## HELEN MANNING

b. 1919 • Aquinnah
Teacher, Gay Head, Oak Bluffs, Washington
Director of Education, Wampanoag Tribal Council, Aquinnah

# I Knew That We Had a Special Place

## Childhood in Aquinnah

I was born in Gay Head, September 24, 1919. My mother was Evelyn Moss. Washington, D.C. was her home. My father was Arthur Herbert Vanderhoop from Gay Head. Now Aquinnah.

I started going to Washington for the winter when I was seven. I did most of my schooling there. I lived here for six months out of the year and then I lived in Washington for six months. My parents would stay at Gay Head and I would go to Washington to be with my mother's mother and my aunt and her husband. My grandmother and my aunt would see to it that I always returned to Gay Head for summer vacation. I always wanted to live on Gay Head, and I was very sad when I'd have to leave in the fall.

I'm an only child, but I had lots of cousins here. They looked forward to my coming and I guess it was something new for them. We always had a good time. And going to each of these homes, I was treated as one of the family. Whatever they did, I was included in everything. It really was very nice. It was very close knit. It was really fun.

My father was in the restaurant business. First he ran the Vanderhoop Restaurant, which his mother and her husband had run, and then he had the Not-O-Way. It was seasonal; after Labor Day most of the businesses just died down.

The Vanderhoop restaurant was there when the ox carts would be coming up from the steamboat landing — that was a little before my time. There was also a restaurant right at the dock, I've heard them say, which they called the Pavilion. They used to have a band, and people danced and they served food. There were many restaurants. In fact, Edwin DeVries Vanderhoop built a hotel that had nineteen bedrooms, nineteen rooms! That was where what we call the Haunted House is now, here at the Cliffs. But it burned down, I'm not sure what year.

So, the Vanderhoop Restaurant was in existence when I was young. But that building burned down also. I was nine years old when my father took over

the Not-O-Way. It was built by a man by the name of Gennochio. He was not a Gay Header, he was from New Bedford. And why he built it no one ever knew because he never, never opened it, never used it. But he stocked it with all these dishes that said "Not-O-Way" and so forth.

I think he was somebody involved in the rum running or something. He had that look. And he knew how to buy up land, too. All over Gay Head. In fact, the Coast Guard station was on land that he had bought, and the Coast Guard had to lease it from him!

The Not-O-Way was right across from the Gay Head Lighthouse, on the outer edge of the circle, right across from where I live now. In fact the steps, I think, are still there. It was an inn and a restaurant. They had about, let's see, one, two, three, I think there were six rooms upstairs. And of course the family and the help took care of three, so that meant they had three rooms, accommodated two people each.

My mother was in charge of feeding the people who came for the inn. She supervised the kitchen, and she did the laundry. For fifty cents you'd get a delicious lobster sandwich and you could get quahog chowder, a bowl for a quarter.

The dining room was very nice too, because they had plate glass windows that looked out on the Atlantic Ocean. And my mother had a friend who raised canaries, so there were canaries all around the dining room, chirping away.

I remember one thing we had. Anyone who came in through the kitchen — friends and family — there was a great big long table. And that long table was always covered with lobsters, cooked lobsters. And you just stand up there and open lobsters and eat them just like you do salted peanuts. So that was great.

My father generated his own electricity, one of the first in Gay Head. He had rigged up a Delco system — he had many, many batteries. We had to really be conservative with electricity because those batteries were only good for so long and then you'd have to run the motor to recharge them. Many times we used the kerosene lamps rather than use the juice from the Delco. And we'd read the paper and read the Sears Roebuck catalog, which was the most popular book. We called it our dream book.

At the Not-O-Way he also had a garden. It was approximately where the big parking lot is now. My father always had a cow, he always had a pig, and he had chickens he kept about a mile down the road. And people who lived here used to go blueberrying and they used to come up and sell the blueberries to my father. So there was always good, fresh food. And big crowds would come every evening to have dinner. And we served lunch.

I was just thinking the other day, he really worked very hard, carting water and doing all those things. There was no running water. We had a pump in the kitchen and a barrel outside for catching rain, but that could only be used for washing the dishes and laundry. So he had to go down to Cook's Spring and get the water for people to drink.

As there was no running water, there was no bathroom, and they had to use chamber pots. We had to do the emptying and see to it that everything was clean. And two outhouses. That was one of my jobs, to go out and wipe off the outhouse. The Ladies', I didn't have to go to the Men's.

Then in the evening, the big deal was to walk to the post office. So we'd go and you'd gather up more people as you went. And then when you got to the post office, everybody would decide what we were going to do that night, whether we were going to have a beach party or whether we were going to be up around the Loop. We had a lot of beach parties. We'd have a fire on the beach, usually at Lobsterville. It was before the '38 hurricane, so all the fishing shacks were still there. And the Not-O-Way had a big porch on it, and we'd be on the porch. Everybody had to be home at least by ten or eleven o'clock. We just talked and fooled around.

The post office was at Leonard Vanderhoop's house. And that was really a social gathering because everybody came up and it was like being at the steamboat wharf — you're talking back and forth to people. Another gathering place was the Baptist church across from his house. On Sundays there was an evening church service, and a lot of people went to that. And us kids would go, too.

I feel personally that the Cliff area, where the lighthouse is and where my house is, I feel that that's very sacred territory. It's sort of hard to explain why. It's something I feel within me. That's where I belong. The Cliffs and that area, they've always been the main resource of the Gay Head Wampanoag people. It gave them an income. For years people sold tons of clay for the making of china and stuff.

Just being a Gay Header was synonymous with being Wampanoag. I knew that we had a special place, a sense of being a Wampanoag. And I carried that with me, too, when I went to Washington. Everybody in the school knew that Helen Vanderhoop was an Indian. It wasn't something that I just had when I was here, it went with me.

I got that sense from being with my father. He was that way too. I mean he was always the Indian. I followed my father everywhere, wherever he went he couldn't get rid of me! I think it was the way that he was treated when he went down-Island to buy supplies for the restaurant and so forth. It was always with a certain amount of respect.

Later, when I was teaching in Gay Head, I kept instilling in the kids how proud they should be to be an Indian, you know. And they all are. They're very proud.

My mother wasn't a Wampanoag. She was just what they call now black. But she had Indian blood in her because her mother had been born in West Virginia, but she never knew what tribe it was.

I have had a rich background in black history and it is something to be proud of. You know, a lot of times people, especially Wampanoags, feel as though to be black is just to be like the worst thing in the whole world. And they'd do anything to get away from it. Anything to be less cognizant of what they really are. I think it's this thing of prejudice against one or the other. That's what needs to be broken down, so that they can really get together and really accomplish something without losing identity.

When I was in Washington, I was very conscious of blackness. Not so much any stigma about being black, but about the people who had made

211

advancements who were black, who had done things like Carter G. Woodson and Harry Burleigh, the tenor and collector of spirituals.

Harry Burleigh used to come down here and every Sunday he would come up to the Cliffs and he'd bring some celebrity with him. He'd bring Ethel Waters and he'd always introduce us. My father had a small stand up there on top of the Cliffs. And that was my job to keep it. I sold candy and soda. I remember Harry Burleigh would come and we'd all hide behind the door. Just plain, silly kids!

I taught in Gay Head for twelve years. At the one-room school. I started in '56, and I think we closed in '68. When I first started, it was first to sixth grade. I think there were about fifteen students then.

It was difficult, but it was a wonderful experience. It was an experience I think all teachers should have, because there was so much interaction with everybody, and everybody taught each other and helped each other. If something came up in the news that happened in Gay Head, we could all get in the car and go to the scene of whatever it was. It was really like a big family. We had a lot of people to come in and help do things. Like Mrs. White from Vineyard Haven used to do clay, and another woman who did great big charts on anthropology, and we had a music teacher who came up. It was great.

My mother taught at the Gay Head school, too, for quite a few years. They always had some big play, and I always wished that I could see these plays because you'd hear them talking about it. I think they did *Alice in Wonderland* and then on Halloween they'd go down to what we used to call Big Tree and she'd make all kinds of scary things down there.

Big Tree was sort of like a little park, and people would go down and play in that area. The trees were so huge, all covered with a canopy of leaves. There was one big tree — it just fell down maybe three or four years ago, it rotted out. But some people were a little frightened of it. People told ghost stories about it and if you were out walking after dark you really stepped up a bit when you got by Big Tree, as if you knew something was going to jump out at you.

There were some older people who knew a lot about medicines. And there were some people that they used to say could "root" you with different things.

We'd always like to go and visit the old folks and we'd sit and talk and they'd give us cookies and milk. When we went to visit this particular lady we would never take any of the nourishment from her. We'd say, "No, thank you" because she was supposed to be one of these people that could root you. You know, they'd either leave certain roots in your path or stick them in your pocket or something like that. You have to have some kind of contact with it. If you were rooted, people could make you do what they wanted you to do. That's what they said. But I don't know of anybody who was ever rooted. We never really believed it, but we were careful.

The revived interest in Wampanoag culture started here, I think, in the '60s and '70s, when everybody was very conscious of what their heritage was.

After we had gotten federal recognition, we had many people who were not aware of what their history was. Some things were passed down in families, but not much. There didn't seem to be an exchange, a sharing of the information. My goal as Education Director for the Tribe was to find out as much as I could, and then pass it on to others. And also to encourage as many people as possible to continue the education and to get back the Indian ways and learn about the Indian. And not only learn about them, but, use them, do them, prepare them.

Now, more Indians are more conscious of what an education can do. I mean they used to think all they needed to do was be Indian. You know, that was enough. And that's not enough. Not in these days. You got to be something, do something.

To be Wampanoag, in the first place, it's inside you. It's really something that you're very proud of and you want to be. You want everybody to be the best that they can be so that they can be important and stand for something and not just be running their mouths. It's a sense that you can come into a room and you can pick out your relatives. You can just look at them and you know. It's a feeling that they belong to the Wampanoag.

*Interviewed 1998*

## ROSALIE SPENCE
1905 — 1988 · Tisbury
Homemaker, Housekeeper
Daughter of Zeb Tilton, Captain of *Alice S. Wentworth*,
last coastal schooner active on the eastern seaboard

# He Didn't Care for Land Work

## *Sailing with Zeb Tilton*

In those days, my father was never there, you see. He was on the boat, the *Alice Wentworth*, all the time. He was at sea and once in a great while he'd come home. He used to come home and take his boat and anchor up in Menemsha, and walk down from Menemsha to where we lived in Chilmark. That's quite a long ways. He'd walk down, maybe stay one night, and then the next morning he's up and gone again, you see. I think he was very happy when he was home, but he had to go because he didn't care for land work at all. He didn't care for farming. His love was the sea, and that's the way he earned his living, and that was his life.

So my mother had practically it all to do by herself to bring us up. There were ten of us. Do the shopping and cook and clean and everything. We had a big garden. Of course we always had a cow, so we had a cow to be milked. I think we mostly had a pig, had to feed that all the time. And getting in the wood, cutting the wood. We had chickens, guinea hens. So there was always a lot to do, you know.

She used to make bread for practically everybody in Chilmark. And my mother preserved a lot of things. All sorts of vegetables and fruit and blueberries. We'd have hundreds of jars of things done up in the cellar by the time winter came. I used to sit up until eleven or twelve or one at night helping her doing up preserves. The rest of them were all sleeping. And I'd be up with her helping her because I was the oldest.

We lived up there in Chilmark and we didn't go anywhere except to school and home and that was it, you know. Never went to church up there. Church was too far away. We didn't have a car. My mother used to go with the horse and wagon and go shopping around West Tisbury a couple of times a week. We never went to the beach when we were young. We'd have to walk four or five miles. And Mother wasn't about to hitch up that horse and take us. She had too much to do, you know. So I never learned to swim. It was primitive times in those days. We lived away from everybody else. We weren't close to anything.

We were always really happy to see my father. Of course, I was always very close to him anyway. He used to wear those suspenders, you know. They didn't wear belts like they do now. They'd wear those suspenders. He used to come lay down alongside me 'til I went to sleep when I was a little girl; and I remember I'd wind my hands around those suspenders and figure, "Well, he's not gonna get away without me knowing it." And when I woke up in the morning, he'd be gone. He'd get my hands out and be gone, back on the boat. And I used to be so heartbroken when I'd wake up in the morning and he'd be gone, you know?

Because I was very close to my father. Being with him was my main thing in those days. My happiness was to be with him and being on the boat and going different places and seeing different people. I went with him a lot when I got older. And my children went a lot with him, especially my oldest boy, he went with his grandfather on the boat a lot.

When I was on the boat I used to help him steer. I used to cook and clean the cabin. Oh, yes, I used to have to work on there. I probably might not have had any responsibilities, but I took them, you know. I helped hoist the sails. A good many times we'd hoist them up by hand. And they were big sails, too. There was no power in the boat, and he used to say that was the beauty of going because we didn't know when we were going to get there, had to depend on wind and weather, you know, to get places. Many times I'd steer the boat for him. Whiles at night, if he wanted to lay down and take a little rest, why, he'd tell me to steer the boat for a certain object, for a light or something that you could see in the night. He'd know how long it was going to take to get there and by that time he'd wake up.

## HAROLD ROGERS
b. 1912 • West Tisbury
Farmer
Highway Surveyor, Town of West Tisbury

# A Little of This, a Little of That

## Farm Life and House Moving

My father had a mill, out back here. Ground corn. He raised his own corn, raised his own hay and, of course, vegetables and all that. Didn't have much to buy, really. My mother made the bread. I remember when I was a kid, going to New Bedford on the boat and we would buy a barrel of flour and half a barrel of white sugar and half a barrel of brown sugar. In the fall. That's about all we needed to buy.

We had a dozen or eighteen sheep. My father would do the shearing himself. There was quite a few sheep on the Island, and the farmers used to get together, put all the wool together and just make a big shipment.

They only got about fifty cents a pound, as I remember. Be about six pounds on a sheep, ordinary sheep. Of course, the big sheep — we had one we used to cut fifteen or sixteen pounds. But even at fifty cents you aren't getting rich.

My father also went out carpentering and he had a clock and watch business. He made grandfather clocks and he used to repair clocks and watches for people. He had a little bench right in the other room here in the house.

We had house raisings and barn raisings and all the neighbors would help. Neighbors used to build stone fences, stone walls. Neighbors would work all together. Build somebody's wall, then go on to the next neighbor's. And come haying time, the neighbors would all help each other out. All working together. No money was passed. They used to work from sunrise to sunset.

Just the way farm life was those days. A little of this and a little of that.

We used oxen for everything on the farm — plowing, harrowing a row, cutting hay, mowing hay, everything. I used to have a team to go plowing farm gardens all over town.

My father used to make the yokes for our oxen from sassafras. It's a light, strong wood.

Oxen are slower than horses. A little more powerful, but much slower. The last team of oxen I had until 1938. I bought a tractor then and used it ever since. The oxen were too slow.

But oxen could do things a tractor couldn't. Like go down to the beach and pick up seaweed to fertilize the gardens. They go where a tractor never could. And they were good and also intelligent. I had a Model A car in the '30s. In the spring when the road was muddy and the car got stuck, I'd take the oxen to pull out the car. The oxen were a lot more dependable than the car.

We used them for plowing the road. They would sink in the snow, but they would plow right along. Very patient. And they used them to move houses. Was one house I heard of, moved before my day, they used sixteen yoke of oxen for it.

They put it on wheels and pulled it right through the scrub oak. That was Daniel Hull's house across from the fire station in West Tisbury. Moved from down where the Scottish Bakehouse is.

When my father was young, and before, they used to move houses everywhere, all the time. People used to get tired of where they were living, decide to move, jack it up and move — house and all. They would use horses or oxen. Sometimes they'd float them on barges or boats.

When they moved my father's house down the hill, it was moved on rollers. Planks and rollers. His half-brother, he was in the house and when they went down the hill the house got away from them and the doors got jammed. And he couldn't get out. Luckily, it didn't go anywhere. It just went down the hill, went off the rollers and it stopped.

Of course the land was all clear then. It wasn't all these trees. Everything was open pastures and hills.

*Interviewed 1983*

the boat there to jump into or hold on to. They'd come across, do their shopping and all, and turn around and push the boat back across the ice. That's the way they got there.

In fact, I've walked across to Chappy on the ice. When I was a small boy, I walked across and my father went ahead of me with some other people. He had an axe and he would chop every so often because going across the harbor was very treacherous. It could be thick in one place and thin in another. Because, the way the current goes under, the water would melt the ice. So you had to be careful.

There was a wonderful pond for skating out here behind the house. Oh, the skating parties were great. We had a man who worked with my father on the farm, and he would take the cobs of corn after the corn had been ground off it and put them in bags and put them on the pond and pour kerosene on them and light them. So we'd have these wonderful bonfires and go skating around the bonfires and all that. My mother was very good about having hot cocoa for all of us afterwards. The pond was not very deep, so it wasn't dangerous. You couldn't fall in or anything like that.

In the summer there were lots of frogs and turtles and red-winged blackbirds, and it was beautiful around there. But all that came to an end back in the '20s when they put oil on the ponds and drained them. There used to be a lot of mosquitoes. Now, we don't have many mosquitoes because they did all that, you see.

I'm not sure. Perhaps it would have been better to have had the mosquitoes, I don't know. A town man who was working one time, he saw me and he called me over and he said, "See that little pool of water there?" And I said "Yes," and he said, "Well, watch it very closely." And there'd be these little worms that would come up in the water and then go down again. Another one would come up and go down. He said, "They're coming up to breathe and pretty soon they will all be mosquitoes." And he said, "Now, I put this oil on here and now watch them." And they stopped coming up, and that was the end of them, you see.

There were movies, and my sixth grade teacher,

Doc Adams, used to play the piano. And, of course, they were silent movies. He would sit there and play and he'd look up at the movie, you know, and whatever it was, he would adapt his playing to fit in with what was going on. If it was robbers and cowboys, he would be playing the piano with those fellows galloping and all. If it was a sad thing, he would just play very sad. It was the Elm Theater, later called the Edgartown Playhouse. It was on Main Street. There were two great elm trees and that's why it was named the Elm Theater. It burned. There was a fire. Some people said it was the best show they ever had there. Now there's just a park there.

Now, Jim Chadwick's bathing beach over on Chappy, that was a very good commercial enterprise. He had two launches, the *Irene* and the *Esther*, that he would use to pick people up near the Yacht Club and then go on down to the North Wharf and pick more people up, and go over to his bathing beach where he had a pier, and they'd get off there and go swimming. You'd hire a bathhouse. Some people had them for all summer. And then there were other men who would take people over in their catboats. Summer people who would come down. They'd have their captain, who would take them over to the bathing beach and wait while they went swimming and all, and then bring them back again. Those were the same boats that went scalloping in the fall.

Jimmy Chadwick, who owned the bathing beach, used to insist on bathing costumes that were way out of date. Women had to wear these undercostumes and then these very flouncy silk costumes. I remember my mother wearing one. When she would come out of the water, it was all she could do to stand up. The water would roar out of her costume because it was so full of water, so heavy, you see. And yet they had to wear their arms covered and these long, black stockings and that sort of thing.

The steamboat was quite different from the way it is now. We called it the steamer in those days and not the ferry. It would start in Edgartown about five o'clock in the morning, go up to Oak Bluffs, then into Vineyard Haven, then over to Woods Hole, then over to New Bedford. And then it would start back from New Bedford to Woods Hole, to Vineyard Haven, Oak Bluffs, and then come down here at night. There were two boats generally doing that. Also, it went to Nantucket. It cut out Edgartown finally because it was easier to get off the steamer in Oak Bluffs and take a car down to Edgartown. Much easier than to stay on the steamer and go to Edgartown, you see.

My grandparents used to watch the steamer come in, and it had a very powerful searchlight. And the steamer would search the light over here to the house if my father and grandfather were on board. That would let the women at home know that they were coming. And so they would harness up the horses — they had a man to do that — and go down and meet them down at the steamer.

When I was young we had gaslights, carbide gaslights, and the gas was manufactured down in the red-roofed garage down here. You could only run the carbide gas during the six months of the year, when it wasn't freezing. When it was freezing, we had to use kerosene lamps. How the gas was made — there was a machine, and you would put down cans of carbide, and the carbide would trickle down into water in this great tank. And then, because of the mixture of the carbide and the water, it produced a gas, a carbide gas.

Now, when I was a small boy, I used to go into the bank same as anybody else did and everything. I never expected I would be president. But there is a lesson I learned as a child. I was just never athletically inclined. And whenever there was a game, a scrub game or anything like that, and they chose up sides, I was always the last one, you know, to be chosen because I was no good in athletics. However, I was rewarded in this way. They formed a boys' club and I was elected president. And I thought, "Now how is this? I can't do anything athletic or anything." And they said, "Well, we elected you president because you can run a meeting."

The Martha's Vineyard National Bank was founded in 1855 in the brick building at the corner of Water Street and Main Street. And then in 1905, there was a man who lived in Vineyard Haven who got control of the bank and he decided he was going to move it up to Vineyard Haven, which he did. And that left the brick Edgartown National Bank building vacant. So Beriah T. Hillman and my grandfather, Julian W. Vose, who had bought this property, and some others formed the Edgartown National Bank at that time. And now the Edgartown National Bank is the oldest bank on the Island. All the others are either merged or changed or something. It's the only bank that was founded here and is still here and hasn't changed its name or location or anything.

I'll tell you, I think I'm one that does not like to see change very much, unless it's a change for the good. I've had lots of people want to buy the Edgartown National Bank, but if they bought it, I'm sure it would change. It would be a tremendous change. It would no longer be the Edgartown National Bank. They'd merge it with something else, you see.

A man came to see me and said, "I'm in charge of mergers and acquisitions for the First National Bank of Boston. I want to talk with you. I want to take you to lunch." And I said, "Well, that's good, but I'll take you to lunch." I didn't want to be under obligation to him, you see. So we went to lunch down at the Kelley House. When we got up to dessert, I said, "Now, you're in charge of mergers and acquisitions for the First National Bank of Boston." And he said, "Yes." And I said, "Well, we don't want to merge with anybody. And right now I think the First National Bank of Boston is too big for us to acquire, so I don't think there's much we can talk about." He said, "I can make you a lot of money." And I said, "Don't even tell me how much because I don't want to know how much I'm turning down. I want to keep it the Edgartown National Bank."

And then when people were moving up to the Triangle because that's where business was going, I said, "No, I think we'll stay right down in the center of town because I don't want to leave a great vacant space here." For the business of the town, you see.

*Interviewed 1997*

230

## DANIEL ALISIO

b. 1902 • Tisbury
Farmer, Musician, Barber,
Contractor, Gardener

# Name It, We Had It

## *The John Hoft Farm*

I was born in Bristol, Rhode Island, in 1902. Where the Herreshoffs and the Howes and the bigwigs hold forth. Sailing yachts. I used to go in the shed there and watch them do the varnish and shellac. Those boats were beautiful. I came to the Vineyard in '27. I've been here a long time and I've seen a lot of changes.

My father was from the province of Salerno, a town called Scavatti, somewhere around Naples. Prior to coming to this country, he was a boiler engineer in a factory in Italy. Then he became a rubber worker in Rhode Island.

When I was young, I went to work in the Livingston Worsted Mill, where my sisters were. And I learned every operation, from the loom to the finishing and shipping of the cloth. During the First World War, we made uniform cloth for the Navy. We made the finish cloth for the officers. We made the khaki for the soldiers. And we made the worsteds for the officers. And I can go through every operation. As a matter of fact, I almost got killed during the last operation of the cloth when they give it a steam bath. It comes out of this oven on this great big roller. And I went after a wrinkle and I got my arm caught. It pulled me up through and I went right through it, this way. Went right through and got wracked into a steaming roller. I got my ear split and my bones got wracked. Got all burned on my cheeks. Had that been a stationary roller, I would have been a dead duck, but it gave way some. Well, I didn't go back to that anymore.

I moved out of Bristol in 1921 and enlisted in the Marine Corps. A group of boys went down to Quantico to set up a six-regiment band. Well, I came from a musical town. Bristol is a musical town. Everybody, the Italian people and Portuguese, plays music. I play clarinet and saxophone. We didn't stay there very long. When I came on back home, I went to work for the U.S. Rubber. We used to cut the materials for the Keds and the Campfires and Sister Sue. As a matter of fact, I can make any one of them. I know how to do all of that work. Four buckles, galoshes, name it. I can do it.

There was a private band in the U.S. Rubber. And I played clarinet in that band. The solo clarinetist, who was a veteran of the Italian Army Alpine Forces, he had a barber shop. And he said to me, "Dan, why don't you come in and help me?" I said, "I can't do any of that work." He said, "Won't be long before you can." So I went in and helped him. So I became a barber. And a musician. Then there was an ad in the *Providence Journal* for a barber in Vineyard Haven, Massachusetts. So I went out and made a call, and I got this appointment to come down here and get this job. In the barber shop. And I got it. It belonged to a Mr. Penney. He was a first-class barber. I finally ended up owning the barber shop where the Gourmet Shop is now. Next to Leslie's Drug Store — used to be Bangs' Market.

I met my wife Marguerite when she came to work for me. She was a beautician and she worked in the back shop. We had two sections. I went away and got a beautician's license. We were the first people that had air conditioning on the Island. It was printed in the *Gazette*. It was a great big hullabaloo, "Everyone's going up to Alisio's Barbershop." But not for treatment, but to look at the air conditioners. We had two. One for the back and one for the front. Oh, it was beautiful. I was working for twenty-five dollars a week. I never wanted for anything. I always had money in my pocket because I was a barber. But I also cut a lot of hair and did a lot of shaves for nothing.

My wife was born on the John Hoft Farm in Lambert's Cove. She's the third generation. She had two children. And that's how I become acquainted with the farm. When I married her, we moved to the farm, because I like farming. Seems all my family worked around the gardens and things. They liked the ground, you know?

We went to work every day, milked six cows by hand, my wife and I and the boy. I'd bring my milk down to Anna Davis in town, what I didn't make cream out of. Then I'd go to work in the barber shop. Every day.

We kept it up until we made the Cooperative Dairy. All the farmers pooled their interests and brought all their milk to the Dairy. We didn't peddle milk anymore. We'd take the milk out to the road. Then the van would come and pick it up for the Dairy. And we've been through that field knee-deep in snow. My wife and I with two twenty-gallon cans of milk. One on each side. Plowing through that snow and over to the gate. Then the dairy went bust, and that was the end of the cattle.

The farm was set up by Marguerite's grandfather. He was shipwrecked off Pasque Island. He was a cabin boy from Hamburg, Germany. And from the ship he was brought to Vineyard Haven and stayed here. He worked and got enough money to buy a little piece of land. That was the beginning of the farm. Then another lumber schooner got stranded, and he and a friend of his went out and salvaged it. And they got a thousand dollars. And he bought another piece of land. And that's how the farm grew. Now there's eighty acres in there, and I own twenty acres adjacent to it.

His son, John, was Marguerite's father. He set up an orchard here. He had a thousand fruit trees on that farm at one time. He had peaches, pears, apples. He had the most beautiful apples, and melon, and everything. He couldn't give them away. There was no market for them. The trees got old and they died. So after the '38 hurricane, they were all laid down, and I yanked them out with my old tractor. I had a '38 International Harvester. I made fields out of them. That's where we kept the cattle.

We drove a herd of cattle up to Chilmark up next to the Tea Lane Farm, and we drove them back in the fall. We tied a lead cow onto the back of an old, dilapidated Model A coach. It took us three or four hours. We had to block off every outlet. A turnoff — somebody had to run and block it off. And I remember we got there to the Correllus place and we had to stop because the cattle were getting away.

We rounded them up, and when we started the car the lead cow wouldn't move. So Mr. Correllus happened to be going up to the house from the barn. And he says, "What's the matter, Don?" He called me Don. "The cow don't want to go?" So he called his dog in Portuguese and he motioned to him. The dog nipped the cow's tail and it started off. I remember that just like it happened yesterday. He was a nice man.

When we first moved up to the farm, there were two active cranberry bogs, and a third old bog. There was three bogs on the farm. But the bogs were just let go because of the labor situation. No price for cranberries. As a matter of fact, Mr. Hoft lost a whole shipment of cranberries. Didn't get a nickel out of it. And where the reservoir is, off Lambert's Cove Road, there was once a peat bog. They burned peat out of it. I think it's 1908 they made the reservoir. Mr. Hoft built it. He was an engineer in his own right.

They used to harvest the cranberries then by hand. They used a hand picker, which I have one in the cellar. Then they had a scoop. The Portuguese women from Oak Bluffs used to come over there and do them all by hand. And, you see, there wasn't this new machinery that they invented later on. Everything was hand labor. Now they're going back to doing it that way.

Those bogs can be restored with very little work. They can uproot those trees and take them out of there and just take a blanket right off there and re-sand the whole bogs and just plant them. Open the ditches, get the flow of water coming through to freeze them in the winter. The Evan Bodfish Bog, Cranberry Acres, which was sold to the Open Land Foundation — our spring feeds those bogs. And that spring is still in effect, but it needs to be cleaned out. It come down through the ditches of the old bog, and there was a sluiceway across there. And that's where the water came through, to help flood those Cranberry Acres bogs.

We didn't go into crop farming. I did plant crops for my chickens. I had a thousand chickens up in the barn. I raised a thousand chickens and sold broilers to everybody. Mrs. Dixon, who had the nursing home, she said she never had a decent broiler since I quit. I used to raise *broccoli de rapé* for them, you know, high protein, and feed 'em mash with skim milk.

I had a crawler tractor, I had a corn binder, I had the whole business to cut the corn and bind it and put it up into the storage. I raised enough grain to keep six head of cattle and six hogs. Oh, yes. We worked like Trojans. We've had a lot of happy days there.

I sold eggs to everyone. But I'll tell you a story about a chicken. Now, this is true. And this has a lot to do with pollution. They've got everybody scared. You can't eat this, you can't eat that, you've got to eat food that's raised from organics. Well, that's true. I'll prove it. Now, I had chickens in the loft laying. I had them in the first floor. I had a chicken that didn't look too well and the comb was pinkish, wasn't that fiery red. And it would walk and fall down. So this may sound cruel. I got her and picked her up by her legs and I opened a window and I just heaved her out and I said, "You're on your own. If you make it, okay, if you don't ..." She lived through the winter. She went down in the barn and she lived off the droppings and what the cows left. That spring, she was laying eggs and she was the healthiest chicken I ever saw. And her comb was redder than a cockerel's. It was bright red. Now, she was on the point of death, because she had a liver ailment. That's where they get hit the hardest, liver. That's the first thing you look at when you clean a chicken. If their liver is nice and red and shiny. The liver will tell it all. That's the truth.

And turnips, I grew turnips as big as a basketball. I would plant them thick, three plantings to a row. And the Portuguese people and the Cape Verdes they would come up and thin them. And I would let them take all the greens. That's one of the specialties for them. I would store my turnips in the barn in seaweed and they would last until Easter. They'd be sprouting by then. You make a big pile in the middle of the barn, cover over with seaweed — rockweed, with the bubbles — not the kind that rots. The salt keeps the turnips from freezing. When you want to eat, just reach into the pile. They were delicious.

We made cream and sold it to the West Chop people during the war. They made butter out of my cream. They couldn't buy any butter. We had everything we wanted during the Second World War. We had a locker full of butter, beef, chickens, eggs. Name it, we had it.

*Interviewed 1995*

## MAXEMENA MELLO

1899 – 1991 • Edgartown
Homemaker
First Portuguese Member of the Edgartown Women's Club
Member, Town Finance Committee, Edgartown

# Too Many Manuels

## A New Bride's First Day in Edgartown

They think it's so funny that I came from the city and married this man with three children, but he was handsome, my husband. He was a very, very good-looking man, and he had a boat and a house.

My mother said, "Look, Maxi, if you don't marry that fellow you're a fool, because he has a home. Of course he's a widow, but never mind, he needs a woman. You'll have a nice home, all paid for. And a boat!" And she says, "You'll have a new life."

I said, "Well, if I like the man all right, I'll marry him. But if I don't like him I won't, Ma."

After our honeymoon we came here, to the Vineyard, to Edgartown.

I wanted to stay a little longer in New Bedford — I mean Dartmouth. That was where I had grown up. That was where my family was. After we came from our honeymoon, we landed there. And I said, "Dad, I want to stay here a little longer."

He said, "No, I have to go because my boat is going on the railways."

Well, I didn't want to play dumb. I said to myself, "The railways?" The only thing I ever had on the railways was my carload of flour, or vinegar — my family had a bakery — whatever we had, flour or molasses or sugar. We never had boats on the railway. I said, "I'd better keep quiet; I don't know what it is."

Well, as soon as we landed here he had to go down and see his *Miramar*. That was the first thing he did. And I had never been in the house I was going to live in.

Oh, he left me at the house. This is the house. And he had three children, three little boys. I said, "Now, boys, I'm going down with your father."

They said, "The women don't go down to the waterfront, only Patty Pease." Patty Pease was from an old family, but she was always down there meet-ing all the boats, you know. And they sort of con-nected everyone that went down there as waiting for the boats, all the young girls when the steamboats came in.

I said, "Well, that's funny. I think I'd like to go down to the boats." And I said, "Daddy, I'm going to go down."

He said "No, Maxi, I have to go. My boat is out at the stake. It's not near the shanties."

Well, that was all new to me. But I went down with him anyhow. I thought, "This is the first time. I've got to get him on a, a ... I've got to get my ways in somehow." Because he was born on the other side, you know, in the old country. And he had a lot of his old-country ideas. You can't get rid of them, any more than I could get rid of my American-born ones.

So we went down to the waterfront. You know, where all those little piers are, between the Yacht Club and that restaurant, the Shanty. Well, there was a row of shanties in there — I have a painting of them — and there were about eight little boat houses. And they used to tie their boats all up through there.

It was the prettiest sight! We got down there. It was about five o'clock in the evening in October, and the sun was setting, and you could see Chappaquiddick, with all the golden lights, you know. It was the most beautiful thing I had ever seen ... that water ... I love the water.

He says, "You can't go with me. I have to go in the rowboat."

I said, "I don't care for the rowboat. I'll wait here for you."

He said, "Well, that's an awful thing for you. You don't know ... I don't like this."

I said, "Well, I'm having fun."

So he gets in his rowboat. He had to go up to his stake, which was way up near that ... well, between Cronkite's and Tower Hill. That's where he anchored his boat.

Within one hour, I met five Manuels down there. The same night I first came here.

Mr. Terra, I knew, Captain Manuel Terra. And he had the deepest blue, blue eyes. Big white mustache. And his skin was all, all tan from the water. He looked a typical seaman, you know. He came over and he started talking to me.

And then along came another Manuel. And he said, "Hi, Manuel."

And Mr. Terra said, "Hi, Littleneck." That was his nickname.

I said, "Is that his name, Littleneck?"

"No, everyone calls him Littleneck. He's Manuel...I can't even think of his last name," Mr. Terra said. "We all call him Littleneck."

I said to myself, "Well, that's fine." So there were two Manuels, and mine was three. And pretty soon another one comes slouching around from Water Street, onto this little pier there, in front of their shanties. And a new Manuel came on.

Of course they saw me there. It was quite surprising.

"Is that Manuel's wife?"

They said, "Yeah, that's the new bride."

And Mr. Santos goes. "Hi, Rebon."

And Rebon says, "Hi, Manuel." Rebon was his nickname. He was Manuel Perry. But there were so many, many Manuels. Each one had a nickname.

That was four, wasn't it? Three...no, that was four. So they all came over and shook hands. It was my first night. First day I was in Edgartown.

But when my husband came, there was his wife, his new bride, surrounded with four men. That was funny, wasn't it? And on our way down-street we passed...my other house is right in back of Manuel Roberts, Manuel Swartz. We always called him Manuel Swartz. And when we walked

down the street to the boat he comes out of his house, with his hands like this on his suspenders, and he says, "Hey, Manuel, is this the new woman?"

He says, "Yep, this is the new lady."

And he says, "Oh, wait a minute," and he hollers to his wife, "Hey, Louisa, come out and see Manuel's new wife."

So poor Louisa came out. Manuel Swartz was definitely Portuguese, but Louisa wasn't. She was, I think, of Scotch ancestry. Poor woman came out, all shy, with her apron on. She was cleaning her mouth. It was supper time.

And she said, "Oh, I'm so glad to know you."

And I said, "Well, I am, too. I'm going to be right in your backyard. Do come over and see me, because I don't know anyone here."

"I'll do that," she said. "I'll be over tomorrow with a cake." And she came over with a cake the next day. She was a nice woman. That was the first Mrs. Swartz.

And that was six Manuels!

And Manuel came and said, "Are you satisfied?"

I said, "I had a lovely time. I've met so many Manuels. So when we have our first child, he's going to be Manuel."

"Over my dead body! There's not going to be another Manuel in this town. Every other person is Manuel. There are too many Manuels. That's enough. Enough is enough!"

And then we came up Main Street. We got to the corner by the bank, and another Manuel comes by, Manuel DeLaura.

I said, "Manuel, for goodness sake, you are right. Every other person is a Manuel. But after all, they are Portuguese."

And we met ... in one day I think I met seven or eight Manuels, that first day!

But I had a wonderful time on the waterfront.

So when we got home, he says, "Now you don't

go down there alone! You didn't see any women down there, did you?"

I said, "I saw one girl with a bag."

"Well, she was waiting for the fishermen to come in, and she was waiting for fresh fish."

That was Patty Pease.

*Interviewed 1983*

## LYDIA CLEVELAND
1898 — 1989 • Tisbury
Nurse, Homemaker

# Just to Get Ready for the Next Day

## Growing Up on a Farm in West Tisbury

My father never had a tractor. He always done with a horse. The plows and the harrows and everything was done by horse.

Every year it was the same routine — walk for miles to put the seeds in, and some of the men would come along and cover it. Potatoes, corn, done by hand, everything. No tractors.

The men would dig holes so far apart in rows wide enough to harrow it, but that was done by horse and wagon.

I'll never forget, one day I was planting corn. Seemed to me it was about ten acres to walk and when I got down to the end of a row and I was tired, I dug a hole and put the rest of the seeds all in there. Eventually they all came up and my father saw what I had done.

We raised vegetables on the farm, anything that could be kept over the winter, such as potatoes and turnips and corn. We had cows, and milked them. Eggs, we had hens. Then, of course, in the summer we raised vegetables and we kids took them to Oak Bluffs to sell to families. Drove down with the horse and wagon.

When we got home, we'd get ready for the next morning. See, we had to leave, I suppose, by five o'clock in the morning to be there by the time people were getting up.

There was corn to pick, several hundred ears, beets to be picked and washed, and chickens to be killed, scalded and dressed. Then load up the horse and wagon.

Just to get ready for the next day.

*Interviewed 1983*

## MARY LOUISE HOLMAN
b. 1906 · Oak Bluffs
Director, Hattie B. Cooper Community Center, Boston, MA
Social Worker, Teacher
Foster Parent

# I Had My Opinion and I Spoke My Mind

## A Black Woman's Experience in Oak Bluffs

I was born in a small town in southeast Georgia, Waycross, Georgia, August 31, 1906. My maternal grandparents were slaves. I lived with my Grandma Butler. The slaves took the names of the families who had them as slaves. She was with a family named Butler, and they were house servants. My grandmother told me that they had a better opportunity and were treated better than the slaves who had to work in the fields. The house slaves took care of the madam's and master's children.

My father was a Methodist minister, and he believed in his children having an education, so they sent me to a boarding school that was run by the Woman's Home Missionary Society of the Methodist Episcopal Church. I remained there until I finished the elementary grades. I was the valedictorian of the class. Then I came to Boston to live with my older sister, Mattie, in the South End and finished high school. In high school, I wanted to take a college course, and one teacher said to me, she said, "Well, why don't you train to be a maid?" I said, "For your information, I am not going to be a maid, I'm going to take this college course and I'm going to college, and you'll see me teaching right here in Boston." And that's what I did.

I was successful in getting a scholarship for college through the Methodist Episcopal church to the Boston University School of Religious Education. When I finished, I went to the man that gave me the scholarship, and I said, "Do you want me to repay that money that you gave me to go to school?" He said, "No, you just go and help people." And that's what I've tried to do. I got a job called National Promotional Worker, and I travelled throughout various states organizing groups, children's groups for the Methodist church.

I starting coming down here when I was a teenager. My sister had a job working for a family who had a cottage up on the waterfront. I would come and visit her and I got jobs. I came back and worked every summer to get money to help me do college.

I worked at Pollard's in the Highlands. She had a restaurant, but she only catered to whites. She served three meals every day. Most of the people she served were up there in the Highlands. They had maids, but the maids didn't do the cooking. So the families would come to her dining room and eat. The food was wonderful. That cook was a swell cook! She was black. Oh, she was a wonderful cook.

She had male waiters from Morehouse College, a black college in Atlanta. The guys came up every summer and they came to waiter, and I helped the cook in the kitchen. I worked over there for quite a while. I've had all kinds of jobs on this Island. I worked for a restaurant in Vineyard Haven for a while, washing dishes in the kitchen, not waiting tables, washing dishes. Anything that I thought would give me a dollar, I'd take it. My folks taught me, if you earn a dollar, you save a dime. So I always had a bank account.

I went back to Atlanta University School of Social Work and got my master's degree in social work. I came back to Boston and I got a job teaching. I taught what we called "Special Class" — children that were difficult to teach. They said the children couldn't learn, and I said they could.

I bought a house in Boston on West Canton Street and for about fifteen years I was a foster mother for girls, delinquent girls from the Youth Service Board. They lived with me in my home. We called it Two-Thirty. It was 230 West Canton Street, and that's where we lived. I had quite a number of girls.

In the meantime, my brother and I had bought a place down here in Oak Bluffs for the summer. And when I retired from teaching, I bought this house and moved down here. And I used to rent rooms. My house was like Grand Central Station — people were coming here from May 'til November.

it. But I did ride the horse for my father to cultivate his garden to guide the horse up and down the rows when they cultivated. And I rode the horse to go after the cows. The Portuguese boys drove them out to the Plains in the morning because they wouldn't want to go, but at night they were anxious to get home and get their feed, so it was all right to send me because the cows would come home anyway.

I wanted to be a nurse. I went into training through a Dr. Whitmarsh, whose home was in Providence, and went to his hospital. And I trained there. I was gone three years from the Island. The nurses all lived in a nurses' home, they called it. And we wore our dresses two inches from the floor, a blue and white striped dress. It had a white apron, white cuffs, and a white bib. And we had the high button shoes.

When I finished training, and I was given one floor of the hospital, I was to run that floor. But my father was sick, and my father wanted my mother with him. And she couldn't be with him and run the farm. So I had to give up my work in the hospital and come home and run the farm until he was able to come back home. But I didn't have to run it for any length of time. You see, my father was only sick for two years. He died and my mother did come back and take over.

But at that point I wasn't given the opportunity to go back. The doctors here kept me busy, so that I never was free to go back to Providence. I had work enough here on the Island, so I never went away again.

I went into the Red Cross Health Center in Vineyard Haven and I was there three years. It was downstairs in Captain Alvin Cleveland's house. You had no doctors at the Center. You just lived there and answered the telephone, so that you get your calls to know what the doctor wanted. At that time every doctor had his own parishioners, and all the doctors made house calls. When I was at the Red Cross Health Center, I took care of Vineyard Haven, West Tisbury and Gay Head, up that way.

So you went to people's houses. It was sort of a home nursing affair. But you only went when the doctor was back of you. You didn't go on your own.

There were several doctors on the Island. Whichever one asked you to take care of their patient, you did. You went wherever and whenever you were called.

I can remember walking up the State Road in a snowstorm at three o'clock in the morning because there was a baby being born. Three o'clock in the morning, and I went way up to my knees going up the road which wasn't dug out. But there was a baby coming and I had to go. There was no place to go to have a child. You had it in your home or else you went to your parents' home. You had to have it at home until the hospital opened in 1929.

When the hospital opened, they gave up the Red Cross Health Center because the doctors thought it was more convenient to take the people to the hospital than it was to take care of them at home. They didn't have to drive from door to door or from town to town. They had day nurses and night nurses and they had a woman to run the hospital, who was a nurse. It was in the same place it is now, but it was a house that they bought and fixed over. Of course, it started small and was known as the Cottage Hospital.

Before, when there was no hospital, everybody took care of their own. You weren't supposed to put your family out. If there was an old person in your family, you just took care of them in your own home. Every family had doctored themselves for years, and treatments were passed from grandmother to mother, and so forth.

I remember my grandmother planting sassafras so as to always have sassafras roots to make tea. My Grandmother Vincent always thought onions were very good for a cold. You stewed up — I don't know how much — onions and ate them. And I remember having a cold, and my mother used salt pork rind. You put pepper on the salt pork and heated it and you tied it around your throat.

They don't use medicines now that they used back in my day. The doctors acted as their own druggists and mixed up the medicines that they prescribed. I had a doctor tell me they put a yellow coat on and call it one thing; they put a chocolate coat on and call it something else. "But," he says, "underneath it is the same old medicine." That's the way he doctored.

I always did private nursing. Sometimes I worked in the hospital, but it was on private cases. Then I was a school nurse. And then my day was planned for me; certain days to go up-Island and certain things I had to do in the schools, according to what the Superintendent of Schools laid out for me. I got through nursing in 1965.

In 1954, I joined the Grange. I was president twice, three years one time and two years the other time. And I have been secretary ever since I joined, except for the years that I was Master. The Grange was very active. They had over two hundred members in the West Tisbury Grange when I joined. And they had a Grange in Edgartown and they had a Grange in Chilmark. The Grange was a farmers' organization and the farmer, his wife, and any child over fourteen years old could belong to the Grange. They didn't have the outside amusements to take their interest. So a man and his wife took their family and went to the Grange. But now they don't do that. I think it is a thing of the past.

If there was a mishap in any family, we'd help out. We've built barns, we've taken care of the sick; we've done all kinds of things to help out in case of need in a farmer's family. And we got the credit under community service. You got credit for the number of hours that you spent, not the money that you gave, but for the hours that you spent helping. More community spirit, I think, then, because whatever you did, you did free for your neighbor. You did it because you were friends.

You grew up in a community which was close-knit. The family and the church. I think most of the older people of my generation were hardworking and independent. But circumstances have changed. It's a change of the times. There's more people and less time to do things. You skim the surface these days. You don't go down and get the fundamentals.

Anybody that was born in the years I was born and grew up as I did is all out of place in the world of today. We lived on the farm. It supplied all our needs. Each family had their own cows and so forth. They didn't have big farms. You had what you thought that you needed to have. We had what we needed. Money is the basis now of most everything. In my day, money didn't count. You had it or you didn't have it. Didn't make any difference.

It's a nice growing up to look back on. Everybody was friends. I like those memories. I wouldn't want to live without them. I think it'd be a very dry world. I don't know what the kids of today are going to carry in their life, what they will have to look back on when they grow old. I suppose there'll be things for them to remember just the same as there were things for me. Probably the things I remember weren't the things that my parents thought of. Everything changes as the years go by. The way of the world has changed.

*Interviewed 1982*

## ETHEL WHIDDEN

1888 — 1992 • Chilmark

Artist, Poet

Member of the Blackwell family, a family active in
Women's Rights, and Chilmark's earliest summer residents

# A Trunk Full of Trees

## *Journeying Up to Quitsa Circa 1908*

And when we finally got to Oak Bluffs after three boat rides on the lovely old ferries — with their rocking beams, state rooms, and orchestras — from New York to Fall River, New Bedford to Woods Hole, Woods Hole to the Island — there was a big crowd, and the men were yelling, "This way to the Pawnee House. This way to the Wesley House. Edgartown ..." and so on.

But we always found Bart Mayhew. And he had a coach with three or four seats. And we loaded on the cat and the dog and the cook and everything we brought with us and guests if we had any with us. And he had two horses, and we drove up-Island on a dirt road.

Parts of it were deep sand ... deep, deep sand. And the grown-ups would get out and walk. And Mother always had crackers because we would say,

"When, oh, when are we going to get there?"

Finally, towards the end of the day, we would arrive in Chilmark at our Quitsa home. And we would immediately take our shoes off.

But one of the things I remember so clearly was the "*baaah ... baaah*" of the sheep which we heard as soon as we came to Chilmark. Especially in the evening they would call out.

The hills were lovely, just like the waves of the ocean. They had no trees, but they had huckleberry bushes and sweet fern. And the stone walls went winding over the hills. It was so lovely and endless. No trees ...

Grandma, instead of bringing her clothes, would bring a trunk full of trees to plant.

*Interviewed 1983*

## ALFRED EISENSTAEDT
1898 — 1995 • Chilmark
Life Magazine Photographer

# Everything Was Like the Beginning of the World

## *The Vineyard Through the Photographer's Eye*

I was introduced to the Vineyard in 1937 by Mr. Roy Larsen, who was, at that time, the second man at *Time*, Inc. He brought me here with a speedboat and landed in Edgartown Harbor, where I spent the night at the Great Harbor Inn. And I liked this enormously. Edgartown was very elegant; you had to be dressed up. At the Old Sculpin Gallery was Mr. Manuel Swartz, and I photographed there. Oh, he was wonderful. He was a carpenter. His boats were beautiful, yes.

I liked the Vineyard so much that I came back two months later and spent my time with the Indians at Gay Head. There was only one road to Gay Head and only one or two people ever came by. And I walked to Gay Head with a little folding chair and read, and the only thing I heard the whole day was a dog barking in the background. It was heavenly, beautiful. At that time, I met Thomas Benton and Max Eastman and Eliena Krylenko, his wife. She was a Russian dancer. I came back almost every year and photographed them. I have many, many pictures of Benton.

I photographed in 1937 in Chilmark, Gay Head — Indians and tribes, you know. I have beautiful pictures in black and white. I photographed Bertha Robinson, who lived in Gay Head and worked with clay. And then others were wonderful. There was a man with two oxen and he went with the oxen to the beach and brought up stones, you know. And it was fantastic. Unbelievable. Wonderful!

I stayed at the Totem Pole. And I came back almost every year; I liked it very much. At that time they had a telephone. I think it was eleven people hanging on the phone. You never could make a private call. I stayed there until I married in 1949, and in 1950 we started to come to Menemsha. And I have never lost a year since 1950. Every year here. Even, I cut an expedition short at the Galapagos Islands, about a week, and came here.

But, at that time, it was heavenly, beautiful!

There was no marina at Menemsha. It was beautiful. I photographed extensively without wires and no interference. I photographed in Menemsha, the father of Mr. Poole, Donald Poole.

I was here after the 1954 hurricane. I photographed at that time Menemsha Harbor. Menemsha was wonderful. In Menemsha, I took many pictures of flowers against the sun. Beautiful things, before the marina came and spoiled everything. I like nature very much. I never got many nature assignments because the editor thought I should stick with people, so I got all these people to photograph.

My God, there are so many I have photographed — hundreds, hundreds. I photographed Mr. Hersey in Vineyard Haven and so on. Ruth Gordon and Kanin. Lillian Hellman, very difficult. She moved always. I photographed an English writer, Somerset Maugham. He was very good, very nice. He stayed actually in Edgartown. I photographed them. I know in the first minute how to handle them, you know. You see right away whom you can approach very familiar or not.

You see, I photographed extensively here. Other people play tennis and do all kinds of things, you know. And I photographed. I experimented with films and filters all the time. I took all lenses and filters and everything along to make tests here. I learned quite a bit, you know, with different filters and so on. I saved all those negatives. That's the reason I have two books of the Vineyard. And they were done out of love and it was not an assignment. So, I could take my time and wait and get the right light and so on.

They don't know the type of pictures we took years ago. Natural light. This type of photography hardly exists anymore. Most photographers, they can't see daylight anymore. Today, everything has changed, everything is staged. Everything is done with color, strobe equipment, very heavy equipment, and you need assistants to carry at least two

We sold yard goods of calico, different things women would make dresses from, and linings, men's suspenders and all kinds of underwear. Some mentionable and some not. And when my father was selling out, I took one set of women's underwear and hung them up between the large posts we had on the veranda there. My sister, who was a little older than I, was quite shocked. And I was reprimanded. And she put them away. But not until we had sold that particular outfit for quite a bit of money. They had the famous name — I shouldn't mention it, but I've said worse things — they had the famous name of "Split Drawers." I hung them up by the laces to two posts.

Well, that was the original store. And then Mr. Rotch, my uncle, decided that store was too small. He was doing good business. So, in 1876 he sent a man to Maine to get a shipload of lumber, and then he built the new store. The old store, now called the Ice Cream Room by some people, became the storage place for grain he sold the farmers, and farmers' tools and so on.

Then, when farming ceased to be active down here, my sister, who was in her teens, decided to sell ice cream there. So we took half the room first, but she was so busy, she had to take the whole room. So for years we had ice cream there.

Around 1916, I guess it was, I had the idea of jacking up the rear wheel of a Ford and putting the handle of the ice cream freezer, ice cream maker, in the spokes of the wheel. If properly aligned, it was able to turn it faster than I could. And of course, no such thing as it getting tired. Also, it tickled my imagination to watch my machine going. Oddly enough, we couldn't fill the freezer as full of cream and raw materials as we would ordinarily because it would go so fast, it would fluff up. I think I invented air being put into ice cream. Everybody loved that soft ice cream.

Well, I had the car going as slowly as it could go, because even that was too fast. And I'd sit there a full hour with the thing and add salt and water and salt and ice to it. An airplane went overhead one day, and I turned to see the airplane, and that car began getting faster. I turned that ice cream just

about an eighth of an inch, and the wheel — it went out of line. Took that freezer way up into the tree. Eventually the thing came down, broke into a million pieces. Naturally, my sister didn't enjoy it very much. I got the usual bawling out.

The County Fair over there at the Hall was our big event. We could hardly wait for it to come and mourned the last day when we wouldn't see it again for a year.

People raised more vegetables than they do now. The farmers would bring in as many varieties as they could, and the best things they could. Lots of kids would exhibit. People would hand in their hens there and geese and turkeys and pigs and rabbits and so on. Gay Headers would bring down their working pair of oxen. They would start before daylight and the oxen would meander their way down here. And the judges would judge the farmers' fields, how they did their plowing. They would go out to the fields and judge the plowing lines, symmetry of the field.

They had athletics at the Fair. We used to enjoy that; they don't have that now. They'd have a rope pull, and other years they'd have Edgartown playing Vineyard Haven in baseball. Those were real savage games, they were played for blood, not for money. Running, jumping and weight throwing. And I used to look forward to the time when I would be old enough to compete there. I remember Norman Benson used to pole vault over there and Emmanuel Campbell and Bert Cahoun and some others would compete at the Fair. And I'd go in, short and chubby, knowing I'd be last. But I'd say, "My time will come." So I just lumbered along. We had lots of fun.

And as a result, those of us who went on to school and college used our experience here to good advantage in college. I've seen world records broken. Very interesting. It started right here at the Fair. We had Bayes Norton in Vineyard Haven, went on to Exeter, one of the Phillips academies. And he made good. He was on the Olympic team, captain of the Yale track team in 1924, I think it was. So the Islanders had some pretty good experiences in track. Johnny Mayhew, whose son John is teaching at the high school, Johnny Mayhew's all-American backfield at Brown around 1908 or 1909. And my brother, the year he died, 1919, was considered the best track man in the state of Maine. He was at Bates College. I finally got my growth and had my share of fun.

The rope pull, the last one I remember, they asked me to get up the single men's team. And somebody else gathered the older men. I probably was in my middle twenties. So I gathered together I think eight men, one or two were widowers, but we were all single at the time. On the other side, they had two or three of the Tilton boys. And they're heavy. So I kept a straight face and said, "Now, we'll go over to the town scales." We used to have town scales over where the gasoline station is. "Go over to the town scales and weigh in." Because I realized, and it turned out, that seven of those fat men, the older men, weighed what eight of us skinnier fellows weighed. And they fell for it!

So I was captain of the team. I said to the boys, "Now, in another thirty seconds, I'll make some sort of call and you let go of the rope and then tighten up again." They let go of the rope and the fat men fell over in a heap. And we young fellows just pulled them right back. That's a legitimate dirty trick. All's fair in love and war. Of course, the crowd laughed. We did look small and skinny aside of those great big seagoing fellows, but they were old and overweight. No matter, it's amusing.

The competition in terms of jams and jellies and pies was very interesting and sometimes almost savage. Women are — perhaps you were too young to have seen the movie, *More Deadly Than the Male*, bringing out the savagery of the female in competition. Well, the story's told — I didn't see it — the story's told of a woman at the Fair who had entered the cheese-making contest. They used to make cheese here.

And this woman, particularly, was on the savage end of life. She sat there with some friends. They were sitting there, the cheese cases or big glass showcases were right in front of her. Then, when the judges came to taste the cheese — in those days they put the name right on of who made it; now it's just a number, so you can't tell whose cheese or whose turnip you are judging. And when they came to the cheeses, she said in a loud enough voice for the judges to hear, "You know Martha has such sore hands, she loves to make cheese." Martha was a good cheese maker and this lady was competing against Martha, so she was hoping, I suppose, to let the judges kind of get their minds made up. It was the idea of the picture of this woman making cheese to make her sore hands feel good. Little things like that, you know.

Most of the board games were run, almost all, by off-Islanders. They weren't always ethical either. We used to go and watch them fellows. They'd come over and sell all kinds of trinkets for a dime. A dime was a lot of money in those day. And they'd sell little whips and funny trinkets. One year they had money out on a table, oh, about four feet square. You were supposed to throw a ring over the money, and if you got the ring over the money, why, you'd get it. One of the selectmen came in and accused them of a gambling game. I don't think it was gambling, but a game of skill. But he took his foot and kicked the board over! And all the money went in a heap.

The rides were brought in in the '30s when the Fair began to die out and they didn't get in enough young people to run the Fair. The older people didn't have the time or energy to get the Fair together. So, they had to do something to revive it, for they were about to give it up. So they put in the whirligigs and all that noise stuff you could hear miles away. And that ruined the Fair as far as some of the older people were concerned. Now they're cutting down on that and plan to get a happy medium. I think they're doing pretty well.

You know, people would look forward to seeing people once a year. There was a place where people would say, "Oh, I haven't seen you since last Fair time," and "Where were you last year, I didn't see you." Old friends and even sisters sometimes perhaps would say, "Why, I haven't seen you since last year!" 'Twas a very essential get-together, I think.

*Interviewed 1983*

## MARY COLES
b. 1903 • Edgartown

Artist

# I Was Crazy About Anything to Do with Painting

## Art, Edgartown and Blindness

When we first came here to Edgartown in the summer, we stayed at Tower Hill. There was an old-fashioned boarding house run by a very elegant lady from Boston, a Mrs. Goell. The view across Chappaquiddick, I can remember it, over to Cape Pogue. Because we used to watch the lights from Cape Pogue, two white and one red, I think. And then to the left you saw the whole town of Edgartown.

Oh, it was wonderful! You've never known of such food. Ladies used to sit there. All these large, fat ladies, I can remember. They'd sit, in what we called the rocking chair fleet, and look out. And they'd just wait for the next meal. Every lunch — I've never known — I can't imagine — the luncheons were three or four choices, generally two meats and one fish or something like that. Plus hors d'oeuvres or soup or something. No liquor, of course. And desserts. Three or four pies. All of that. The supper was a little less. And, of course, always baked beans and brown bread on Saturday night.

Everyone swam at the bay over on Chappy then. They had catboats you hired from one of those elegant Portuguese gentlemen who had them for fishing and scalloping. They used to take us across to the bathing beach where there was a big pier that you tied up on. What is now the Beach Club used to be owned by some people from here. They just had long rows of rickety cabins. And everyone went there. My mother and her friends, I can see them now. Always with skirts. My mother had a hat which had a big brim of rubberized stuff. And they'd stand in the water and talk, gossip. And we, as children, used to dive underneath and pinch them. I can smell the bathing suits. Long black stockings. Corsets. And that damp smell. They'd be hung up in the bathhouse overnight, you see, and then they'd have to get into them the next morning.

We spent the morning at the beach, and in the afternoon, we used to walk into town. There was an ice cream and a paper place up on Main Street. There was a wonderful woman — Maude Tilton. She had been in some of those Lillian Russell-type choruses in the old days and she'd married a Tilton from the Island. They had ice cream there in little cardboard boxes with little silver tin spoons that came with them. They only had chocolate, vanilla and strawberry, and occasionally pistachio. And we had a cousin who was a very slow eater. He loved pistachio. We'd get our own and then we'd dig into his. Also, this was during Prohibition, and the men knew how to get around. When they got their *New York Times* in the morning, the gents went into the back room there and bought some liquor.

As children we'd always go to Manuel Swartz's shop and watch him building his boats. We loved hanging around there. My brother would tease him and we'd play around in his shop, shuffling around in the wood shavings. He never seemed to mind, he was a good-hearted man. Such a gentleman. And a beautiful boat builder.

We'd go down in a catboat to Katama. South Beach was so different then. The ocean never broke through to the bay. There would be a shack there, and there was a man there who had this spindly dock. The family would tie the catboat up there or sometimes drop an anchor. And he would come out, and he had clams on the half-shell, and we'd eat that. The family would. He sold those there. They had sort of duck boards to walk across the dunes to the water, where we had picnics. No one swam. We weren't allowed to. It was considered far too dangerous.

Oh, we had a wonderful time in the catboat with my father. We'd sail down to Cottage City. All of us would go, and we'd eat popcorn, we'd have ice cream sodas — we had everything. Coming back in the catboat, we'd all throw up if it was in any way rough. And my father used to go wild over those Japanese shops on Circuit Avenue. He would buy kimonos and he would buy wonderful boxes with inlaid wood. Pictures of Fujiyama. I remember those things. And those flowers. Those things that you dropped in water, and they'd come out into flowers.

I had polio when I was about eight. I can't use my left arm at all. I sometimes used to have nurses — I needed a lot of care, you see. One of them used to draw those awful, terrible heads with big ribbons and stuff. And I thought that was wonderful. I used to copy them. For Christmas, a family friend gave me a small oil set, and she showed me how to do skating scenes with stick men, sort of, tiny little line things with oil colors. And that's when I got interested in art.

When we moved up to our house on North Water Street, I didn't care for it too much. My brother and sister, they all were in the Yacht Club. My father was one of the founders of it, you know. And I didn't sail. I got bored with the hoity-toity social scene here. But there was a lively arts community in Edgartown.

And I was crazy about anything to do with painting. There were always artists here, and always people who had classes. I used to study with various people. I studied with Miss Helen Wheeler, and Vaclav Vytlacil was there too. Miss Wheeler was a very, very advanced woman. And there were other artists here. There was one on Davis Lane, a very famous sculptress, Enid Yandelle, who fascinated me. She had been in Paris. Anything to do with art just fascinated me, you see.

I didn't come back to Edgartown after 1920. I went to dramatic camp in Vermont and then to study art in Provincetown. And then I went to Smith. I had a wonderful art major at Smith. And then from there, I went to Europe to study and paint. I lived in Paris and then in Majorca. In Paris I lived with a friend from Smith in a room four flights up in the Latin Quarter. My friend used to help me. After she moved away, I was alone in a hotel and I learned to dress myself. I just needed a little concentration. When I was twenty-six, I got a picture accepted by the Salon, which was exciting. The first summer I was in France, I went to Concarneau, which is in Brittany. And that's — oh, that was a place. The fish nets were sort of cerulean blue, and all the fishermen wore these wonderful — their trousers and things were red, sort of. They were sort of an earthy red. And as they became worn out, they faded. The wives would patch them. The new patches would be white, with sort of earthy red, and the rest would be almost pink, or something. Wonderful colors. I started water colors there. I came back to this country in '39, just before the Second World War.

I used to draw in the canteens and hospitals during the war in New York City, portraits of the soldiers and sailors who'd come in. I could get a likeness quickly. And then when I came back to the Vineyard, they had a USO here in Edgartown because the military practiced at the airport. It was right down on Main Street, near the Yacht Club. The men would go in there. I guess there was some entertainment. I'd draw there, and I drew out at the airport, too. I did portraits of the men, some of them.

They also practiced at South Beach. You weren't supposed to go there, that was all hush-hush at that point, but I had a friend who was in the Navy, and he let me watch. I couldn't draw while I was there. But I did a lot of pictures from that. Because I could memorize it. That's the only reason I can do things now — because I studied that thoroughly, working from memory.

During all that time my eyesight was getting worse. I'd always been near-sighted. And then finally they diagnosed it as glaucoma. They couldn't control it. I had twelve percent vision in one eye when I went to Haiti in '49. I had about six operations. Oh, it was just no good. Nothing. So now I'm totally blind.

I came here to live in '57. Because I knew it as a child, I remembered it. I couldn't live in New York City anymore. Then I went to the Seeing Eye and got my dogs. And that helped me. Up until just a couple of years ago, I could go out with them alone, but, now that I'm old, I don't want to break my legs.

I kept going, I just kept painting. I came here,

and it took me a time. But I did keep going. Luckily I have a good memory. They call it total recall. And instinctively I know composition. I feel it. So I could do that. I cannot see what I'm doing. I can't see a thing. I know what I have in mind when I'm doing it, and whether it comes off ... Well, people have encouraged me, but you either have it, or you don't have it. I'd love to be able to see it now. It just burns me up that I can't.

Interviewed 1995

## CRAIG KINGSBURY
b. 1912 • Tisbury
Selectman, Naturalist
Gardener, Shellfish Warden, Tisbury

# I Didn't Bring Any Skunks to the Island

*Chestnuts, Critters, Cranberries and the Noble Experiment — Tales from an Island Legend*

What skunks? I didn't bring any skunks to the Island, Sweetie. I didn't bring 'em. But I'll tell you what it is — pet skunks. Now a skunk, or any wild animal, when they're little fellows are cute, and they are pets. But when they reach maturity, then they become rugged individualists. Then they become ornery. In fact, I know a boy up at Seven Gates had one that he let go when it got mean and bit him. You can't pick them up when they get big. Over-familiarity, they become dangerous. Your gregarious herd animals you can keep, but your rugged individualists, your solitaries — skunks, foxes, bobcats — they grow up, and they don't want anything to do with you. You're no longer their mama. So that's how they got here.

Only thing is, a couple of them showed up here at this place. I know they were tame because they were deodorized. They were a diffent pair from the ones at Seven Gates. They had white stripes. The Seven Gates ones were all black. I let them hang around. Some of the jackasses saw them, and they sent a fathead up here, one of the state boys, wanted to catch them. I said, "You sonofabitch, you, you lay a hand on one of the animals on this place, and I'll blow you to hell. So get out of here!"

First skunks I saw, Sis, was in 1962. I saw the tracks of one up-Island. And in 1963, the pair of them came here. And there was a female up at Cagney's, and she had a litter, so there must have been a male handy up there somewhere. But they were all deodorized. Pet skunks that got mean and were let loose or escaped. They'll follow you like a puppy up 'til they're four months, but then they'll leave you. But now this place is full of them. Every night I come out, and there are two or three of them fooling around in the yard. But, hell, I didn't bring them here.

Now, one thing I did do, I've been propagating native chestnut trees, and that's been quite successful. Evidently the chestnut blight didn't hit here or some of those trees escaped. There's a few of them on the Island that I know about. There's one up at Matt Tobin's place. It's about that big, now. Nice, straight tree. Then there's one over back here in the woods. And another one up in Norton's woods. And one up at Seven Gates. The trouble with them is, they had no pollinators. And that's probably why they're alive today, they were isolated and didn't get smacked, or something. But they don't bear. I didn't get any viable nuts 'til Mrs. White planted the Chinese chestnuts up there at Tea Lane.

Now this goes back to 1938, when Ozzie Fischer and I cleaned up the Tea Lane nurseries for Mrs. White. Ozzie says, "Hey, what the hell kind of a tree is this?" I said, "It's an American chestnut, and I don't believe it. It's a beauty." It's probably sixty, seventy feet tall, enormous thing. Mrs. White planted Chinese chestnuts and hybrids, and the American chestnut is off to one side. And they pollinated the American. So, now you've got trees, but they're mongrels, they're not consistent. Some go for the Oriental and some go for the American, and then there's intermediates.

Up at Peter Greenough's — I didn't plant it, the squirrels planted it — is a perfect American chestnut from the ones I've planted along there. Last year, I must have had a bushel and a half off that tree. I planted the walnuts and the chestnuts there the same day. The chestnuts have been bearing now for seven years, and I would say the biggest one is a good thirty feet tall. Then that squirrel planted one. It's the tallest of any now, a good thirty-five feet, and real American, one hundred percent. So, crossbreed stuff is pretty hard to figure out.

How did I learn about that stuff? Well, when I was a little kid in New Jersey, the other kids used to pound on me. And I read in a book how the Japanese, even though they were very small, could knock the hell out of any big six-footer. And there were two Japanese gardeners on an estate nearby, so

I went up there and talked to them, said I'd come and help them every Saturday and after school, if they would teach me how Japanese fight. Which they did. Every fair chance I had, I went and worked with these Japanese gardeners. And they taught me a lot. How to make bonsai and all the rest of it. Air propagation, and stuff like that.

And then there was an old boy over in Oak Bluffs. Old man Ferreira, little wizened-up old Portuguese guy, he showed me a lot of stuff. He liked me because he caught me stealing his strawberries when I was little and beat the hell out of me. Took a garden stick and played Yankee Doodle on my ass. "Now, you little bastard, no more steal, I kill you!" So I figured, there's a good old guy. So I went, I brought him a big string of fish. "Hey, thank you, my boy! You not mad 'cause I break your ass?" I says, "No." I says, "If I hadn't been stupid and let you catch me, I wouldn't have got my ass broke." "At's a boy! That's a good thinking! You no get caught, you do it, but you get caught, you gonna get your ass broke!" But, hey, those old boys were not a bit backward about walloping you.

He showed me a lot of stuff. His favorite was a dahlia bush. Beautiful! Three different dahlias on one bush. He showed me how to take a tuber with a sprout on the end, and another one of a different kind, three together in all. Then when they came up, he would carefully cut them and put them together about that high, then let them go. You'd have a red, a yellow, and a lavender, all on the same bush.

Then he carried on about pollinating trees, making them self-fertile. He would take two seeds, put them together. When the little ones come up, same thing. Keep splitting the bark and binding them together 'til maybe that high, then let them go. Then you've got a self-pollinating tree. That's stuff he learned in the old country. He was illiterate, like a lot of those old-timers. Everything he had was in his head. Anyhow, those were the ones I got my knowledge from.

We used to have a lot of native black ducks and things like that around here, but they are way down. Your salt ponds, they have been messed up. And on top of that, nobody hunts snapping turtles any more, and they are a hell of an enemy of ducks. They pull them right under. Mainly they feed on fish or whatever they can get, but if you've got ducks and like that, they are going to go after them. I've seen some old whackers... I mean, some of those damn things will get as big as a dishpan. There's a huge one over on the south side down at Watchee. The damn thing has a head the size of a musk melon. It'll be there long after I'm gone, if nobody kills it. They're very long-lived.

I used to hunt snapping turtles myself. We used to ship them to Philadelphia. You got some pretty good money out of it down there. I used to catch them with what you call a drogue. It's a float, and then underneath there is a treble hook with a piece of meat. And it's tied to the bank, of course, something solid. Mr. Turtle comes up underneath and grabs, and he's hooked!

You pick your right day, kind of cloudy, overcast. Bright sun, they don't move much. Towards evening, of course, or early in the morning. You lay out a line of them, and then, you know, take it easy, maybe go fishing, and watch. And when one hits, you can tell. You see your float begin to jump around. And then you'd ship them off. You'd pack them live in crates they'd send you. Those places in Philadelphia, they had big tanks they'd chuck them in until they were ready to use them. The best I ever got was sixty bucks for one shipment. That was about fifteen turtles.

Another way to catch them is you use a hook to feel them out in the mud and the cold. Then you hook them under the shell and yank and haul them right up. But you only do that in winter when they're sluggish and logy. A lot of guys went turtling in the winter. In the summer, the minute you start prowling around like that, they are going to scoot.

And there were plenty of cranberry bogs on the Island when I was younger. There was one, two down by Lake Tashmoo, then the big one, Evan Bodfish's on the Lambert's Cove Road. Then the next one around was Howland's. Chase bog's up this way. Then the Will Look bogs. And I don't know who owned the Goethals' bogs before they bought the place there. Then A.C. Smith was a big four-acre bog up there on the North Shore. Then old Mr. Alley had one down by the Mill Brook in West Tisbury. And then there were big bogs down in Oak Bluffs, over at Kidder's Cove, right next to Felix Neck. Then you had Dutton's bog, a big bog, just as you go into Edgartown. There's big trees in there now — it doesn't take long for the trees and brush to take over. Then the Flynn bogs on the South Shore. And then there were the Gay Head bogs — they were wild, natural grounds. There were a lot of little wild bogs. And the wild bogs over in Eastville, by that Crystal Lake — the hurricanes and the salt water killed those, and they filled up with sand.

Of course, they were all wild bogs 'til people levelled them off, and weeded and ditched them so they could drain them when they needed. You'd make ditches and dikes, and sluice gates so you could let the water out, or hold it in and direct it. That was the whole thing. When it got dry in the summer you'd raise the water level for a couple of days, and give the plants a drink. Otherwise you'd be harvesting buckshot.

The bog men had regular help. But when it was time for picking, anybody who wanted to could come up and pick, and get so much a box. It was mostly women did the picking. I'll tell you a funny thing, now, when it comes to fine work on the crops, the women have always been best at it. Better than men. There'd be eight or nine people out there, picking by hand, with a scoop. Then they'd take the berries up to the shed. And the guy'd be there, counting your boxes for the day, and they'd pay you fifty cents a box. Then they put them in the big winnowing machine. They'd get the twigs and the bugs and the rotten ones winnowed out of them. And then they were packed in barrels for shipment.

I went picking a few times, and I weeded, and I wheeled sand in winter, and stuff like that. After the berries were picked, you'd go in and weed the bog as much as possible. Then they were flooded for the winter. You put water on them to keep them from chilling and winter kill. Spring, the water was taken off, let to dry a few days. And then go in once more to make sure you got as many weeds as possible, and then that's it. Don't even go walking on them until picking time.

About every two or three years they were sanded. About half an inch of sand thrown over them, to mat the bushes so they'd root and make new bushes instead of just these long scraggly old vines that you couldn't handle. Then you get nice young shoots, with the berry. And it also helps to keep the weeds down, and helps to hold the water. You want a short vine that you can run the picker through.

You have to sand them when there's ice on the bog. Because how in hell are you going to get a wheelbarrow full of sand through some nice, soft, marshy muck? You and it are going to be up to your respective ears in muck. So you either have to use planks or ice. Otherwise, you'd go down, *squish*. And not only that, wheeling that wheelbarrow over those lines, you'd raise hell with it. Wouldn't encourage them a bit. For eight years, though, there was no ice. So that was another thing that screwed them up. Mild winters. You're not going to go around and around with a wheelbarrow full of sand on that ice unless it's at least two inches thick, or you're going to go swimming.

I picked in Duarte's bogs, and then I picked a section of wild stuff for my own use. Go out there and get some of the wild berries. They were very dark, almost black, and smaller, but I think they're better. I'd pick a bushel for the winter. A lot of people did that, picking the wild bogs. But don't go into the private bogs, you'll get your arse kicked. There was a law then, that picking bogs was the same as breaking and entering. You could get a fine up to a hundred dollars if they caught you. So that was it.

Was it fun, picking? My dear lady, no, it was not, believe me. Down on your hands and knees in the god-damned muck, and the mosquitoes and flies are out to keep away the dull times. No, it was not fun! I was never interested in cranberries. I was chasing muskrats.

Now, back in the early thirties, when I was big enough to be into mischief, there was quite a lot of cockfighting on the Island. There were big barns around and places. I've had some in my barn. You don't really organize a cockfight. You just get the news out that some guys, maybe from away, wanted to have a main, or there'd be some bid down here, or some guy would challenge, that's all. Ten, fifteen people, because there weren't that many of us fighters here. It was a couple of bucks to enter each bird. And that goes to the guy who has the pit and stuff, just to cover expenses and trouble. That's pit money. And then the guys would call their bets, "Five on the blue! Two-fifty on the spangled!"

The cockpit is twelve feet across, and you just set up something so it's portable, canvas, and stuff. You'd count how many birds were coming in, and then you'd challenge the other fellow, and you put the birds in the ring and let 'em rip. And then you'd pick 'em up. We used to run on two-minute rounds and two minutes rest. Some of these well-matched birds would fight bejesus. They'd have to go into the drag pit — that's where you put birds that were still willing to fight, but wobbly — to let 'em finish it off. That was so the next contenders could come in. Not tie up the pit for an hour. That's how long sometimes those old bastards would fight. I had a rip-roaring good fighter, old Geronimo, he won eleven fights. And then I retired him.

Fighting cocks are handsome birds though. Look some different from these barnyard seagulls, God-damned things. And more damned breeds to them than you can shingle hell a mile with. Some of them had the names of people that brought 'em up. A famous strain of birds were the Jackson Greys. It's claimed they're descended from roosters old Andy Jackson had. Then there was the Gordon Greys — Sir Alex Gordon from Scotland — his strain. God, been so long since I've even thought of them. I had nothing but the Gordon Greys.

When a cock is what they call a stag, under a year old, some guys will fight 'em to test 'em out, but not serious. See how they shape up. And the ones that don't shape up are gotten rid of. And the good ones are kept and continued with training until they've gone through their stag moult and have reached the adult moult. And the spurs have

got to be big enough so that you can put the heels on them. Because the heels go over the spur and get strapped on. The steel spurs.

The Mexicans and those people fight 'em with their natural spurs sharpened and dressed. But the natural spur makes a terrible wound. Ripping. Scotties fight 'em natural spur, too, and Irish. But the steel spur is just a punch. If it doesn't reach a vital spot, why, in four days the bird is over it. The old-fashioned spur that comes out in a drop, that's the favorite one, with variations. But the Filipinos and the Orientals use slashers that are like miniature swords, sharp on the point and sharp on the sides. So the loser gets slashed up — make their own chop suey on the hoof.

Sometimes one of the cocks gets killed. That's up to the owner. But if he's a fine bird, and just bad luck for this particular time, you holler, "Pick up!" And, of course, you forfeit your money.

To condition the birds, you'd walk them and you'd fly them. To walk a cock, you just take your hand and you push him back and make him work his legs. And then you flight him — pick him up and let him fly down — to strengthen his wings. And then a lot of guys had a wheel, like a hamster wheel, they put him in and let him go it.

Then for grain, you fed them hard, ripe corn. For food, each guy had a different thing. One had rather high protein and low fat. Guys used to feed them hamburgs, fish, birdseed mixture cooked in beef juice and Lord knows what, and each guy had his own particular brand of food. But that's gone, with the oxen, and them days. Me and Bob Nevin, I guess, were the last two cockfighters alive.

During Prohibition here, life was goddamned lively, I'll tell you those. Because this was a way station. Also, we had a lot of geniuses here cooking up their own bug juice. The old-time Portuguese people, Italians and them, they were well into the winemaking and brandy. And the New Englander was apple jack and hard cider. Then, of course, we had a bunch of boys that found out recycling you make a pretty good brand of bug juice out of a mixture of swill and molasses. And then, after it was cooked, you could feed it to the pigs! You got double use out of it. Use anything that will ferment. Good garbage would ferment. And the really good stuff, like they make down South, is made with corn, rye, wheat, stuff like that. Rum, of course, is made out of molasses.

The still can vary, but the whole thing is, first, you got your tank where you put your mash or mix. Under that is a fire. The lid comes on it, and then there's like a spout comes out and hooks to a copper tubing — the worm — which goes round and round and round into a big barrel of cold water. And the alcohol vaporizes much before the other stuff. So that steam goes out down through the condenser and runs out the end. And there's your moonshine.

They'd buy one of these hot-water heaters. Take the gizzards out of that, and then instead of having hot water come out through the coil, you'd have that going through cold water, and that was the still. You could make one of them over for a still with not too much expense. You could also get these family stills, small ones — small stills you could rig up that worked from the kitchen stove.

The real cheapo stuff we used to make with a washtub and a horse blanket and a clothes wringer. Catch the steam in the blanket, wring it out in the clothes wringer, and sift out the blanket fuzz and stuff, and there you were. No coil at all, just the blanket. Blanket catch the steam.

And you tested the quality. You went in — everybody had a coal stove — you take the lid off, spit a mouthful of the stuff in the stove and see how high the blue flame came. And that would show you the strength of the moonshine. Just a little feeble flame — "No, John, that stuff's half water. Come on! Not a buck. I'll give you sixty cents."

Oh, you could make some money. It was a cottage industry. One old boy used to peddle moonshine out of a baby carriage. He come down on the street, Silk Sock Sam, he comes down on the street, and the baby is sitting up maybe that high. Then as the day goes, the baby goes down, down, down. And the racket was that the baby was roosting on several pints of booze, moonshine. My aunts used to always say, "That lovely little man, he's always wheeling his little child there."

Hey, when Prohibition was going good, be a hard job to throw a rock and not hit on a booze establishment somewhere. What they called a blind pig. That's what they used to call the places, you know, a dispensary. Christ, they had the old Yankees that knew how to make rum and whiskey. Then you had the Portuguese who knew how to make a blend of stuff they called *cachaca* which was a dual-purpose thing. You could run a lawnmower on it. You could blow up rocks with it. And you could drink it.

The boats with liquor were coming from beyond the twelve-mile limit. All along the Atlantic coast. There were big vessels out there, hove to. And you go out there and pick up a load of what you wanted, pay for it, and then try to get it through.

We had these hijackers out here, would try and grab the guys running in and rob them, take their booze. Had one old captain, famous old whaleman, had a little schooner. Now there was a lot of whaling gear around New Bedford then, because the last whale ship didn't come in 'til 1926 — the *John R. Manter*. And the old man got a whaling harpoon gun and mounted it on the stern.

It had an exploding tip, and I guess the captain doubled the dose. He wasn't worried about blowing it into a whale. See, you put too much in there, you're working against yourself. It would blow the harpoon right out of the whale. Blow a great big hole in the animal. But he loaded it up in good shape. He probably used smokeless powder, too.

Dog Meat Francis was a witness, he was telling about it. He said, "Goddamned hijackers come after the old captain. Cap'n says, 'Going to screw around with me but one time.' Tells me, 'Easy. Take the wheel and just hold the vessel steady.'" And Dog Meat says, "I done it. I looked right ahead." He says, "Next thing you know, jumpin' Jesus — *ka-Boom*! He blowed them goddamned hijackers two-hundred feet into the air, guts and giblets was raining down all over." It was a gang from Rhode Island. Charlie the Chink's gang. Sherman, Dilroy and them. Yeah, I remember that one, boy. A noble experiment.

I never drove a damn car 'til I was, I think I was

sixty years old. When I was young, I swore to Jesus I'd never drive a car until I had been sober and hadn't had a drink for five years. Because I saw so much of smash-ups and killing and crippling and a bunch of rum-dumbs behind the wheel. I walked and I had a big, rugged bike. And if I was going for a load of stuff, I would take either my horses or the oxen, whichever I had at the moment. So, that was one sensible thing I did in me life! Haven't had a drop of booze since 1972.

I remember I once had a load of wood to deliver down to West Chop. I had my oxen and the wood loaded in the wagon behind. So, that's fine. I go to West Chop with the wood. Then they had these people serving cocktails and that, and of course I got drunker than a bloody piper. The next thing you know, somebody's screaming to the cops that there's a madman with a couple of crazy bulls on the loose. So up comes Mr. Cop and tosses me in the clink. State cop. So then comes a fuss, because them damned oxen wouldn't move for anybody. They were up there on Franklin Street. See, they only respond to their own master. Some

stranger can't do anything with them. They had to let me out of jail to go up and get the oxen home.

We come home, and my sow's having little pigs. I says, "Hey. You can't put me back in jail. We got to get through with these pigs. Now, give me a hand!" So I make the cop get in the pigpen with me. I was hoping the boar hog would bite him, but he didn't. And I get the little pigs all delivered.

The next day I'm in court and the judge, old George Braley says, "Well, what's he done now?" "Well, your honor, he was drunk and creating a disturbance and an uproar," and blah, blah, blah. "And very uncooperative." Old Abner listens. Now, he asks me, he says, "Well, what were you driving? Were you driving a horse or a car or a truck or what?" I says, "No, your honor. Driving a team of oxen." And the old judge grabs a book and he's this way. I see his shoulders jumping, and then he put the book down. "No law in the statutes against driving an ox cart as long as the oxen were sober. Case dismissed."

*Interviewed 1994*

# Index

A&P, Oak Bluffs 111, 149, 164
Adams, Frank 126
Adams, Lillian 61
Adams sisters 120, 128, 175
African-Americans 34-36, 106-8, 162-66, 211-212, 260-62
Agricultural Fair 62, 94-96, 143, 170, 180, 214-15, 275-76
Agricultural Hall 143
Agricultural Society 155
Airplanes 47, 275
Alisio, Dan 231-34
Alisio, Marguerite 232
Alisio's Barbershop 232
Allen, Joseph Chase 124
Allen, Sarah 124
Allen, William 124
Alley, Antone 118, 284
Alley, Betty 7-10
Alley, John 96, 118
Alley's Store 50, 94, 142 (see also S.M. Mayhew Store)
Amaral, Dr. Clement 164
Animals 18, 31, 42, 43, 66, 74, 78, 102-103, 114, 124, 130, 135, 154-155, 168-70, 178, 179, 190, 200, 222, 228, 233-234, 247, 254, 265, 282-283, 285, 287 (see also Horses and Oxen)
Aquinnah (see Gay Head)
Armitage, Lorraine 65-68
Artists 106-8, 270-71, 278-80
    art 26-28, 95, 278-80
      Edgartown Artists Community 279
      Martha's Vineyard Artists Association 106
Athearn, Leonard 49-52, 216
Athearn family 94
Automobiles 40, 47, 120, 127-28, 144, 148, 163, 175-76, 222, 228, 275, 286-87
Azores 8, 74, 168, 190, 204, 240, 264

Ballou, Phoebe Ann 106
Bang's Market 50, 111, 201, 205, 232
Barney, Ethel 78
Barney, Mr. 78, 84
Basset, John 18, 155, 179
Bean, Judge Roy 30
Beetle, Capt. Henry W. 60
Belain, Bertha 26
Belain, John 26
Belain, Joseph 26
Benson, Franklin 192, 249-51
Benson, Norman 246, 250-51, 275
Benton, Thomas Hart 182, 270
Bernard, George 162
Berrying 4, 169
    blueberrying 19, 146, 169, 201, 211, 241

Bethel, The (see Church)
Bird, Rev. Henry 54
Blacksmith 28, 60
Blue Barque Tea House 19, 175
Boarding houses 34, 36, 38, 106, 120, 157-58, 174-75, 260, 270, 278
Boatbuilding 70-72
Boathouse, Oliver 46
Boats 14, 70-72, 186, 196, 240 (see also Ferries)
    *Alice Wentworth* 186-87, 218-22
    *Annie Jackson* 228
    bum boats 224
    catboats 43, 71, 114, 117, 229, 278
    coastal schooners 2, 82, 186-87, 218-19
    fishing boats 15-16, 24, 32, 121, 130, 183-84, 202, 256-58 (see also Fishing)
    *Hazel M. Jackson* 15-6, 227-28
    *Madison Edwards* 186
    "Menemsha" 71
    sailboats 71
    "Vineyard 15" 71
Borgen, Ole 136, 246
Boston Fire Brick & Clay 30
Bradley, Susan 162
Bradley's Livery Stable 139, 224
Braley, Judge George 287
Brewster, Kingman 57
Brickman family 111, 112
Bricks/brickyard 31-32, 219
Bryant, Nelson 57
Burleigh, Harry T. 36, 106, 211
Burt, Otis 248
Burt, Alice 223-26
Burt, Erford 69-72, 226, 248
Burt's Boatyard 200
Butler, Capt. 122
Butler, David 18
Butter making 67, 168-69

Cagney, Jimmy 32, 182, 282
Cahoun, Bert 275
California 94, 134-35
Call, Maude 136, 246
Camp Meeting Grounds (see Oak Bluffs)
Campbell, Antoin 142
Campbell, Emanuel 275
Catboats (see Boats)
Cape Pogue 228, 278
Cape Cod Canal 162, 224
Cape Verdeans 234
Carriages (see Transportation)
Cattledrive 154, 233
Cavert, May 19
Cavert, Cora 19

Cavert, Helen 19
Cedar Tree Neck 121
Cedars, The 155
Cemeteries 40, 127, 139
    Chilmark Cemetery 18
Chadwick's Bathing Beach (see Chappaquiddick Bathing
    Beach)
Chamarita 8, 75, 182, 201-2
Chappaquonsett 48
Chappaquiddick 26-28, 120, 228-29
Chappaquiddick Bathing Beach 120, 229, 278
Chicken Alley 183, 200
Childbirth 9, 94
Chilmark 18-19, 21-24, 30-32, 88, 124-28, 138-39,
    182-84, 218-20, 268, 270-71
Chilmark Brickyard 30
Chilmark Tavern 23
Chilmark Town Hall 23, 182
China Clay Company 30
Christmas 8, 34, 75, 165, 205, 278
Church/Temple 55, 126-27, 205, 217, 225, 260
    baptism 225-26
    Baptist Tabernacle 38, 165
    Bradley Memorial Church 162-66, 262
    Bradley Memorial Missionary Society 166, 262
    Catholic Church 75, 205
    Gay Head Baptist Church 26, 211
    Grace Church 54, 208
    Holy Jumper 127
    Lambert's Cove Methodist Church 248
    Martha's Vineyard Hebrew Center 111-12
    Methodist Tabernacle 38, 165
    North Tisbury Baptist Church 248
    Old Whaling Church 54
    Seaman's Bethel 2, 162, 172, 186-87, 240
    Union Chapel 38, 163, 176
    Vineyard Haven Baptist Church 224-26
    West Tisbury Congregational Church 117, 163
Circuit Avenue 38, 78, 90, 175, 187, 261, 278
Civil Rights Movement 54-57
Civil War 30, 60
Clambakes 26, 79, 132
Cleveland, Alice 263-66
Cleveland, Capt. Alvin 265
Cleaveland, Henry 116
Cleaveland House 116, 118
Cleveland, Josiah 220
Cleveland, Lydia 253-54
Cleveland, Pheobe 50, 117
Co-op Dairy 155, 233 (see also Dairy)
Coal 80, 84, 200 (see also Heating)
Coast Guard 22, 139, 197, 210, 219
Coast Guard Station 22, 210
Coastal and Geodetic Survey 94, 102
Cobblestones 118
Cockfighting 285
Colby, Bill 71
Coles, Mary 277-80
Conservation 64
    Conservation Society 242

Coon, Nelson 207-8
Cooper family 42
Cooper, Mary 43
Correllus, Manuel 239-42
Cottage City (see Oak Bluffs)
Cottagers, The 261-62
Cottle, Bill 247
Cottle, Eric 13-16, 20-24
Cottle, Lucy 247
Cottle, Marguerite 17-19, 20-24
Cottle, Stephen 94, 274
Coutinho, Alice 203-6
Coutinho, John 199-202, 205, 272
Cranberries
    cranberry bogs 28, 63, 118, 179, 233, 283-84
    harvesting 284
Cranberry Acres Bogs 233
Creekville 32
Crickers 21-24
Crocker, Crosby 47
Cronig, Anne 109-12
Cronig, Henry 112, 150
Cronig, Samuel 110-11
Cronig, Tebby 111
Cronig's Store 110-11, 168
Crossing Jordan 86
Crystal Lake 196, 250, 284
Cullen, Countee 35
Cultivation (see Farming/agricultural procedures)

Daggett, Obed 61, 70, 122
Daggett, Silas 110
Dairy Farms 5-6, 78, 134-35, 154, 157, 159, 233-34, 264
    milk inspector 194
    milk processing 155, 168, 264
    milk routes 5, 80, 127, 130, 155, 157, 168, 194,
    264
Dancing 23, 127, 140, 163, 176, 182, 225
Dancing dolls 205
Darling's Candy and Popcorn Store 85, 149
Davis, Anna 233
Davis, Orlin 155, 194
Davis, Judge Everett Allen 94, 103, 142
Deafness 14, 148
    deaf and dumb 14, 32, 127, 182
DeBettencourt, Nelson 91
Denniston, Amy 162, 166
Denniston, Dean K. 161-66
Denniston, Gerald 164, 165, 166
Denniston, Olive 162, 164, 166
Denniston, Oscar 162-66, 262
Depression, The 63, 98, 112, 166, 201, 241
Ditty bag 162
Doctors 44, 60, 265-66
Downs, Elizabeth 47-48
Downs, Howard 47-48, 50
Ducks 28, 50, 283
    hunting 4, 28, 50-51
    trained decoys 51
Dugan, Bill 71

Duys, Claire 137-40

East Chop 38-39, 174-76, 196-98, 250
    East Chop Tennis Club 174-75
Eastman, Max 270
Edgartown 26-28, 62-63, 98-99, 106, 116, 120-22, 130, 228-30, 236-38, 256-58, 264-66, 270, 278- 80
Edgartown Artist Community 279
Edgartown Harbor 236, 258
Edgartown National Bank 228, 230
Edgartown Post Office 98
Edgartown Yacht Club 279
Edwards, Madison 2, 162
Eisenstaedt, Alfred 269-71
Engley, Roger 146
Evanti, Madame Lillian 106

4-H Club 68
Fairchild, Dr. 43
Farland, Spike 90
Farm Neck 4, 148
Farmers' Market 95
Farming 4, 6, 18, 22, 24, 26, 31, 42, 50, 60, 78, 94, 102-4, 110, 124-28, 130, 134, 142-44, 148, 152, 154, 157, 168-70, 182, 214-16, 218, 222, 228-30, 254, 264, 266, 283
    agricultural procedures 44, 154, 169, 190, 222
    crops 4, 42, 222
    equipment 102-4, 169-70, 214-16, 230, 254
    farm animals (see Animals)
    fertilizer 4, 84, 103, 154, 222, 230
Fences 178, 222
Ferries/Steamboats 39, 61, 74, 114, 116, 120, 130, 134, 174, 229-30, 244, 254, 268
    Chappaquiddick Ferry 27
    ferry strike 214
Fiddles (see Music)
Fiebich, Rudy 139, 149-50
Fire alarm 76
Fire protection 83 (see also State Forest)
Fires 146
First National 201
Fischer, Albert (Ozzie) 154, 155, 282
Fischer, Arnold 50, 51, 153-60, 282
Fischer, Priscilla 156-60
Fisher, Fred 213-16
Fishing Derby, The 98
Fishing shacks 15, 183-84, 236, 258
Fishing 18-19, 15-16, 22-24, 27-28, 31, 50-52, 63, 98, 117, 124, 130, 182-84, 202, 204, 236, 241, 244, 246, 256-58
    bass 27
    bluefish 27
    clamming 27, 104, 132, 168, 278
    cod 183, 257
    dory fishing 183-84
    dragging 202, 257-58
    fishing boats (see Boats)
    eel fishing 50-51, 63, 104, 130-31
    fish pounds (see trapfishing)
    fish weirs (see trapfishing)
    frost fish 5
    hake 5
    hand lining 183, 257
    heave and haul 27-28
    hermit crabs 244
    herring 5, 28, 104, 130-31, 168, 179,192, 240-41
    ice fishing 43
    lobster 15, 31, 132, 202, 210-11, 258
    long lining 257
    quahogging 27, 183
    scalloping 27, 183, 278
    seining 18 (see also herring)
    shellfishing 4, 21, 27-8, 103, 168, 183
    swordfishing 14-16, 27, 58, 63, 202, 256-58
    trap fishing 43, 52, 60-61, 69, 70, 135, 178-79, 192, 246
    trout 44
    white perch 18, 28, 52
Flanders, Robert 247
Flat Point Farm 154
Flying Horses 47, 86
Food
    preparation/baking 74, 95-96, 124-28, 169
    preservation 5, 74, 75, 124, 178, 190-91, 218
    refrigeration 48, 50, 118, 124-25, 155
    storage 9, 31, 67, 74, 118, 125, 168, 178, 191
Freedom Riders 55
Fresh water springs (see Water/Plumbing)
Fruit 18, 74
    fruit bushes 74
    fruit orchards 233
    fruit trees 18, 169
Fuller, Meta Warrick 106
Funerals 26, 82, 163

Games 14, 127, 186, 191, 224, 275, 276
    children's games 46, 83-84, 88, 120, 135, 174, 230
Gardens 74, 190, 200, 205, 208, 211, 282 (see also Farming)
    vegetable gardens 4, 18, 26-28, 66-67, 135, 168, 204, 211, 218, 228, 234, 247, 254
Gay Head (Aquinnah) 26, 31, 39, 42-44, 95, 178-80, 183, 210-12, 261, 270-71
    Gay Head Cliffs 39, 51, 210
    Gay Head families 163
    Gay Head School (see Schools)
Gay Head Herring Creek 178
Geology 242
George's Bank 202, 256-58
Germantown Road (see Old County Road)
Gifford, Willis 273-76
Gifford's Store 50, 117, 274-75
Girdlestone Park 79
Girl Scouts 72, 164, 175
Goell, Mrs. 120, 278
Goff, Le Roy 132, 243-44
Gold Rush 116

Golf Course, Tashmoo 201
Gordon, Ruth 270
Gouveia, Rose 73-6
Grain Mill 42, 222
Grange, The 266
Great Plains 120, 146
Greene, Farmer 111, 247
Griswold, Mary 173-76
Grocery Stores 43, 84, 110-11, 117, 164, 200, 222, 228, 254, 264, 274-76 (see also individual stores)
      grocery wagon, up-Island 46-47, 50-51, 201, 205, 225

Hammett, Sarah 124
Harlem Renaissance 35-36, 107
Harness making 47
Harrington, Gratia 1-2
Harris, Sidney 29-32, 126
Havenside, The 157
Haying 19, 22, 142-43, 148, 154, 157, 169, 214-15, 228
Haynes, Billy 247
Haynes, Mrs. 247
Heating 83, 125, 158, 200
    coal dock 121
    coal stoves 14, 83, 158, 224, 286
    wood/woodlots 4, 14, 28, 30, 66, 67, 78, 154, 168, 287
    wood stoves 4-5, 14, 32, 66, 154
Heath Hens 146, 214
Hellman, Lillian 270
Hemmings, Robert 107
Hersey, John 270
Highland Beach 36, 38
Highland Wharf 38
Highlands, The 36, 38, 165, 260
Hill, Polly 40, 151-52
Hoft, John 233
Holman, Mary Louise 259-62
Holy Ghost Crown 74-75
Holy Ghost Feast 8, 75, 205
Holy Ghost Society 75
Holy Ghost Soup 206
Horses 31, 34, 42, 83, 102-4, 124, 138, 143, 169-70 214-16, 224, 254
    horse races 79, 103, 143
    horse raising 139
    horseback riding 135-36, 138
Horticulture 152, 208
Horton, Harry 112
Hospitals 265-66
    Marine Hospital 200
    Martha's Vineyard Hospital 135, 143, 265
    Cottage Hospital 265
Hotels 106, 148-50, 157, 210, 254, 260-61, 268
Hough, Dr. Gary 60
Hough, Dr. George T. 60
Hough, Henry Beetle 59-64, 96
House Moving 22, 222, 247
Household chores 19, 27, 66, 88, 204, 246

Hovey, Allen 140
Hughes, Langston 35
Humphreys, Argie 144, 256
Humphreys, Bernice 256
Hunting 28, 146, 169, 283
Huntington, Albert 140
Huntington, Gale 139, 185-88, 252
Huntington, Mildred 182, 185-88, 252
Huntington, Willie 104
Hurricanes 70, 256-58, 270
      '38 Hurricane 51, 233
Hurston, Zora Neal 35
Hymns 176, 186

Ice cream 165-66, 169, 275
     parlors 85, 136, 246
Ice 31, 46, 51, 84, 126, 155, 202, 220, 227-28, 257, 272
    ice boxes 125, 224, 251
    ice cutting 118, 250-51
    ice delivery 46, 84, 168, 224
Illness 225, 279
Illumination Night 84
Immigration 110, 190-91, 204, 240
Indian Hill Road 60, 66-68, 222
Inns 82, 94, 116, 210
    Tisbury Inn/Mansion House 168, 204
Issokson, Mr. 111-12
Jackson, Robert, Jr. 100, 255-58
Jackson, Robert, Sr. 15, 256-58
Japanese Stores 85, 278-79
Jeffers family 51
Jeffers, Linus 183
Jeffers Lydia 26
Jeffers, Milton 25-28
Jenkinson, Fannie 87-88
Jenkinson, Sarah 167-70
Jewish life 110-12
    families 111
      Holy Days 111
John Hoft Farm 232-34
Johnson, Anna Francis Adams 94
Johnson, Asa 94
Jones, Lois Mailou 105-8

Kaeka, Shirley 245-48
Kanin, Garson 270
Kaplan, Kivi 57
Karl, Eddie 150
Karl, Ida 147-50
Katama 130, 278
Keegan, Mike 91
Kenniston, Allen 146
Kenniston, Betty 160
Kerosene (see Lighting)
King, Martin Luther, Jr. 54
Kingsbury, Craig 281-87
Knowles, Peg 119-22
Krylenko, Eliena 270

Lagoon, The (see Ponds)
Lambert's Cove 176, 232-34
Lamplighters 46, 82
Landscapes 26-28, 50, 130, 136, 152, 154, 222, 271
Lane, Dr. 48
Language 8, 74, 148-49, 190, 200, 204-5, 224, 240, 252
        sign 15, 32, 127, 148
Lee, Jonas 107
Leonard, Connie 45-48, 50, 90
Leonard, Freeman 46, 89-92
Lewis, Gladys 37-9
Lighting 14, 84, 142, 210-11, 230, 234 (see also Lamplighters)
Lighthouse boat 196
Lighthouses 43, 196-97
        Cape Pogue Light 228
        East Chop Light 38, 196-98
        Edgartown Light 121
        Gay Head Light 39, 43, 46-47, 196, 210
        Nantucket Light 196
        West Chop Light 197, 244
Lilienthal, Peg 54
Livery Stables 84, 224
        Bradley's Livery Stables 139, 224
        Renear's Livery Stable 61, 244
Lobsters (see Fishing)
Lobsterville 43, 114, 117, 180, 183, 211
Look, Jim 50-51, 158
Look, Artie 248
Luce, Carey 154, 157
Luce, Ethel 154
Luce, George Hervey 60
Luce, Ham 3-6
Luce, Henry 148
Luce, Otis 70

Manning, Helen 209-12
Mansion House/Tisbury Inn 168, 204
Manter family 94
Manter, Daniel 51
Manter, Rebecca 32, 42
Manter, William 126
Marchant, Edward 62
Martha's Vineyard Artists Association (see Artists)
Martha's Vineyard Airport 202, 279
Martha's Vineyard Hebrew Center 111-12
Martha's Vineyard Hospital (see Hospitals)
Martha's Vineyard Herald 63
Martha's Vineyard Little Theater 99
Martha's Vineyard National Bank 230
Martha's Vineyard Shipyard 71, 200
Martha's Vineyard Sinfonietta 139-40
Martha's Vineyard Summer Institute 38
Masons 98-99
Mattaer Brothers 149
Mattakesett Creek Co. 130-31
Maughm, Somerset 270
May Day/May Baskets 9, 142, 160
Mayhew, Bart 18, 42, 61, 254, 268

Mayhew, Ben 15, 16
Mayhew, Carlton 15
Mayhew, Ernest 15
Mayhew, Fred 61
Mayhew, Grace 117
Mayhew, Johnny 104, 275
Mazer, Milton 54
Mazer, Virginia 54
Mead, Ruth 106
Medeira 200, 205
Medeiros, Barbara 123-28
Medicine 43, 186, 264
        herbal remedies 43, 246, 265
Mello, Maxemena 235-38
Menemsha 14-16, 21-24, 58, 107, 114, 122, 218, 270
Menemsha Coast Guard Station 22
Menemsha Creek 15
Military 92, 202, 279 (see also Civil War, WWI, WWII )
Mill Brook 50, 103
Mitchell, Delly 143
Morgan, Jimmy 15
Mosher Photo 68
Moss, Evelyn 210
Movies
        film operations 90-92
        theaters 90-92, 163, 165, 229
Murphy, Polly 54
Music 10, 46, 85, 91, 127, 138-39, 148-50, 163-64, 182, 204-6, 229, 232, 247-48
        fiddles 182-83
Music Street 117, 126, 274

NAACP 54-57
Navigation 220
Neubert, Eleanor 155
New York Yacht Club 72
Newhall family 94, 102, 142
Newhall, Edwin 94
Newhall, Jane 93-96
Night Watchman 83
Nip 'n' Tuck Farm 214-16
Nobnocket 46
North Road 21, 23, 32, 58, 124, 143-44
North Tisbury 47, 61, 136, 152, 246-48
North Tisbury Post Office 61
Norton, Mayhew G. 60
Norton, Orin 28, 121
Norton, Robert 155, 193-194
Nursing 264-66

Oak Bluffs (Cottage City) 4-6, 36, 61, 78-80, 82-86, 90-91, 106-7, 142-50, 162-66, 168-70, 190, 260-62, 278-79
        Camp Meeting Grounds 62, 78, 82-83, 148, 164, 174, 240, 261
Oak Bluffs Beach 85-86, 121
Oak Bluffs Pumping Station 79-80 (see also Water/Plumbing)
Oak Bluffs Skating Rink 86, 148
Oak Bluffs Water Works (see Water/Plumbing)
Oakland Mission 162

Old County Road 74, 154
Old Holmes Hole Road 111
Old South Road 42, 178
Oliver, Jesse 75
Open Door Club 261
Opening the Pond/Beach 52, 103, 118
Operator (see Telephone Company)
Osborne, Charles 61
Owen, Barry 48, 224
Oxen 19, 22, 31, 52, 95, 143, 178-80, 216, 222, 270, 275, 287
     ox carts 42-43, 179, 210
     ox training 52, 179-80, 216

Painting 106-8, 278-80
Pastures 42, 178 (see also Landscapes)
Pavillion, The 42, 210
Peakes, Harry 155, 250
Pease, Buddy 250
Pease, Chester 120
Peat bogs 233
Peddlers 46, 274
Perlstein, Harry 112
Photography 68, 270-71
Pig slaughtering 8, 74-75, 178, 190-91, 287
Pilot Hill 154
Pilot's Landing 42
Plumbing (see Water/Plumbing)
Police 287
Pollution 63, 229, 283
Polly Hill's North Tisbury Arboretum 152
Ponds
     Black Point Pond 103, 142
     Chilmark Pond 19
     Fisher's Pond 127
     Lagoon Pond 78-80
     Mill Brook 50, 103
     Mill Pond 51, 117-18
     Old House Pond 250
     Parsonage Pond 102
     Poucha Pond 28
     Priester's Pond 247
     Sengekontacket Pond 4
     Tisbury Great Pond 50-52, 102-4, 117-18
     Watcha Pond 283
Poole, Donald 122, 270
Popcorn Harry 120
*Port Hunter* 31
Portuguese 8, 64, 74, 148-49, 162-64, 182, 183, 190, 200, 204, 233, 234, 236-37, 264, 283, 285, 286
     food 8-9, 74-76, 204-6
     holidays 8-9, 74-76, 204-6
     language 190, 204-5
     names 8, 190, 237-38
     songs 8, 205
Post, Emily 19, 99
Powell, Adam Clayton 106
Pratt, Sadie 91
Preachers 127, 164 (see also Church)
Priscilla Pearls Company 130, 240

Prohibition 176, 278, 285-86
Purdy, George Walter 196
Purdy, Mary Jane 196
Putnam family 126, 135-136, 138-39
     Putnam, Dr. Charles Russell Lowell 135, 138
     Putnam, Mrs. 135, 138-39

Quansoo 40, 51, 118, 143
Quenames 142
Quitsa 254

Racism 27, 36, 106-7, 164-66, 240-42, 260-61
Rausch's Ice Cream Parlor 39, 85
Ray, Alice Purdy 195-98
Red Cross 149
Red Cross Health Center of Martha's Vineyard 265
Reed, Maude 15
Restaurants 26, 150, 261
     Lewis' Restaurant 261
     Not-O-Way 210-11
     Pollard's 260
     1785 House 150
     Vanderhoop Restaurant 43, 210
Riggs, Dionis Coffin 115-18
Ritter, Henry 106
Roads (see Transportation)
Roaring Brook 31, 42
Roberts, Bill 99
Roberts, Manuel Swartz 71, 99, 121, 236-37, 270, 278
Robinson, Captain 248
Rogers, George A. 61
Rogers, Harold 221-22
Rum Running 31, 100, 172, 210, 286

Sam Cahoon's Fish Market 70
Sanchez, Elizabeth Marchant 11-12, 62
SBS 47, 111, 135, 225
School 21, 27, 32, 75, 112, 117, 128, 138, 150, 157, 182, 187, 204, 240, 241, 260
     Cape Higgon School 32, 126
     Chilmark School 15, 21, 32, 139
     Dukes County Academy 117, 125-26 (see also West Tisbury School)
     Gay Head School 211, 212
     Locust Grove School 67
     Oak Bluffs School 78, 164, 166
     Regional High School 159
     Vineyard Haven High School 21, 32, 68
     Vineyard Haven School 46, 75, 111, 112, 241
     West Tisbury School 117, 157-60, 274
School Orchestra 150
School Plays 125-26, 164, 211-12
School Teachers 15, 67-8, 125, 157-60, 182, 212, 246
School Committee 32, 126, 158-60, 164
School Superintendent 150, 164, 265
Schooners, coastal (see Boats, see also Shipping, cargo)
Seven Gates Farm 61, 66, 70, 127, 134-36, 174, 282, 248
Shaler, Professor Nathaniel 61, 134
Shearer Cottage 106-7, 262
Shipping, cargo 31, 50-2, 102, 114, 130, 155, 187, 228, 240

Shipwrecks 2, 83, 233 (see also Hurricanes)
Sibert, General 139
Siefert, Carl 74, 169
Silva, Virginia 194
Sinfonietta (see Martha's Vineyard Sinfonietta)
Singing 127, 176, 182, 188, 204
Skunks 282
Slavery 34, 260
S.M. Mayhew Store 50, 67, 94, 117, 142 (see also Alley's Store)
Smith, Elisha 77-80
Smith, George 78
Smith, Henry 129-31
Smith, Hollis 145-46
Smith, Lucy P. 264
Smith, Nancy 54
Smith, Woollcott 55
Snapping Turtles 283
South Beach 121, 278
South Roader 21-4
Sparkman and Stephens 72
Spence, Rosalie 217-20
Spring Point 136, 138
Spinning Wheel House, The (see Adams sisters)
Squibnocket 178, 183-84
State Forest 146, 240-42
    fires 240, 242
    forest management 242
    heath hens 146, 241
    hunting 242
    land-use 241
Steamboats (see Ferries)
Steamboat Wharves/Landings
    Edgartown Memorial Wharf 116, 121, 130, 230
    Highland Wharf 39, 86
    New York Wharf 196
    Oak Bluffs Wharf 35, 85, 268
    Pilot's Landing 42, 210
    Vineyard Haven Wharf 2
    West Chop Wharf 62
Stevenson, Henry 224
Stills 286
Stonewalls/building of 201, 222
Stonework 66
Storms 2, 88, 187, 219, 257-58 (see also Hurricanes)
Storytelling 142, 219-20
Sunday restrictions 38, 62, 186, 226
Sunday School 2, 163, 226
Supernatural 212
    Big Tree 212
    ghosts 139
    rooting 43, 212
Swartz, Manuel (see Roberts, Manuel Swartz)
Swimming 15, 46, 61, 85, 134, 175, 246, 278
Swimming Suits 85, 225, 229, 278

Tabernacle, The 240
    Baptist Tabernacle 38, 165
    Methodist Tabernacle 165, 240
Tarpaulin Cove 70, 136

Tashmoo Herring Creek 240-41
Tea Houses 19, 120, 128, 175
Tea Lane 139, 282
Teaming 50
Telephone Company 75-76, 226
    telephones 76, 190
    telephone party lines 139, 158, 244
Tennis 34, 174
Thatcher, Eban A. 219, 224
Theatricals 99, 175
Thimble Farm 79
Thurman, Wallace 35
Tilton family 21, 182, 188, 248, 276
Tilton, Almon 127
Tilton, Alton 194
Tilton, George Fred 21, 188, 219, 252
Tilton, John R. 188
Tilton, Maude 278
The Singing Tiltons 182, 188
Tilton, Tom 171-72, 186-87
Tilton, Welcome 21, 182, 188
Tilton, William 21, 188
Tilton, Willard 127, 188
Tilton, Zeb 21, 31, 154, 186-88, 218-19
Tilton Rentall 261
Tilton's Drugstore 47
Tisbury, England 208
Tisbury (see Vineyard Haven)
Tisbury Inn (see Inns)
Tivoli, The 22, 38, 86, 148, 176, 201, 261
Tom's Neck Farm 26, 228
Totem Pole 270
Tower, Austin 186
Tower, Miriam 186
Transportation 42, 48, 92, 114, 134, 142, 143-44, 163, 218, 254 (see also Walking)
    automobiles 40, 48, 143, 148, 175-76, 222, 228
    buggies 34, 78
    horse and wagon/carriage 48, 66, 84, 154, 169, 214, 218, 224, 254
    roads 61, 120-21, 142, 143-44, 169, 222, 268
    trolleys 62, 149, 240
Trees 135, 152, 208, 212, 240-42
    Chestnut trees 30, 282
    harvesting 241
Tucker, Charlie 57
Turner, Charlie 142
Turtle hunting 282
Turtles 192, 229

Utilities 14, 19, 82, 83, 158, 168, 210-11, 230 (see also Water/Plumbing)

Vanderhoop, Alfred 177-80
Vanderhoop, Arthur Herbert 210
Vanderhoop, Charlie 47
Vanderhoop, Leonard 41-44, 211
Vegetables (see Gardens)
Vincent, Chester 146
Vincent, Dan 14

Vincent's Drugstore 121
Vincent, Nellie 146
*Vineyard Gazette* 12, 34, 64, 99, 61-4, 124, 208, 232
Vineyard Haven 2, 46-48, 60, 74-76, 91-92, 110-12, 114, 72, 186, 194, 200-1, 204, 205, 208, 224-º26, 240-41, 265, 272, 282-87
Vineyard Haven Harbor 2, 38, 186, 240, 272
*Vineyard Haven News* 63
Vineyard Haven Shipyard 200
Vineyard Haven Yacht Club 71
"Vineyard 15" 72
Vineyard Open Land Foundation 233
Vose, Donald 227-30
Vose, Julian W. 230
Vytlacil, Vaclav 279

Wadsworth, Mildred 81-86
Walking 19, 74, 83, 85, 114, 120-22, 126, 135, 211, 218, 225
Wampanoag
        culture 42-44, 210-12
        people 26, 31, 42-44, 95, 178-80, 183, 184, 210-12, 262, 270
Washburn and Call 110
Water/Plumbing 14, 19, 21, 28, 67, 78-80, 82-83, 118, 124-25, 143, 168, 169, 224
        fresh water springs 4, 211, 233
        outhouses 19, 83, 125, 211, 229
Waterpumps (see Water/Plumbing)
Waters, Ethel 106
Webb, Willoughby 127, 134
Webb's Campsite 246
Webster, Daniel 94
Welch, David 189-91
Well water (see Water/Plumbing)
Wentworth, Eddie 91
Wentworth, Sarah 162
Wesley House 261, 268
West Chop 107, 244, 287
West Chop Post Office 244
West, Dorothy 33-36
West, Josie 14-15, 182
West, Katie 182

West, Pat 58, 113-14
West, William 126
West Tisbury 50-52, 94-96, 102-4, 116-18, 134-36, 142-44, 154-55, 157-60, 214-16, 241-42, 254, 274-76
West Tisbury Post Office 50, 117
West Tisbury Town Hall 159
Whales 67, 246
        whaling 43, 60, 95, 104, 116-17, 182, 252, 264, 274, 286
Wheeler, Helen 279
Whidden, Ethel 267-68
White, Ruth 212, 282
Whiting, Allen 94, 159
Whiting, Emma 142-43
Whiting, Everett 95, 143
Whiting, Henry Lawrence 94, 102
Whiting, Jane 95
Whiting, John 95, 101-4, 143
Whiting, Johnson 94-95, 102, 103, 142, 143
Whiting, Nancy 53-57
Whiting, Virginia 94, 142
Wilde, Alfred 97-99
Wilder, Thornton 99
Wilkie, Margot 133-36
Wine making 9, 200
Winter sports 46, 84, 118, 127, 196, 225, 229, 272
WPA 166
World War I 31, 47, 83, 148, 149, 169, 175, 208, 232, 228,   240-41
World War II 22, 63, 92, 112, 132, 150, 158, 234, 279-80
Women
        fishing 23
        roles 236
        whaling wives 116, 264
Wood (see Heating)
Woodaman, Ray 142
Woods, Edwin Newhall 141-44
Writing 35-36, 98-99, 116-18, 208

Yates Drugstore 80
Yates, Jimmy 27
Yendell, Enid 279